the EASTERN EUROPEAN COOKBOOK

the EASTERN EUROPEAN COOKBOOK

KAY SHAW NELSON

Dover Publications, Inc., New York

Published in Canada by General Publishing Com-
pany, Ltd., 30 Lesmill Road, Don Mills, Toronto,
Ontario.
Published in the United Kingdom by Constable
and Company, Ltd., 10 Orange Street, London
WC2H 7EG.

This Dover edition, first published in 1977, is an
unabridged and unaltered republication of the
work originally published by Henry Regnery Company, Chicago, in 1973.

International Standard Book Number: 0-486-23562-9
Library of Congress Catalog Card Number: 77-86259

Manufactured in the United States of America
Dover Publications, Inc.
180 Varick Street
New York, N.Y. 10014

To my husband,
Wayne Nelson,
for all his help and interest

Contents

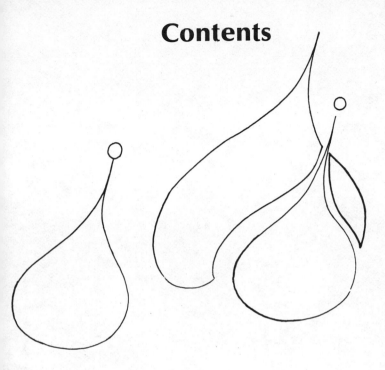

Introduction

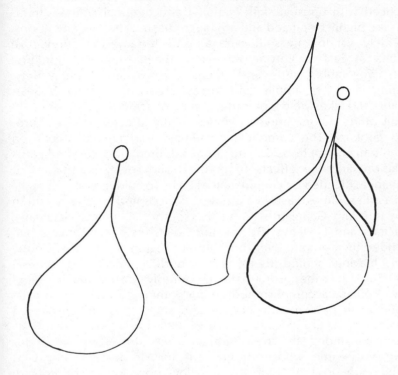

The cookery of Eastern Europe, an historically complex area that now comprises nine nations, is as fascinating to explore as it is delightful to savor. For in this collection of distinguished cuisines may be found a wealth of culinary treasures carefully evolved over the centuries by creative cooks. Indeed, the kitchens of these countries have produced some of the world's most cherished delicacies, as well as flavorful, down-to-earth hearty dishes that have enduring appeal. Such gastronomic specialties, which are challenging and rewarding to prepare, are intriguing additions to the culinary repertoire, either for everyday dining or for special occasions.

It is no accident that the cuisines of Eastern European countries —Russia, Poland, East Germany, Czechoslovakia, Hungary, Romania, Bulgaria, Yugoslavia and Albania—are so beguiling. The ancient proverb, "a man is made by the food he eats," is widely accepted in these countries, and the art of good cooking is practiced with unusual skill. National and regional culinary traditions are highly respected and are taught to succeeding generations. Widely varying in soil, climate and terrain, the productive regions of Eastern Europe have long been blessed by nature. Fruits, vegetables, nuts and grains exist in abundant variety. Grazing lands are ample, and forests are rich with game. Seas, streams and lakes yield a plentiful variety of seafood.

Still other factors, however, have greatly affected Eastern European cookery. The complicated culinary heritage is interwoven with the history of invasion and conquest, the influence of religious affiliation, and the effects of political and social orientation or allegiance, dictated by circumstances or by royal decree.

In earliest times Eastern Europe was occupied by the northern Germanic and Celtic tribes and the southern Illyrians, Scythians, Thracians and Hellenes. By the time of Christ, the Romans had extended their empire over the southern regions up to the Danube River, leaving behind them lasting and significant agricultural gifts. Barbaric tribes from Asia temporarily erased many of the early Roman accomplishments, but other peoples eventually moved in to permanently occupy and settle these much-desired areas.

Primary among the new settlers were the Slavs, an Indo-European people whose origins are lost in history, but who settled early in the Oder River valley, now a part of Poland. From there, beginning about the third century, the Slavs spread eastward to Russia and westward to the Elbe River. By the tenth century the Slavs had crossed the Danube River to take over almost all of the Balkan Peninsula and had established the linguistic and cultural pattern for most of Eastern Europe. Thereafter these lands were occupied by the northern and western Slavs (Russians, Poles, Czechs and Slovaks) and by a southern group (Slovenes, Croats, Serbs, Macedonians and Bulgars). The Hungarians, Romanians, Illyrians of Albania and East Germans were exceptions, being non-Slavic in origin.

Slavic culinary preferences, therefore, although representing a mixture of tastes, distinctly influenced most of the Eastern European cuisines. But other invaders and conquerors, such as the Tartars, Magyars, Turks, Austro-Hungarians, Germans and Italians, all, at one time or another introduced various foods and dishes and left their imprints on the cookery of Eastern Europe. General admiration of Western European royal courts, notably the French, also exerted some influence, as did the choice of religion—Roman Catholic, Eastern Orthodox, or Islamic.

In any event, the cookery of Eastern Europe is ample evidence that the people, whatever their regional or cultural differences, share a fondness for fine food. It is a tribute to these people that, despite the rigors of a checkered history and the effects of political grouping and regrouping, the cuisines of the various countries retain national and, in some cases, regional characteristics that make them interesting and distinctive.

Brief reviews of the factors contributing to the culinary heritage of these nations are intended to enhance understanding of the cookery. This representative collection of recipes for each country provides you with an opportunity to experience and enjoy some of the best culinary accomplishments of Eastern Europe.

the EASTERN EUROPEAN COOKBOOK

CONVERSION TABLES FOR FOREIGN EQUIVALENTS

DRY INGREDIENTS

Ounces	Grams	Grams	Ounces	Pounds	Kilograms	Kilograms	Pounds
1 =	28.35	1 =	0.035	1 =	0.454	1 =	2.205
2	56.70	2	0.07	2	0.91	2	4.41
3	85.05	3	0.11	3	1.36	3	6.61
4	113.40	4	0.14	4	1.81	4	8.82
5	141.75	5	0.18	5	2.27	5	11.02
6	170.10	6	0.21	6	2.72	6	13.23
7	198.45	7	0.25	7	3.18	7	15.43
8	226.80	8	0.28	8	3.63	8	17.64
9	255.15	9	0.32	9	4.08	9	19.84
10	283.50	10	0.35	10	4.54	10	22.05
11	311.85	11	0.39	11	4.99	11	24.26
12	340.20	12	0.42	12	5.44	12	26.46
13	368.55	13	0.46	13	5.90	13	28.67
14	396.90	14	0.49	14	6.35	14	30.87
15	425.25	15	0.53	15	6.81	15	33.08
16	453.60	16	0.57				

LIQUID INGREDIENTS

Liquid Ounces	Milliliters	Milliliters	Liquid Ounces	Quarts	Liters	Liters	Quarts
1 =	29.573	1 =	0.034	1 =	0.946	1 =	1.057
2	59.15	2	0.07	2	1.89	2	2.11
3	88.72	3	0.10	3	2.84	3	3.17
4	118.30	4	0.14	4	3.79	4	4.23
5	147.87	5	0.17	5	4.73	5	5.28
6	177.44	6	0.20	6	5.68	6	6.34
7	207.02	7	0.24	7	6.62	7	7.40
8	236.59	8	0.27	8	7.57	8	8.45
9	266.16	9	0.30	9	8.52	9	9.51
10	295.73	10	0.33	10	9.47	10	10.57

Gallons (American)	Liters	Liters	Gallons (American)
1 =	3.785	1 =	0.264
2	7.57	2	0.53
3	11.36	3	0.79
4	15.14	4	1.06
5	18.93	5	1.32
6	22.71	6	1.59
7	26.50	7	1.85
8	30.28	8	2.11
9	34.07	9	2.38
10	37.86	10	2.74

Russian Cookery

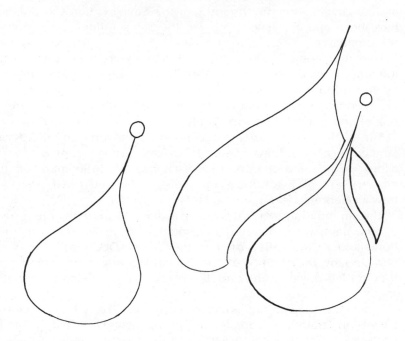

Russian cookery has some exotic and exciting contrasts, because it is derived from the gigantic jigsaw puzzle of climates, land-scapes, soils, peoples, customs and foods that constitutes modern Russia. Each of the fifteen republics that today comprise the USSR has created its own colorful cuisine, which for centuries has nourished both spirit and flesh. Everyday life in Russia revolves around zestful and hearty dining.

Here we will explore the traditional cookery of only the regions of the USSR that lie in Europe, west of the Ural Mountains. In this historic crossroads the modern country of Russia, its culture and cuisine began, matured and expanded.

Today European Russia is a mosaic composed of Estonians, Latvians and Lithuanians on the northern Baltic Sea; Armenians, Azerbaidjanis and Georgians in the southern Caucasus; and Slavs in Great Russia, the Ukraine, Byelorussia and Moldavia. Each of these nationalities has its own proud tradition in culture, cuisine and language. Since the majority of the Soviet Union's population have been and are Slavs, however, the Slavic influence in cookery predominates.

Like all national cuisines, those of Russia were born of necessity, influenced over the years by foreign contributions and enlarged by the adoption of dishes of peoples that were absorbed into the country. Consequently, the Russian culinary repertoire is one of unusual richness and variety.

The ancient and intricate recipes bear the imprint of Russia's tangled history. Many centuries before Christ, nomadic Asian tribes roamed the steppes of Russia, but left little mark on the cookery except a fondness for grilled skewered meat, shashlik, now a celebrated international favorite.

The foundations of Russian cookery began with the arrival of the Slavs, who migrated to central western Russia from their homeland in the valley of the Oder River. Doubtless they were attracted by the fertility of the flat and gently rolling land, and they settled down, converting the black soil into fields of essential foods.

From the beginning, Russian cookery, like all others, was based on grains or cereals, but it necessarily relied primarily on those grains that could withstand the severe climate. Although wheat, barley and millet were grown and used, the great favorite for making breads became the reliable rye. Dark, coarse-grained breads made with rye have been the most important foods of Russia throughout history. What would a Russian meal be like without large thick chunks of black bread? From fermented rye the early people also made a mildly alcoholic everyday tipple called kvass, still a staple drink on the workingman's table.

It was another hardy, quickly grown grain, buckwheat groats, native to Siberia and Central Asia, that became so important to the everyday Russian diet that without it many people would not have survived. A cooked porridge, kasha, usually made with buckwheat groats but also made with other grains, has been a staple Russian food for centuries and is eaten in various forms for daily meals. The Slavs learned to like sunflower seeds. They chewed the seeds for nourishment and pressed them for the oil, which is still a favorite cooking ingredient. Although the corn of the New World did not gain general popularity, cornmeal is used in southwestern Russia. In the Ukraine corn on the cob is very much enjoyed, which is unusual in Europe.

Fortunately, the early Russian settlers had an abundance of fine foods from field and forest, which they used creatively to form the basis of their cuisine. Wild honey, nuts and mushrooms, which were readily available in large variety, became kitchen staples and were cleverly combined with other foods to add flavor and diversity. Berries and fruits were used to make the jellies and jams for which the Russians have an inordinate fondness. Game was and still is plentiful in Russia, and its cookery is interesting and good.

Although the early Russians did have beef, the most important food animal was the domesticated pig, which was kept in every farm backyard and provided the favorite holiday suckling pig and a variety of smoked and fresh pork creations. In the southern areas, however, the lamb of the Near East became the favorite meat.

From the streams, lakes and rivers came a plethora of seafood, which provided everyday soups and stews as well as regal party fare. In Russia the most popular fish has long been the sturgeon, enjoyed fresh or smoked and prized for its luxurious roe, which the world has come to know as caviar. Salmon was another readily available gastronomic treat, and other fish species ranged from the northern smoked eel and herring to bream, trout, carp and pike.

The Russians quickly learned to rely on those vegetables that could be grown in the short summer season and that could not only be eaten fresh but could also be preserved for winter use. The early cooks became experts in the art of pickling, and today no meal is complete without such foods as pickled mushrooms or cucumbers. The latter is one of the most popular foods, either eaten by itself or mixed with other ingredients. Root vegetables, which can be stored through the long winter months, came to be traditional ingredients for the all-important soups. Beets, cabbage, carrots, turnips, and later the New World potatoes are used often in Russian cooking. The versatile herb dill is by far the favorite Russian flavoring. With these foods the Slavs developed a basic cuisine that was wholesome, hearty and plentiful, that was suitable for a cold climate and hard-working people and that has survived many centuries.

Changes and refinements in this basic cuisine came with

political entanglements and territorial expansion. The first of many outside influences was that of the northern Vikings. In 862 A.D., the agriculturally oriented Slavs, feeling the pressures of impending invasions, invited a Viking ruler, Rurik, to form a protective city-state for them. Thus Novgorod, or "new town," became the first Russian capital, and the name of Rurik's warriors, Rus, or "of the earth," was taken for the settlement and eventually for the country.

The Slavs also acquired from their northern neighbors some significant culinary and dining customs. They adopted the Viking practice of using preserved fish, especially herring and eel, in hot and cold dishes. They developed the Scandinavian fondness for chilled fruit soups and adopted the customs of serving cooked fruits, particularly tart berries, with poultry, game and meats and of using dried fruits, such as prunes and apples, for stuffings. The Russian preference for pancakes is also believed to have been derived from the northerners.

Most significantly, however, the Slavs became enamored of the Viking convivial premeal spread, or cold board, enlivened by potent spirits. In Russia the smorgasbord became *zakusky.* At first zakusky relied heavily on salted herring and other fish, game and meats, but it was expanded to a galaxy of the finest fare. The Russians loved spirited, robust eating and drinking, and relished the frequent toasts in which they downed in one gulp small glasses of their favorite vodka. Certainly the zakusky tradition is one of the greatest Russian dining customs.

Vodka, now internationally known, is the preferred Russian alcoholic drink. "Little water," as it means, is an unaged grain alcohol distilled from wheat, although it may also be made with corn, rye or potatoes. Vodka is generally colorless; however, the Russians also enjoy vodka in several colors and flavors. One pinkish variety is infused with berries, and a yellowish type, called *zubrovka,* is colored with buffalo grass.

A successor of Rurik, Vladimir the Saint, made further changes to the basic Russian cuisine when he enlarged his kingdom by conquering the southern Slavs and their capital, Kiev. In addition, by the time of his conquest, numerous Byzantine influences had infiltrated northward from Greece. The most important Byzantine influence was the Eastern Orthodox faith, which Vladimir accepted in 988 A.D. for all his people. For centuries thereafter the Russian Orthodox Church, the official state religion, regulated the year-round ritual of rigid fast days and colorful religious festivals. The principal feast day was the beloved Easter, "the holiday of holidays and the celebration of celebrations," when lengthy traditional meals with symbolic foods were carefully prepared and joyously eaten.

In southern Russia, the Slavs and the people of the Caucasus acquired from the Byzantines, and later from the Turks and other Near Easterners, a liking for foods and dishes not known in the north until modern times. People in the south had a greater variety of fresh vegetables, for example, and they especially liked tomatoes, peppers and eggplants. Many varieties of stuffed vegetables are specialties of the Armenians and Azerbaidjanis. In some regions, rice replaced the northern buckwheat groats, and pilafs, enhanced with poultry, game, fruits and nuts, became everyday fare. Sour cream gave way to yogurt, and rich nut and honey pastries were typical desserts. Flavorings such as garlic, onions, mint, pine nuts, lemon juice, olive oil, coriander and spices played significant roles in cookery development.

Further culinary impressions were left by the Tartar invaders from Central Asia, who overran and conquered most of Russia in the thirteenth century and remained for some 200 years. The Tartars left behind lasting oriental traces in Russian culture and cuisine. From them the Russians acquired a taste for sour foods and flavorings. Sour cream, for example, is a national passion, which leads many visitors to Russia to believe that nothing in the cuisine could be prepared or served without the rich, tart *smetana*. The Tartars also introduced the use of curd or cottage cheese in many dishes—as a stuffing for unsweetened pastries and as a filling for dumplings, for example. A tart beverage, *kumiss*, was made from fermented mare's milk.

One of the most significant Tartar contributions was the secret for fermenting cabbage, or sauerkraut, which ever since has been a Russian staple, eaten as a snack, cooked in soups and used as a stuffing.

Because the Tartars ate raw meat, an embellished ground or scraped beef specialty eventually became known in the western world as steak tartare. It is generally acknowledged that these easterners also introduced the Russians to the national pastime of drinking tea, an all-day preoccupation, as well as to the samovar, the ornate urn in which the water for tea was kept boiling.

Ivan III, the first grand duke of Muscovy, regarded as the founder of the Russian Empire, finally repelled the Tartars. He imported architects from Italy, who not only enlarged the Kremlin but who also introduced the Russians to noodles, macaroni, sherbets, ice creams and pastries, which thereafter became cherished foods. Court banquets at this time were boisterous celebrations, with emphasis on quantity rather than on quality. Ivan's grandson, Ivan the Terrible, despite his cognomen, enjoyed luxury, attempted to introduce refinements in cookery and dining, and himself preferred dainty dishes to more hearty meat specialties.

Peter the Great, who ascended the throne in the late seventeenth century, devoted himself to the modernization of Russia by decreeing the introduction of West European civilization in all aspects. In his newly built capital, Saint Petersburg (now Leningrad), the czar imposed western-inspired modes in dress, manners and etiquette. A gargantuan diner, Peter was so interested in culinary affairs that he sought out foreign dishes while traveling, imported French chefs and even entered the royal kitchens to prepare some of his own meals. He became particularly intrigued with such Dutch food products as cheeses, white breads and honey cakes, and because of his close associations with the Prussian court, he is credited with the introduction into Russia of such German fare as sausages, roast goose and duck with red cabbage. By Peter's time there also had been a number of culinary exchanges with Poland, and the Polish origin of many dishes that are well known in Byelorussia is still debated.

By the late eighteenth century reign of Catherine the Great, there was a definite Russian upper-class preoccupation with the enjoyment of lengthy and lavish meals that were as expensive and expansive as possible. Although born a German princess, Catherine became a devoted Francophile who enthusiastically adopted French culture and established among the aristocrats a vogue for French chefs and cooking. Most of the rich Russian sauces and puréed or creamed soups can be traced to French influence. The greatest gourmet among Russian rulers, Czar Alexander I, continued the French culinary craze and retained the world-famous chef, Antonin Carême, to supervise the imperial kitchens. For the czar, Carême created the now-famous charlotte russe, among other elegant desserts.

Strangely enough, the preoccupation with European chefs, dishes and modes in entertaining did not really alter basic Russian cookery. It merely added some refinements to the cuisine and embellishments to the decor. Even on the royal tables, buckwheat groats, pickled foods, hearty soups, sausages, herring casseroles, stuffed pastries, dark breads and vodka were served along with more elegant continentally inspired food and wines.

In the Soviet Union the lavish entertaining of bygone czarist days was definitely frowned upon, but this did not alter the national desire for good food and convivial family and holiday meals. The traditions of the fifteen republics that comprise the USSR continue to flourish. Gradually the exchange of foods and dishes within the country has increased. Northern city restaurants have begun to feature Caucasian and Central Asian specialties. Home cooking has become more versatile as a greater range of ingredients has become available.

Today the love of good eating and drinking continues in Russia as it has for centuries, reflecting the traditional esteem for the art of cooking and the pleasure of dining in good company. This selection of recipes gives you an opportunity to experience the best in Russian cookery.

ZAKUSKY

A very typical and pleasurable Russian dining custom, which takes place before the main meal, is the enjoyment of cold and hot appetizers, zakusky, accompanied by vodka. Believed to have been adapted from the Scandinavian smorgasbord when Rurik became the first czar of Russia, zakusky became particularly lavish during the nineteenth century, when the nobility gathered daily in handsome homes to partake of regal repasts.

Zakuska, the singular of zakusky, means literally "bite down," and the tradition is to drink a glass of vodka neat and then to "bite it down" with one or more appetizers. The simplest and most common zakuska is herring in one form or another. Generally, however, the herring is accompanied by other foods such as pickles, sausage, cheese, vegetable salads, other kinds of fish, breads and butter. Traditionally the zakusky and vodka are set up in the living or reception room on a cloth-covered table with small plates, implements and glasses. Each person, customarily standing, helps himself to the food and vodka during this premeal social hour or two.

From humble beginnings, the zakusky array expanded considerably to become one of the world's most appealing appetizer assortments, distinguished by artful seasonings, colorful garnishes and inviting culinary contrasts. Imperial Russian tables groaned with sumptuous displays of as many as sixty or seventy creative dishes, which were eaten with a wide selection of vodkas downed in considerable quantity.

Today the Russians do not concentrate on the opulent settings of the bygone czarist days, but they do continue an elaborate dining tradition with the enjoyment of zakusky. The repertoire for a special occasion might be expanded to include cold meats and poultry, preserved fish, stuffed and pickled vegetables, pâtés, fish in aspic, galantines, vegetables in sour cream, savory souffles, filled pastries, casseroles, salads of cooked vegetables and fish or meat and a particular favorite, buckwheat pancakes. The noblest of all the foods, however, is caviar, offered in variety and quantity to the extent the pocketbook permits.

Generally speaking, Americans do not have or choose not to have the dining capacity of the Russians, so they often do not favor the serving of a galaxy of dishes before a meal. However, you may wish to serve a few of these appetizers with drinks before dinner or one or more as a first course at the table. Or, an array of the zakusky would be good fare for a buffet supper or dinner or cocktail party.

The recipes in this section are a few of the many characteristic Russian zakusky dishes. Recipes for some of the salad and vegetable creations that are often served as a part of zakusky, are on pages 36 to 40.

Estonian Herring Salad

Russians almost always eat the humble salt herring, caught in large quantities in the North and Baltic Seas, with vodka. The salted or preserved fish may be served merely with oil and vinegar in a marinade or made into many kinds of inventive dishes. This preparation, a cold vegetable-herring salad called rossolye, is traditional fare in Estonia as well as in the neighboring Baltic republics.

3 medium potatoes, boiled, peeled and cut into ¼-inch cubes	1 medium tart apple, cored, peeled and diced
	1 medium onion, peeled and chopped

2 medium dill pickles, diced
1 fillet of pickled herring,
  diced
4 canned beets, cut into
  ¼-inch cubes
2 hard-cooked eggs, shelled
  and diced
1 cup (about) sour cream

2 tablespoons wine vinegar
2 tablespoons sharp mustard
1 teaspoon sugar
Salt to taste
Garnishes: cooked beet
slices, hard-cooked egg
wedges

Combine first seven ingredients and mix lightly. Mix together sour cream, vinegar, mustard, sugar and salt and spoon over the other ingredients. Mix. Use enough sour cream to bind the ingredients. Serve in a mound on a plate or in a bowl. Garnish with beet slices and egg wedges. Serves 6.

Pickled Mushrooms

Mushrooms are a staple in Russia, eaten in great quantity and variety. In the autumn families gather many kinds of wild mushrooms, which they dry or preserve for use throughout the year. One of the most popular dishes is pickled mushrooms, an important zakuska.

1 pound small fresh
  mushrooms
  Salt
  Water
⅔ cup red wine vinegar

1 small bay leaf
6 whole peppercorns
3 whole cloves
2 teaspoons salt
1 tablespoon vegetable oil

Clean mushrooms by removing any dirt with wet paper towels or by rinsing quickly under running water. Remove stems and save for use in some other dish. Put caps in a saucepan with lightly salted water to cover. Bring to a boil and simmer 5 minutes. Drain and cool. Spoon into a jar. Put vinegar, bay leaf, peppercorns, cloves and salt in a saucepan and bring to a boil. Pour over mushrooms. Spoon oil over them and cover jar tightly. Leave for at least 3 days before serving. Remove from marinade to serve. Serves 4 to 6.

Radish Salad

Raw vegetables in a sour cream sauce or marinade are customarily served as a part of the zakusky.

2 hard-cooked eggs, shelled	2 cups sliced red radishes
1 cup sour cream	2 tablespoons fresh parsley
Salt, pepper to taste	or dill, chopped

Cut eggs into halves and remove yolks. Mash yolks with a fork; chop whites. Mix yolks with sour cream, salt and pepper. Put radishes in a small bowl and spoon sour cream mixture over them. Sprinkle with chopped egg whites and parsley. Chill. Serves 4.

Bliny

Buckwheat yeast pancakes, called bliny or "bleeny," are great Russian favorites, usually eaten as appetizers. Although bliny may be served stuffed or folded over, the preferred way is to spread the small thin pancakes with melted butter, then with a piece or slice of smoked, salted or pickled fish or caviar and then with a dab of sour cream. Other widely used fillings or spreads include mushrooms and cottage cheese. Each year during Maslenitsa, or "butter festival," the carnival week before Lent, the Russians indulge in a bliny binge. Everyone consumes the pancakes in great quantities, as snacks throughout the day or with meals. Bliny batter is made in several variations, but a popular mixture is that of half buckwheat and half white flour.

1 package active dry yeast;	3 eggs, separated
or 1 cake compressed yeast	1 teaspoon sugar
1 cup lukewarm water	1 teaspoon salt
2 cups warm milk	3 tablespoons melted butter
1½ cups sifted all-purpose	2½ cups sifted buckwheat flour
white flour	Butter or shortening for
	frying

Sprinkle the dry yeast or crumble the cake yeast into a large bowl. Add water (use very warm water for dry yeast and lukewarm for cake yeast). Let stand a minute or two and then stir to dissolve. Add milk and white flour. Beat well and put in a warm place. Cover with a clean light towel, and let dough rise until doubled in bulk, about 1 hour. Beat egg yolks until creamy and add sugar, salt, melted butter and buckwheat flour. Stir into the yeast mixture and set again in a warm place, covered, to rise for 1 hour. Beat egg whites until stiff and fold into the mixture. Pour a little batter onto a hot greased griddle or heavy skillet and cook until lightly browned on the bottom. Turn over and cook on the other side. Keep warm while cooking the others. Makes about 3½ dozen. Serve on a platter accompanied by a small bowl of melted butter, one of sour cream and a plate of chopped salt herring, sliced smoked salmon or caviar.

Salat Olivier

This well-liked zakusky dish, a chicken and vegetable salad, was created by Olivier, Czar Nicholas II's French chef, and named by the czar in his honor. The ingredients vary considerably, but generally they are a rich medley combined with a flavorful sauce and garnished ornately.

1 cup cooked white chicken, shredded or cubed	½ cup mayonnaise
3 medium potatoes, boiled, peeled and diced	½ cup (about) sour cream
	2 tablespoons drained capers
2 medium carrots, scraped, cooked and diced	1 tablespoon chopped fresh dill
1 cup cooked green peas	Salt, pepper to taste
½ cup dill pickles, diced	Garnishes: pitted black olives, tomato wedges,
6 green onions, with tops, cleaned and chopped	hard-cooked egg wedges

Combine first six ingredients. Mix together mayonnaise, sour cream, capers, dill, salt and pepper and add to chicken-vegetable mixture. Serve shaped as a mound or pyramid on a plate or in a bowl. Garnish with olives, tomatoes and eggs. Serves 6.

Caviar

The choicest zakusky specialty is caviar, the roe that is carefully extracted from four species of sturgeon. The roe is called *ikra* in Russia; outside of Russia, it is called caviar, from the Turkish word *khavyah*. Appreciated as an expensive delicacy for decades, the "black pearls" are still luxury fare and served only on affluent tables. The roe of the Volga sterlet, the legendary gold caviar once reserved only for czars, is the most highly prized caviar and has the finest flavor. The biggest of the sturgeon, the beluga, produces the largest of the choice firm fresh eggs, which are named for it and which may be either black or gray. The medium-sized osetrova and smaller sevruga sturgeon yield medium and small choice eggs, which also are named for these two fish.

A primary reason for the high cost of caviar is the necessary roe extraction process, which must be done by hand and by experienced workers. The eggs have to be taken immediately from the freshly caught fish, and they must be removed just before the roe is fully ripe or ready for spawning. Then the roe is sieved by hand to remove any mucus and membranes. The best quality eggs are lightly salted, which in Russian is called *malossol*. Thus many persons consider beluga malossol the most desirable type of caviar. Damaged or less choice eggs are pressed and sold more cheaply. Another reason for the high cost is that fresh caviar is difficult to ship, as it must be specially packed in airtight containers, sealed and stored or transported at carefully regulated temperatures.

Although only the eggs of sturgeon are considered truly worthy to be called caviar, the name is also applied to the roe of other species of fish. Particular favorites in Russia are the red or pink eggs of fresh and salt water salmon, which when served on buttered pumpernickel and garnished with a dab of sour cream make appealing appetizers.

Caviar connoisseurs dote on dispensing advice about the selection, serving and eating of this prized delicacy and many of their opinions have been personally well researched and are respected. Suffice it to say that if you are lucky enough to have some of the "black gold," which sells for about $80 a pound, it should be spooned and eaten directly from the original ice-packed container without any adornments or accompaniments. Some persons, however, prefer to serve caviar on lightly buttered toast or black bread, with a small sprinkle of fresh lemon juice. Purists frown at the custom of embellishing fresh caviar with chopped hard-cooked eggs or onion.

The following two recipes use less expensive or pressed caviar.

Caviar-Stuffed Eggs

Cut 8 hard-cooked eggs in lengthwise halves. Take out yolks and sieve. Spoon black or red caviar into the egg shells. Sprinkle with fresh lemon juice and the sieved yolks. Top each with a dab of sour cream. Serve as a part of the zakusky or as a first course. Serves 8.

Eggs à la Russe

Cut 6 hard-cooked eggs in lengthwise halves. Place, yolk-sides down, on small individual plates or on one large plate. Cover with a sauce made by combining 1 cup sour cream, ½ cup black caviar, 2 tablespoons lemon juice, 3 tablespoons chopped chives and freshly ground pepper. Chill. Serves 6.

Forshmak

During the reign of Catherine the Great a number of hot dishes inspired by German tastes were introduced into the zakusky array. One of these dishes is called forshmak, which means "warm appetizer." This dish is still very popular and can be served with a hot tomato sauce, if desired.

1 medium onion, peeled and minced	1 pickled herring, minced
2 tablespoons butter or margarine	3 medium potatoes, boiled, peeled and mashed
2 cups chicken, ham or veal, diced and cooked	3 eggs, separated
	1 cup sour cream at room temperature

¼ cup fresh dill or parsley,   Fine dry bread crumbs
  chopped
Salt, pepper to taste

In a small saucepan, sauté onion in butter until tender. Mix in a bowl with chicken, herring and mashed potatoes, which preferably should still be warm. Stir the egg yolks until creamy and mix with chicken combination. Add sour cream and dill; season with salt and pepper. Beat the egg whites until stiff and fold into the mixture. Spoon into a buttered soufflé or baking dish and sprinkle the top with bread crumbs. Cook in a preheated hot oven (400°F.) for 25 minutes, or until hot. Serve warm. Serves 4 to 6 as an appetizer.

Mushroom-filled Pirozhki

Small oval or round plump pastries made with nonsweet dough and filled with various food combinations are called pirozhki. The term is derived from an old Russian word *pir*, meaning feast. Pirozhki are made with both raised dough and plain pastry, and can be filled with mixtures based on mushrooms, cabbage, chicken, ground beef or fish. Pirozhki are popular appetizers and also are served with soups. Generally those that will be used with soups are made a little larger, about 5 inches in diameter.

1 envelope active dry yeast   4½ to 5 cups all-purpose flour
  or 1 cake compressed yeast   3 eggs
¼ cup lukewarm water   Mushroom filling
½ cup butter or margarine   (recipe follows)
1 cup lukewarm milk   1 egg yolk
1 teaspoon salt   2 tablespoons cold water
2 teaspoons sugar

Sprinkle the yeast or crumble the cake into a large bowl and add water. After a minute or two stir to dissolve. (Use very warm water for dry yeast and lukewarm for cake yeast.) Put butter in milk and leave until melted. Add butter and milk, with salt and sugar, to yeast. Stir in 1 cup of flour and then eggs, beating well after each addition. Add the remaining flour, enough to make a soft dough. Turn out on a floured board. Knead dough until smooth and elastic. Form into a large ball and put in a large greased bowl. Turn the dough over so it becomes greased on both sides. Cover with a towel and leave in a warm place to rise until doubled in bulk, about 1½ hours. Punch down dough. Turn out onto a floured board and knead until smooth and elastic. Cut off small pieces of dough and flatten into thin circles, about 2½ inches in diameter. Place about 1 teaspoon of Mushroom Filling (recipe follows) in the center of each circle. Bring up the dough around the filling to secure completely and shape into a smooth round. Place on a greased cookie sheet. Let rise, covered with a light cloth or towel, in a warm place for 20 minutes, or until pirozhki are light and somewhat larger. Mix the egg yolk with the water and brush the tops with it. Bake in a preheated hot oven (400°F.) for about 20 minutes, or until the tops are golden and the dough is baked. Serve warm. Makes about 3½ dozen.

Mushroom filling

½ pound fresh mushrooms	Salt, pepper, nutmeg to
½ cup chopped green onions,	taste
with tops	3 tablespoons chopped dill
3 tablespoons butter or	or parsley
margarine	¼ cup sour cream, at room
	temperature

Clean mushrooms by rinsing quickly or wiping with wet paper towels. Cut off any tough stem ends. Chop finely. Sauté chopped green onions in butter until tender. Add chopped mushrooms and sauté 4 minutes. Season with salt, pepper and nutmeg. Remove from heat and stir in dill and sour cream. Let cool.

Salmon Kulebiaka

This delectable filled dough, which can be made with a short pastry or yeast dough, may be filled with white fish or salmon or a combination of the two, and can include buckwheat groats instead of rice. Kulebiaka is an excellent buffet dish, appetizer or first course.

1 package active dry yeast or 1 cake compressed yeast	3½ cups (about) sifted all-purpose flour
⅔ cup lukewarm milk	Salmon filling (recipe follows)
¼ cup butter or margarine, melted	2 cups cold cooked rice
4 eggs	3 hard-cooked eggs, shelled and sliced
1 tablespoon sugar	
Pinch salt	

Sprinkle or crumble yeast in a large bowl; add some of the milk (it should be slightly warmer for dry yeast). After a minute or two stir to dissolve. Add remaining milk, melted butter, 3 eggs (one at a time), sugar and salt. Mix well. Add 1½ cups flour and beat well to combine ingredients. Add remaining flour, enough to make a soft dough, and beat well again. Turn dough out onto a floured board and knead until smooth and elastic. Form into a large ball and place in a greased bowl. Turn dough over once to grease other side. Leave in a warm place, covered with a towel, until doubled in bulk, about 1½ hours. Punch down and turn out onto a floured board. Knead again. Roll into a rectangle, 20 inches by 14 inches. Spread ½ of the Salmon Filling lengthwise along the center of the rectangle, leaving a 4-inch border on all sides. Place layers of rice, egg slices, and remaining Salmon Filling over the dough. Bring the long sides of the dough together and pinch. Fold the two short sides over and pinch. Seal the edges with water and press to close firmly. Butter and flour a cookie sheet and carefully place the filled dough on it so that the sealed edges are down. Make several small slashes in the top of the dough. Cover with a cloth and let rise in a warm place for about 30 minutes, until light and enlarged. Beat the remaining egg slightly and brush over the top. Bake in a preheated moderate (375°F.) oven about 30 minutes, until the dough is crisp and golden. To serve, slice crosswise. Makes 12 to 14 servings.

Note: The top may be decorated with pastry leaves cut from the dough, if desired.

Salmon filling

2 medium onions, peeled and chopped	3 cups cooked red salmon, flaked
¼ cup butter or margarine	¼ cup fresh dill or parsley, chopped
1 cup chopped mushrooms	
2 tablespoons lemon juice	Salt, pepper to taste

Sauté the onions in butter until tender. Add mushrooms and lemon juice and sauté 4 minutes. Mix with remaining ingredients and cool.

SOUPS

Shchi

In Russia soups are basic foods, ranking in importance after breads and grains. The most common soup is made with cabbage and is called shchi, or s'chee. Over the years the soup has provided sustenance and nourishment to a vast population. It is particularly favored because it does not require a meat base. During the summer the soup is made with fresh cabbage and called "lazy," while during the winter sauerkraut is used, and the name is changed to "sour." All the kinds of shchi are hearty dishes and are very rich in vitamins. The ingredients usually include whatever is on hand. Beef, sausages and smoked pork add further sustenance to some of the cabbage soups. Shchi is often served with kasha (see page 21) and garnished with sour cream. This is one variation.

1 large onion, peeled and sliced	1 stalk celery, cleaned and sliced
1 leek, white part only, cleaned and sliced	½ turnip, peeled and cubed (optional)
2 medium carrots, scraped and sliced ¼ inch thick	3 tablespoons bacon fat or shortening

8 cups beef bouillon
1 head green cabbage, about 1½ pounds, cored, cleaned and shredded

1 can (6 ounces) tomato paste
3 tablespoons chopped fresh dill or parsley

Sauté onion, leek, carrots, celery, and turnip in bacon fat in a large kettle. Add beef bouillon and bring to a boil. Stir in cabbage and tomato paste and reduce heat. Cook slowly, covered, for about 1 hour, or until vegetables are cooked. Sprinkle with chopped dill or parsley. Serves 6 to 8.

Note: After the soup is cooked, thicken with flour browned in butter, if desired. Potatoes, peeled and cubed, may be added about 20 minutes before the soup is finished cooking.

Caucasian Chikhirtma

A characteristic soup of the Caucasus is made with chicken or lamb and has a tart flavor achieved with vinegar or lemon juice. Egg yolks and fresh coriander further enhance the flavor.

6 cups chicken broth
1 cup slivered cooked chicken
½ teaspoon powdered saffron (optional)
1 large onion, peeled and chopped

1 tablespoon butter or margarine
1 tablespoon flour
2 egg yolks
⅓ cup fresh lemon juice
3 tablespoons fresh coriander or parsley

Put chicken broth and chicken in a large saucepan and heat. Dissolve saffron in a little hot water and stir into hot broth. In a small saucepan, sauté onion in butter until tender. Stir in flour and cook several seconds. Spoon into hot soup and stir until thickened. Beat egg yolks in a small bowl and pour in 1 cup of hot broth. Beat well and slowly pour into saucepan, stirring while pouring. Simmer another minute or two until the soup thickens. Taste for seasoning. Sprinkle with coriander. Serve at once. Serves 6.

Fish Solianka

This soup, made with either fish or meat, also reflects the Russian fondness for a tart flavor. In this dish, tartness is achieved with the addition of salted cucumber, capers and olives. In Russia Fish Solianka is traditionally made with sturgeon, but any firm white-fleshed fish will do. There are some stews and vegetable dishes in Russia that are also called Solianka.

2½ pounds whole white-fleshed fish (halibut, haddock)	2 tablespoons butter or margarine
3 medium onions, peeled and chopped	2 large tomatoes, peeled and chopped
1 bay leaf	1 medium salted cucumber, peeled and chopped
3 sprigs parsley	3 tablespoons drained capers
2 whole cloves	12 pitted black olives
6 peppercorns	2 tablespoons chopped dill or parsley
Salt to taste	Lemon slices

Have the fish dealer dress and fillet the fish. Take home the trimmings, heads and bones as well as the fillets. Cut the fillets into bite-sized pieces.

To cook, put the trimmings, heads and bones in a kettle with 1 chopped onion, bay leaf, parsley, cloves, peppercorns, salt and 2½ quarts water. Cook, covered, over a medium fire for 30 minutes. Strain broth and discard the ingredients. Sauté remaining 2 onions in butter until tender. Add tomatoes and cook 2 minutes, stirring. Put this mixture, with cucumber, capers, olives, fish pieces and strained broth, in a large kettle. Cook slowly, covered, until fish is tender, about 8 minutes. Remove and discard bay leaf, cloves and peppercorns. Correct the seasoning to taste. Serve in bowls garnished with lemon slices and dill. Serves 6.

Okroshka

This chilled meat and vegetable soup is a popular warm-weather dish and is sometimes served with ice cubes in it. The traditional flavoring for the soup is derived from kvass, a fermented and slightly alcoholic liquid made from grain and used as a beverage and soup stock. There is no real substitute for kvass, but some suggestions are given.

1 cup cold cooked beef, ham or veal, diced	4 cups apple cider, beer or a mixture of 3 cups beef bouillon and 1 cup white wine
1 medium cucumber, peeled and diced	
½ cup sliced green onions, with tops	2 teaspoons sharp prepared mustard
2 hard-cooked eggs, shelled and chopped	1 teaspoon sugar
	Salt, to taste
½ cup (approximately) sour cream	3 tablespoons chopped dill or parsley

Combine the first 4 ingredients. Mix together the sour cream, cider or other liquid, mustard, sugar and salt and beat well. Add beef mixture and chill. Serve sprinkled with the dill. Serves 6.

Borshch

The second most popular soup in Russia is based on beets and is called borshch, or derivations of that name. Believed to have originated in the Ukraine, the soup is made in many variations. It can be prepared with only beets; it may include additional vegetables, with or without meat; or it may include poultry or game. Borshch can be served hot or cold, and it is generally garnished with sour cream. The kind of borshch that is made in the Ukraine is very hearty. It differs from the other varieties in that it includes garlic, tomatoes and pork as well as beef and a great number of vegetables. All the kinds of borshch are excellent soups and are particularly good when reheated. This is one variation I like. It is a one-dish meal, good for a winter supper.

8 medium beets	½ cup vinegar
Salt	Water

2 pounds soup beef
3 cracked soup bones
½ pound lean fresh pork
1 medium bay leaf
8 peppercorns
2 sprigs parsley
1 garlic clove, halved
3 medium carrots, scraped
and sliced
2 medium onions, peeled
and chopped

2 medium leeks, white part
only, washed and sliced
½ small head cabbage,
coarsely chopped
3 medium tomatoes, peeled
and chopped
1 or 2 teaspoons sugar
1 cup sour cream at
room temperature

Wash beets and cook 7 of them whole and unpeeled, in salted water to cover, with ¼ cup of vinegar. Cook 30 to 40 minutes, until tender. Drain; peel beets and julienne. Put beef, bones, pork and 2½ quarts cold water in a large kettle. Bring to a boil. Skim well. Add bay leaf, peppercorns, parsley, garlic, carrots, onions and leeks and cook slowly, covered, for 1½ hours, or until the meat is tender. Add cabbage, tomatoes and cooked beets; continue to cook slowly for another 30 minutes, or until ingredients are tender. Remove meat and cut up, discarding any bones and gristle. Take out and discard bones, bay leaf, peppercorns, parsley and garlic. Return cut-up meat to the kettle. Season with salt. Peel and grate remaining beet. Place in a saucepan with 1 cup of hot soup stock, the remaining ¼ cup of vinegar and sugar. Bring to a boil. Stir into the soup and warm up, if necessary. Ladle soup into bowls and garnish with a spoonful of sour cream. Serves 8 to 10.
Note: Four peeled and cubed medium potatoes may be added to the soup about 20 minutes before it is finished, if desired.

GRAINS

Kasha

Kasha, a dry porridge made with a grain, usually buckwheat

groats, is eaten in Russia as a staple. Kasha can be also prepared
with oats, barley, wheat or millet. Buckwheat groats, originally
introduced by tribes migrating from Siberia and Central Asia
to Eastern Europe, have been eaten in Russia and Poland for
centuries. They can be easily grown, and they are nourishing,
flavorful and inexpensive. Kasha is eaten with milk for breakfast
and is used as an accompaniment to other foods, as an ingredient
in soups and stews and as a stuffing or filling. Leftover kasha
can be fried and served with melted butter or sour cream. The
basic recipe given below can be further enriched with sautéed
onions and mushrooms or combined with sour cream and cottage
cheese and baked. In the United States, buckwheat groats are
packaged and sold as kasha.

1 cup medium kasha (buckwheat groats)	2 cups boiling water
	1 or 2 tablespoons butter or margarine
1 egg, slightly beaten	
1 teaspoon salt	

Combine kasha and egg in a bowl. Put into an ungreased skillet
or saucepan and cook, uncovered, stirring constantly, until grains
are toasted and separate. Add salt and boiling water and cook
slowly, tightly covered, for about 30 minutes, or until grains are
tender and liquid is absorbed. Stir in butter. Serves 6.

Caucasian Rice with Fruit

In the Caucasus, rice replaces buckwheat groats as the staple
grain. Dishes made with rice are called *plov*, the Russian version
of pilaf, believed to have originated in the Central Asian provinces
and still popular there. The most flavorful combinations are the
so-called "sweet ones," which include in their ingredients raisins
or currants, nuts, fruits, and sometimes honey. Other plovs are
made with lamb, chicken, herbs or vegetables.

1 cup dried apricots	3 cups chicken broth
½ cup seedless raisins	1½ cups uncooked rice
¼ teaspoon ground saffron	Salt, pepper to taste
3 tablespoons butter or margarine	

Cover apricots and raisins with boiling water and soak for a few hours. Drain and cut apricots into bite-sized pieces. Steep saffron in 2 tablespoons hot water. Melt butter in a saucepan. Add chicken broth and bring to a boil. Stir in rice, season with salt and pepper. Add apricots, raisins and saffron. Mix well. Lower heat and cook slowly, covered, about 25 minutes, until rice is tender, grains are separate and liquid is absorbed. Serves 6 to 8.

Armenian Cracked Wheat Pilaf

Cracked wheat, or bulgur, a staple grain in many southern areas of Eastern Europe, consists of small brown kernels, actually hulled and pounded wheat. Bulgur has a delectable flavor and is an excellent accompaniment to roast meats and poultry. It can be purchased in Middle Eastern or specialty food stores. A national favorite in Armenia, bulgur also appears in a cinnamon-flavored lamb pilaf.

3 tablespoons butter or margarine	1 cup medium cracked wheat (bulgur)
1 medium onion, peeled and chopped	2½ - 3 cups beef bouillon or consommé
2 medium tomatoes, peeled and chopped	Salt, pepper to taste

Melt butter in a skillet; sauté onion in butter until tender. Add tomatoes and cook 1 minute, mashing with a fork. Stir in cracked wheat and sauté, stirring constantly, for 3 minutes. Add 2½ cups of bouillon, salt and pepper. Mix well. Bring to a boil. Lower heat and cook slowly, covered, about 30 minutes, or until cracked wheat is tender. If more liquid is needed, add more bouillon as wheat cooks. Serves 4.

ENTRÉES

Sturgeon Baked in Sour Cream

Of the many species of fish enjoyed in Russia, the greatest favorite is sturgeon, which is prepared in many creative dishes. The most characteristic way of cooking sturgeon, as well as other fish, is with piquant sauces sharpened with mustard, capers, pickles, horseradish or sour cream. In America, this dish can be made with any firm white-fleshed fish as a substitute for fresh sturgeon, which unfortunately is difficult to find in our stores.

2 pounds white-fleshed fish fillets (haddock, mackerel or cod)
Flour
Salt, pepper to taste
2 hard-cooked eggs, shelled and sliced
½ pound fresh mushrooms, cleaned and sliced

2 tablespoons butter or margarine
1 tablespoon fresh lemon juice
1 cup sour cream at room temperature
3 tablespoons fresh dill or parsley, chopped

Cut fish into serving portions and wipe dry. Dust with flour and sprinkle with salt and pepper. Arrange in a buttered shallow baking dish and place sliced eggs over fish. Sauté mushrooms in butter and lemon juice for 3 minutes and spoon over eggs. Spoon sour cream over mushrooms and sprinkle with dill. Bake in a preheated moderate oven (350°F.) for about 20 minutes, until fish is tender. Serves 4.

Armenian Fish Plaki

In Armenia, a typical way of preparing fresh fish is to cook it with a topping of several sautéed vegetables. This makes a truly flavorful entrée.

2 medium onions, peeled and sliced
1 or 2 garlic cloves, crushed
½ cup olive or vegetable oil
3 medium tomatoes, peeled and chopped
2 medium carrots, scraped and sliced thinly

2 stalks celery, cleaned and sliced
Salt, pepper to taste
2 pounds white-fleshed fish fillets (halibut, cod, mackerel, haddock)
2 large lemons, sliced
3 tablespoons chopped fresh dill or parsley

In a large skillet, sauté onions and garlic in oil until tender. Add tomatoes, carrots and celery and cook for 5 minutes. Season with salt and pepper. Arrange fish fillets in a buttered shallow baking dish and cover with vegetable mixture. Arrange lemon slices over them. Sprinkle with dill or parsley. Bake in a preheated moderate oven (350°F.) about 20 minutes, or until fish is fork-tender. Serve hot or cold. Serves 4.

Note: Sautéed potato slices may be added to the vegetable medley, if desired.

Bream Stuffed with Buckwheat Groats

A small freshwater fish called bream, which in appearance resembles the carp, is well-liked in Eastern Europe. In the United States the name "bream" is sometimes used for sunfish. Good substitutes for bream are crappie, porgy and sunfish.

2 medium onions, peeled and chopped
6 tablespoons butter or margarine
2 cups cooked buckwheat groats
2 hard-cooked eggs, shelled and chopped
2 tablespoons chopped fresh parsley

2 tablespoons chopped fresh dill
Salt, pepper to taste
6 small white-fleshed fish (porgies, crappies, sunfish), each fish about 1 pound, cleaned
Fine dry bread crumbs
1 cup sour cream at room temperature

Sauté onions in 3 tablespoons of butter. Add cooked buckwheat, chopped eggs, parsley, dill, salt and pepper. Mix well. Wash fish and wipe dry. Sprinkle cavities with salt and fill with stuffing. Arrange fish in a buttered shallow baking dish. Melt remaining 3 tablespoons butter and sprinkle over fish; sprinkle also with bread crumbs. Bake in a preheated hot oven (400°F.) about 10 minutes, or until fish are almost tender. Spoon sour cream over fish and cook another 5 minutes. Serves 6.

Note: If there is stuffing left over, serve it with the fish.

Fish with Apple-Horseradish Sauce

This is another Russian fish dish, with a piquant, flavored sauce.

2 pounds white-fleshed fish (halibut, cod or haddock)	2 sprigs parsley
1 cup wine vinegar	6 peppercorns
1 leek, white part only, cleaned and sliced	Salt to taste
	¼ cup freshly grated or pre-
2 medium onions, peeled and sliced	pared horseradish, well drained
2 small bay leaves	1 cup puréed apples
¼ teaspoon dried thyme	1 tablespoon sugar
	Lemon wedges

Cut fish into serving portions and put in a large saucepan. Cover with the vinegar. Bring to a boil; remove from the stove. Put leek, onions, bay leaves, thyme, parsley, peppercorns and salt, with water to cover, in another saucepan. Bring to a boil. Lower heat and cook slowly, covered, for 5 minutes. Remove fish from the vinegar and add to the vegetable mixture. Then cook slowly, covered, about 5 minutes, or until fish is fork-tender. Remove fish to a warm platter and keep warm. Combine horseradish, apples and sugar to make a piquant sauce. Thin with a little vinegar, if desired. Serve sauce and lemon wedges with fish. Serves 4.

Chicken Kotlety Pozharsky

These tasty and golden fried chicken cutlets are named for the owner of an inn at Torzhok, which was once a popular stopover for travelers journeying between Moscow and St. Petersburg. Originally the cutlets were made with game.

4 slices stale white bread, crusts removed	4 tablespoons softened butter or margarine
⅓ cup (about) milk	Salt, pepper to taste
2 cups finely chopped raw chicken	Fine dry bread crumbs
	Butter or oil for frying

Soak bread in milk for about 20 minutes. Squeeze dry and mix with chicken. Put chicken and bread through a meat grinder. Mix with softened butter; season with salt and pepper. With wet hands, shape mixture into oval patties; cover patties with bread crumbs. Fry in hot butter or oil until golden and crisp on all sides. Serves 2.

Chicken Kiev

One of the best-known and most delectable Russian dishes is this chicken creation, which takes its name from Kiev, the capital of the Ukrainian republic and Russia's third largest city. Kiev was once the capital of Russia, and in medieval times it was one of Europe's leading cities.

4 chicken half breasts	1-2 eggs
6 1-inch squares butter, frozen	Fine dry bread crumbs
	Vegetable oil for frying
Salt, pepper to taste	6 buttered rounds of bread
Flour	

Carefully remove bones from chicken with tip of sharp knife. Remove skin, membranes and fat. Cover each boned breast with a piece of wax paper and carefully pound with a meat mallet or pounder to flatten as thin as possible, about ⅛ inch thick. Be careful, however, not to tear any holes in the flesh. Trim off any edges to make the pieces even oval shapes. Put a frozen square of butter in the center of each breast and season with salt and pepper. Fold each breast into the shape of a drumstick to enclose the butter. Tuck in any ends. Fasten with toothpicks. Do not leave any gaps, or the butter will ooze out while cooking. Roll each piece in flour; dip in beaten egg; roll in bread crumbs. Shape gently to remove any excess crumbs. Chill for 1 to 2 hours. Fry in hot deep fat (375°F. on a frying thermometer) for about 5 minutes, or until golden brown. Keep warm. To serve, fry the bread rounds in butter or oil until golden and arrange one chicken breast over each bread round. At the table, slit the chicken breasts lengthwise with a sharp knife, so that the hot butter will ooze out. Serves 6.

Circassian Chicken

The Circassians were an ancient tribe that inhabited the western part of the Caucasian Mountains, but their name has been used for all the inhabitants of the Caucasus. In the past Circassian ladies were noted for their beauty, and many of them introduced native dishes to the courts of the sultans in Constantinople. Thus this creation is popular in Turkey as well as in southern Russia. It makes an excellent buffet dish.

1 stewing chicken (3½ to 4 pounds)	Salt, pepper to taste
1 small carrot, scraped and diced	2 cups shelled walnuts
1 medium onion, peeled and chopped	3 slices stale white bread
	1 large onion, peeled and chopped
¼ cup chopped fresh parsley	1 tablespoon paprika

Put chicken, carrot, onion, parsley, salt, pepper and 5 cups water in a large kettle. Bring to a boil. Reduce heat and simmer, covered, for 2 hours, or until tender. The exact simmering time will depend on the age of the chicken. Remove chicken from kettle to cool. Strain broth and reserve. Cut meat into shreds.

Put the walnuts through a meat grinder twice. After each grinding reserve the oil separately from the nuts. Soak bread in some of the strained chicken broth until soft. Squeeze dry and mix with ground walnuts, onion and pepper. Put this mixture through a meat grinder two more times. Then gradually add about 1 cup of the strained chicken broth to the mixture to make a paste or sort of mayonnaise-type sauce. Combine ½ of this sauce with the shredded chicken and spread evenly on a platter. Cover with remaining sauce. Garnish with the reserved walnut oil by sprinkling it, along with the paprika, over the sauce.

Georgian Spitted Chicken with Plum Sauce

In southern Russia, a favorite method of preparing poultry is to serve either spitted or broiled chicken with a sauce made with green gooseberries, pounded walnuts, sour cream or fruits. One of the most typical sauces is tkemali, which is made with a base of wild or sour plums that grow only in the Georgian republic. It is not possible to duplicate the recipe outside of the region, but a good substitute can be attempted. This is an excellent entrée for an outdoor meal.

<table>
<tr><td>2 broiler chickens, about
   2½ pounds each
   Salt, pepper to taste
   Butter or margarine
1½ cups puréed cooked plums
1 garlic clove, crushed</td><td>2 tablespoons chopped fresh
   coriander or parsley
⅛ - ¼ teaspoon red pepper
   Garnishes: slices of
   tomatoes and cucumbers</td></tr>
</table>

Wash chickens and wipe dry. Season with salt and pepper. Arrange, skin side down, on a grill or broiler rack. Brush well with butter. Put in a preheated broiler and cook under medium heat for 50 to 60 minutes or until tender, brushing occasionally with butter. Turn a few times during cooking. While chicken is cooking, combine plums, garlic, coriander or parsley and red pepper in a saucepan; season with salt and pepper. Cook on the stove long enough to heat through. To serve, arrange chicken on a platter and garnish with tomatoes and cucumbers. Serve sauce separately to be poured over chicken. Serves 4.

Beef Kotlety

In Russia, everyday dishes are made with ground meat mixtures prepared and served in various ways. Tiny meatballs served with sauces as appetizers or entrées are called bitky. The so-called Russian hamburgers, kotlety, are characteristic everyday restaurant and family fare. Kotlety differ from American hamburgers in that kotlety are golden and crisp on the outside and moist and tender on the inside. In Russian restaurants, they are served plain or with sour cream, mushroom or tomato sauce and accompanied by kasha, macaroni or potatoes.

<table>
<tr><td>3 slices thick, stale, crusty
   white bread
   Milk</td><td>1 pound lean ground beef
2 eggs
1 medium onion, peeled and
   minced</td></tr>
</table>

Salt, pepper to taste
⅓ cup (about) fine dry bread crumbs

Butter, margarine or vegetable oil for frying
3 tablespoons sour cream at room temperature

Soak the bread in milk to cover for about 20 minutes, or until bread is softened. Squeeze bread dry and mix with beef. Put through a meat grinder or mix very well. Add eggs, one at a time, beating after each addition. Add onion, salt and pepper and mix well. Shape into flattened oval patties and roll in bread crumbs. Fry in heated butter, margarine or oil until cutlets are cooked through and golden and crisp on the outside. Remove to a warm plate and keep warm. Scrape ·drippings in the pan and stir in sour cream. Leave on stove long enough to heat through. Spoon over cutlets. Serves 6.

Pork Chops with Cherry Sauce

Russians are extremely fond of pork, which they prepare in interesting variations. One of their great holiday treats is roast suckling pig stuffed with kasha. The recipe for this dish is not included here, since most home cooks don't have the facilities for preparing a whole pig. Other typical pork dishes, such as this one, are those served with fruit sauces. Plums may be substituted for the cherries, if desired.

6 loin pork chops, about ½ inch thick
Salt, pepper to taste
Fine dry bread crumbs
Butter, margarine or oil for frying
Water
1 cup puréed canned sour cherries, pitted

Sugar to taste
½ teaspoon ground cinnamon
½ teaspoon ground cloves
1 teaspoon grated lemon rind
1 tablespoon honey
½ cup Madeira wine

Cut any fat from the pork chops. Season with salt and pepper. Roll chops in bread crumbs seasoned with salt and pepper. Fry chops in hot butter, margarine or oil until brown on both sides. Add ½ cup of water and cook over low heat, covered, 45 to 60 minutes, or until tender. Meanwhile, combine cherries, sugar, cinnamon, cloves, lemon rind and honey and bring to a boil. Lower heat and cook 5 minutes. Add a little water to thin, if desired. Stir in Madeira and remove from stove. Serve over cooked chops. Serves 6.

Beef Stroganoff

The Russian meat dish most known outside Russia is doubtless this creation, which was named for a gourmet and bon vivant of the czarist court, Count Paul Stroganoff. There are many recipes for the dish, and this is one of them.

2 pounds beef sirloin or tenderloin	1 tablespoon prepared mustard
5 tablespoons (approximately) butter or margarine	1 cup beef bouillon Pinch of sugar
1 medium onion, peeled and chopped	Salt, pepper to taste
½ pound fresh mushrooms, cleaned and sliced	2 teaspoons flour 1 cup sour cream at room temperature
3 tablespoons tomato paste	

Remove any fat from meat and cut crosswise into strips about ½ inch thick and 3 inches long. Heat 2 tablespoons of butter in a skillet. Add some of the meat and brown quickly. Remove to a plate. Add more butter and more meat and brown; also remove to plate. Sauté onion in drippings. Add mushrooms and more butter, if needed, and sauté 4 minutes. Stir in tomato paste and mustard. Add bouillon, sugar, salt and pepper. Bring to a boil. Lower heat and cook slowly, covered, for 10 minutes. Add meat and cook 5 minutes longer. Combine flour and sour cream and add to sauce. Leave on stove 3-5 minutes over low heat. Serves 4.

Baltic Beef Zrazy

Stuffed roulades of beef, prepared in several variations, are popular meat dishes in Lithuania, Latvia and Estonia.

2 pounds round steak
Salt, pepper to taste
1 medium onion, peeled and
  minced
2 slices thin bacon, minced
½ pound fresh mushrooms,
  cleaned and chopped
2 large slices dark rye bread

Beef bouillon
1 egg, slightly beaten
Flour
Fat or butter for frying
1 cup sour cream at
  room temperature
3 tablespoons chopped fresh
  dill or parsley

Have butcher cut meat into long thin slices and pound with a meat cleaver to make as thin as possible. (Some markets sell meat already cut for roulades). Trim to make pieces uniform size. Season with salt and pepper. Sauté onion with bacon until onion is tender. Pour off all fat except for 2 tablespoons. Add mushrooms and sauté for 4 minutes. Remove from stove. Soak bread in bouillon to cover and squeeze dry. Add with egg to onion-mushroom mixture. Mix in egg and season with salt and pepper. Place a spoonful of bread stuffing on each slice of beef and roll up. Tuck in meat edges to completely enclose stuffing; fasten with toothpicks or tie with thread. Dust roulades with flour and brown in fat. Add bouillon to cover and cook slowly, covered, about 50 minutes, or until tender. Remove roulades to a warm plate and keep warm. Scrape drippings and stir in sour cream. Leave on stove long enough to heat through. Pour sour cream sauce over roulades and sprinkle with the dill or parsley. Serves 4 to 6.

Shashlyk

A classic southern Russian dish, skewered meat or shashlyk was popularized in America and Western Europe by Russian emigrées who opened restaurants and featured this native specialty, which was very often served flaming. Known as shish kebab in the Eastern Mediterranean and Central Asian countries, shashlyk has many variations. Generally shashlyk is made with lamb, but it can also be prepared with beef, pork, innards or a combination of these. Marinades and seasonings for shashlyk differ according to regional and personal tastes. Georgians prefer to marinate the lamb in pomegranate juice and, when cooked, to sprinkle it with powdered barberis. Others prefer lemon juice, red wine or vinegar as marinades and season the meat only with onions, salt and pepper. Usually, the dish is prepared simply using the flavorings only with the specific purpose of enhancing the flavor of the meat. The marinade serves as a tenderizer for tough meats. Shashlyk can be cooked outdoors over hot coals or indoors under the broiler. It is a good and fun company dish.

3 pounds boneless leg of lamb, trimmed of fat and cut into 1½ inch cubes	Salt, freshly ground pepper to taste
1 medium onion, peeled and minced	2 medium onions, peeled and cut into chunks
3 tablespoons fresh lemon or pomegranate juice	Garnishes: tomato wedges, green onions, lemon slices

Put lamb into large bowl. Add minced onion, lemon or pomegranate juice, salt and pepper; stir. Allow to marinate 2 hours or longer. When ready to cook, thread lamb cubes, interlarded with chunks of onion, on skewers. Broil over hot coals or under broiler for 12 minutes or longer, turning once during the cooking. Serve on skewers on a platter garnished with tomatoes, green onions and lemon slices. Serves 6.

FILLED DUMPLINGS

Siberian Pelmeny

Filled dough or dumplings are basic to Russian cookery, and there are a fascinating number of them, which vary from region to region. In the Ukrainian republic, for example, varenky are prepared with a dough that can be made of white or white and buckwheat flour, to which cottage cheese or mashed potatoes are sometimes added. Fillings for varenky range from the most common cottage cheese-egg kind to meats, fish, vegetables and fruits. The most popular of all the dumplings, however, are pelmeny, or pelmeni—stuffed triangles or half-circles. Although they are Russian in origin, pelmeny have been called Siberian dumplings because housewives in the large cold northern expanse made them in great quantities to be frozen for everyday use during the winter. Pelmeny were also taken to eat on long trips. Given here are two fillings for pelmeny.

Cheese filling

1½ cups pot or dry cottage cheese

1 medium egg, beaten

¼ cup sour cream at room temperature

2 tablespoons chopped fresh dill or parsley

Salt, pepper to taste

Combine ingredients and mix well.

Beef filling

⅓ cup finely chopped onion

1 tablespoon butter or margarine

½ pound lean ground beef

1 medium egg, beaten

2 tablespoons chopped fresh dill or parsley

Salt, pepper to taste

Sauté onion in butter in a small frying pan. Add ground beef and cook, stirring until the redness disappears. Spoon off any fat. Remove from heat and cool. Stir in egg, dill, salt and pepper and mix well.

Dumplings

1½ cups unsifted all-purpose flour

1 large egg at room temperature

½ teaspoon salt

4 tablespoons (approximately) water

Melted butter

Sour cream

Put flour in a large bowl or on a wooden or marble surface; form into a mound. Make a well in center of dough and break egg into it. Add salt and 2 tablespoons of water. Working with the tips of the fingers, mix flour with other ingredients until all are well combined. Add water, a little at a time as needed, to form a stiff and compact ball of dough. Knead on a floured surface 5 to 10 minutes, or until dough is smooth and elastic.

Cut dough into two portions. Roll out each portion as thin as possible. With a tumbler or cookie cutter, cut dough into 3-inch circles. Place a small spoonful of filling in the center of each circle. Dip the tip of a finger in cold water and rub around the edge of dough. Fold over to form a crescent and pinch edges to enclose filling. When ready to cook, drop filled pelmeny, several at a time, into a large kettle of boiling salted water. Keeping the water at a steady boil, cook pelmeny about 10 minutes, or until dough is cooked. Remove with a slotted spoon and drain. Serve warm with melted butter and sour cream. Makes about 36 dumplings.

Note: Pelmeny with beef stuffing are often cooked and served in soups.

White Cheese Patties

A very typical Russian food is a dry cottage cheese, called *tvorog*, which is used to fill dumplings and tarts, to make puddings and pancakes, or to make these simple but good patties. Well-drained cottage or pot cheese can be used as a substitute for tvorog.

2 cups pot cheese or well-drained cottage cheese	½ cup (approximately) all-purpose flour
2 eggs, beaten	Butter or vegetable oil for frying
½ teaspoon salt	
2 tablespoons melted butter or margarine	

Mash the cheese. Mix with eggs, salt and butter. Stir in flour, enough to make a stiff mixture. With wet hands form mixture into small patties, about 2½ inches round; dust patties lightly in flour. Fry in hot butter or oil until golden on both sides. Serve with melted butter and sour cream, if desired.

Note: Another variation of this dish is to make a stiff dough with the same ingredients, but using more flour. After cutting, the dough is boiled in salted water.

VEGETABLES

In Russia potatoes are consumed in great quantities. They are used to make several traditional, excellent-tasting dishes. Mashed cooked potatoes are made into patties and served with sour cream, mushroom or tomato sauces; fried potatoes are cooked with eggs and herbs; sliced cooked potatoes are baked in a sour cream sauce. A favorite spring dish is new potatoes with sour cream and fresh dill. Whole cooked potatoes are stuffed with meat or mushrooms. Grated raw potatoes are used to make pancakes, and in Lithuania a number of puddings, called kugelis, are served. Kugelis were originally created by the Jewish inhabitants of that country. The following are recipes for three Russian potato dishes.

Potato-Mushroom Patties

1 medium onion, peeled and minced
2 tablespoons butter
1 cup chopped mushrooms
2 cups cooked potatoes, mashed

1 egg
Salt, pepper to taste
Fine dry bread crumbs
Butter or oil for frying

Sauté onion in butter in a skillet until tender. Add mushrooms and sauté for 3 minutes. Mix with potatoes, egg, salt and pepper. Shape into flat round or oval patties and roll in bread crumbs. Fry in butter or oil until golden on all sides. Serves 4.

Lithuanian Potatoes in Sour Cream

4 medium potatoes
2 thin slices bacon, chopped
1 medium onion, peeled and chopped

⅓ to ½ cup sour cream at room temperature
Salt, pepper to taste
2 tablespoons chopped fresh dill or parsley

Peel potatoes and cook in salted boiling water until tender. Drain. While potatoes are cooking, fry bacon and onion until bacon is crisp, and onion is tender. Mix in sour cream, salt and pepper. Add warm potatoes; toss. Serve garnished with dill or parsley. Serves 4.

Byelorussian Vegetable-filled Potato Roll

6 medium potatoes	1 cup cooked carrots, diced
2 eggs, well beaten	1 cup cooked green peas
¼ cup butter or margarine	1 cup cooked mushrooms,
2 tablespoons chopped	chopped
fresh parsley	Dash nutmeg
Salt, pepper to taste	

Peel potatoes and cook in salted water until tender. Drain and mash while still warm. Add eggs, 3 tablespoons butter, parsley, salt and pepper. Mix well. Turn out on a flat surface and shape into a long, narrow rectangle about 1 inch thick. Combine carrots, peas and mushrooms. Add remaining 1 tablespoon of butter and season with salt, pepper and nutmeg. Spoon mixture lengthwise along center of potato rectangle. Fold potato rectangle around vegetables to completely enclose them and to form a long roll. Spread top generously with butter. Bake in a preheated hot oven (450° F.), about 10 minutes, until golden on top. To serve, cut in slices. Makes 6 servings.

Georgian Kidney Beans

In the republic of Georgia, the favorite vegetables are beans of all kinds—kidney, white or green. Kidney beans are served most often with a pounded walnut and red pepper sauce or with this simple marinade. The dish is called labio.

2 cups canned kidney beans, drained	½ cup chopped green onions, with tops

¼ cup olive or vegetable oil
2 tablespoons red wine
   vinegar

3 tablespoons chopped fresh
   coriander or parsley
   Salt, pepper to taste

Combine all ingredients and leave 2 hours or longer before serving.
Serves 4 to 6.

Vegetables in Sour Cream

In Russia, one of the most characteristic ways of serving vegetables
is to combine cooked or raw vegetables with a sour cream sauce
or mixture. The following recipe can be used for any number of
cooked vegetables, such as beets, beans, corn, carrots, eggplant or
potatoes.

3 cups sliced or cut-up
   cooked vegetables
1 cup (approximately)
   sour cream (room
   temperature)
1 tablespoon vinegar
   (optional)

2 tablespoons chopped
   fresh dill
   Dash sugar
   Salt, pepper to taste

Combine cooked vegetables, while still warm, with remaining
ingredients and mix well. Heat through over a low fire and serve.
Serves 4.

Sauerkraut Casserole

One of the most beloved Russian foods is sauerkraut, which is eaten
in a number of interesting dishes like this one.

1 large onion, peeled and
   chopped
5 tablespoons butter or
   margarine
2 cups sliced mushrooms

1 medium cucumber, peeled
   and diced
2 pounds sauerkraut,
   drained
¼ cup tomato paste

1 tablespoon sugar
1 bay leaf
   Salt, pepper to taste

Garnishes: lemon slices,
olives

Sauté onion in 3 tablespoons of butter until tender. Add mushrooms and sauté 4 minutes. Melt 2 tablespoons of butter in a second saucepan and add sauerkraut. Sauté, stirring with a fork, for 1 minute. Add tomato paste, cucumber, sugar, bay leaf, salt, pepper and ⅔ cup of water. Cook slowly, covered, for 15 minutes. Arrange half the sauerkraut combination in a baking dish. Spoon the onions and mushrooms over it. Cover with remaining sauerkraut. Bake in a moderate oven (350° F.) for 15 minutes. Serve with lemon slices and olives. Serves 6 to 8.

SALADS

Lithuanian Vegetable Salad

1 cup cooked carrot slices
1 cup cooked beets, diced
2 cups cooked potato slices
1 cup cooked green peas

2 tablespoons dill pickle, minced
1 to 1½ cups sour cream
Salt, pepper to taste

Combine ingredients and chill. Serves 6 to 8.

Cucumber-Sour Cream Salad

Cucumbers are one of the most popular Russian vegetables, and a favorite preparation for them is a simple combination with sour cream. Serve this dish as part of the zakusky or as a salad.

2 medium cucumbers
   Salt
2 tablespoons fresh lemon
   juice

½ - ¾ cup sour cream
3 tablespoons chopped
   fresh dill

Peel and slice cucumbers. Sprinkle with salt and leave to drain for 1 hour. Pour off all liquid and mix with remaining ingredients. Serves 4.

Mixed Vegetable-Chicken Salad

This salad, called vinaigrette in Russia, is a handsome and delectable creation that is a good buffet dish. It can be made with various vegetables, meats, seafood, poultry or game, all of which are marinated in a vinaigrette sauce and then bound with mayonnaise. Piquant foods, such as pickles, capers and anchovies, are also included. Beets are customary. Piled high as a pyramid or mound, this salad is elaborately garnished with colorful foods. Very special garnishes are cooked shrimp and lobster. This recipe is but one of many vinaigrettes, and the ingredients may be altered according to taste.

1 cup cooked green peas	Salad oil
1 cup cooked carrots, diced	Vinegar
1½ cups cooked beets, cubed	Salt, pepper, cayenne to
2 cups cooked potatoes,	taste
cubed	1¼ cups (approximately)
1 cup diced cucumber	mayonnaise
6 green onions, with tops,	2 tablespoons prepared
chopped	mustard
3 gherkins, chopped	Garnishes: capers, tomato
2 cups cold chicken or ham,	slices, olives, hard-cooked
cubed	egg wedges, pickle slices

Combine vegetables, gherkins and chicken or ham. Sprinkle with salad oil and vinegar. Season with salt, pepper and cayenne. Leave to marinate at room temperature for 1 hour. Mix mayonnaise and mustard, using enough mayonnaise to bind mixture. Carefully stir mayonnaise into ingredients. Arrange in a tall pyramid or mound and garnish as desired. Makes 8 to 10 servings.

DESSERTS

Kisel

The best known Russian dessert is a simple fruit pudding made by thickening cooked fruit with cornstarch or potato starch. The preferred fruits are those with tart flavors, such as cranberries, rhubarb, sour cherries or apples, but all kinds of berries are used. The thickness can vary from that of jelly to a bit more runny consistency. Customarily the dessert is served with cream.

   2 cups fruit purée   2 - 3 tablespoons cornstarch

Heat fruit purée in a saucepan. Blend cornstarch, the amount varying according to the desired consistency, with a little cold water to smooth. Stir cornstarch into fruit and cook, stirring constantly, about 3 minutes, or until mixture thickens. Spoon into dessert dishes and chill. Serve with cream, if desired. Serves 4.
Note: Sugar may be added if a sweeter dish is desired.

Honey Mousse

A simple but flavorful dessert.

   4 eggs, separated   1 cup honey

Combine egg yolks and honey in a saucepan and mix well. Cook over low heat, stirring constantly, until mixture thickens. Remove from heat and cool. Whip egg whites until stiff and fold into honey mixture. Spoon into dessert dishes and chill. Serve with whipped cream, if desired. Makes 4 servings.

Ukrainian Cherry Dumplings

Ukrainian dumplings called varenky, which are prepared and eaten for dessert, may be filled with any kind of fruit, but cherries are most often used.

2 cups sifted all-purpose flour	½ cup (about) water
1 teaspoon salt	1 egg white
2 eggs	Fruit filling (recipe follows)

Put flour and salt in a large bowl. Make a well in center of mixture and add eggs. Stir in enough water to make a stiff dough. Knead on a floured board. Shape into a ball and let stand 1 hour. Roll out very thin on floured board. Cut into small rounds, about 4 inches in diameter. Place 1 spoonful of the fruit filling on lower half of each circle. Brush edges with egg white, slightly beaten. Fold pastry over to form a half-circle, and press edges together. Drop, a few at a time, into a large kettle of boiling water and cook briskly for 15 to 20 minutes, or until dumplings come to the surface. Remove with a slotted spoon and drain. Serve warm. Serve with warm cherry juice and thick cream, if desired. Makes about 16.

Filling:

1½ cups canned pitted sour red cherries, drained	1-3 tablespoons sugar

Put cherries and sugar in a small saucepan and simmer for 5 minutes. Cool.

Armenian Shredded Wheat Dessert

6 shredded wheat biscuits	1 teaspoon vanilla
2 cups sugar	1 cup chopped walnuts
1 cup water	1½ cups heavy cream, whipped

Crush shredded wheat and put in a shallow baking dish. Toast in a preheated hot (425° F.) oven for 20 minutes. Meanwhile, boil sugar and water to consistency of thick syrup. Add vanilla. Place toasted shredded wheat on 6 individual serving plates. Cover with syrup. Let cool at room temperature. Sprinkle each serving with chopped nuts; top with whipped cream. Serves 6.

Note: Shredded wheat is a substitute for a native pastry called shredded kadayif.

Fruit Compote

Russians are extremely fond of sweet fruit compotes, which are customarily well-flavored with spices, wines, liqueurs or fruit rinds, and sometimes include chopped nuts. The compotes differ considerably from region to region. The amount of sugar required varies according to the type of fruit and according to individual tastes. Some compotes are made with a combination of fruits, which are cooked separately. This is a general recipe that can be varied to taste. Preferred fruits include pears, peaches, berries, apples, plums, green figs and oranges.

2 pounds fresh fruit
1½ to 2 cups sugar

1 tablespoon lemon juice, wine or rum
1 cinnamon stick

Prepare fruit by washing, peeling, coring or removing any pits. Cut into halves or quarters. Combine sugar, lemon juice, cinnamon stick and fruit in a saucepan. Add water to cover and cook slowly, covered, until fruit is tender but not mushy. Remove from heat and discard cinnamon stick. Cool. Serve cold with fresh or whipped cream, if desired. Serves 6 to 8.

Twigs

These cookies take their name, khvorost, from the Russian word for firewood kindling—twigs or branches—which they somewhat resemble.

½ cup milk
2 eggs, beaten
2 tablespoons rum, gin or vodka
¼ cup sugar
½ teaspoon salt

2½ - 3 cups sifted all-purpose flour
Fat for deep-frying
Confectioners' sugar
Cinnamon

Combine milk, eggs, liquor, sugar and salt in a large bowl. Mix well. Gradually add flour, enough to make a stiff dough. Turn out on a floured board and knead until smooth. Roll out thinly and cut into approximately 36 5-by-1-inch strips. Make a lengthwise slit down the center of each strip, allowing 1 inch on each end uncut. Put one end of the dough through the slit to form a sort of loop. Deep-fry in hot fat (375° F. on a frying thermometer), about 10 at a time, until golden. Remove with a slotted spoon; drain. To serve, sprinkle with confectioners' sugar and cinnamon. Makes about 3 dozen.

Easter Paskha

Paskha is the Russian word for Easter as well as for a marvelous traditional rich dessert to honor that very special holiday. The dessert is a splendid, gaily decorated tall, round or pyramid creation made with sieved pot cheese, butter, heavy cream, sugar, eggs, nuts and candied fruits. Her paskha is the pride of every Russian housewife. In the old days most households had a special four-sided wooden mold in the shape of a pyramid, which was carved inside with a cross and the letters XB (*Khristos voskrese*: Christ is risen). Otherwise an ordinary two-quart flowerpot with a hole in the center for drainage may be used. Very important to the preparation of paskha is the firmness of the dessert, as it must be able to maintain its shape after unmolding. Paskha is regally displayed on the Easter table and served on a plate with another traditional dessert, kulich, a raisin-studded yeast cake.

3 pounds pot cheese	1 cup heavy cream
½ pound sweet butter, softened	½ cup chopped blanched almonds
1 cup sugar	½ cup mixed candied fruits
3 egg yolks, beaten	

Be sure that cheese is completely dry. If it is not, wrap in cheese-cloth and place in a colander to drain off any liquid. Put cheese through a fine sieve and mix well with butter. Mix together sugar and egg yolks and add to cheese mixture. Add cream, almonds and candies, beating and stirring while adding, as the mixture must be as smooth as possible. Line a paskha mold or ordinary flowerpot that has a hole in the bottom for drainage with fine cheesecloth that has been rinsed in cold water and wrung out. Pour mixture into mold or pot and bring the cheesecloth up around mixture to cover it. Put a weight on top of the cheesecloth-wrapped mixture and leave out for 24 hours to drain. Unmold onto a plate. Decorate the sides and top with candied fruits and almonds. Place fresh flowers and green leaves on the plate around the dessert, if desired. This holiday specialty is traditionally ornately garnished. The dessert will keep in the refrigerator for several days. Serves 12.

Polish Cookery

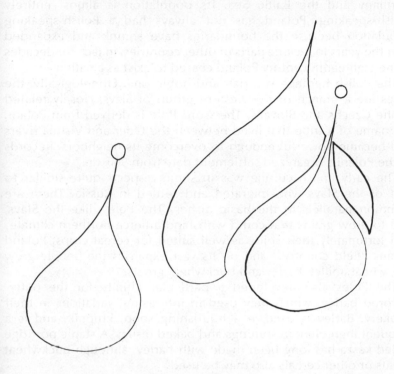

Poland has a distinguished and distinctive cookery, which has evolved over the centuries because a talented people have concerned themselves seriously with their daily fare and still do. Unfortunately Polish cuisine has not been accorded the recognition it deserves in other lands. Americans know little about Polish national dishes, and food writers practically ignore this cookery. Too often it has been confused with that of Russia, Germany, Austria and Hungary.

The Poles, however, developed a cookery that has a character of its own. Basically Slavic with Baltic overtones, the cuisine has been influenced by the country's pivotal crossroads position and by its turbulent history. It is a tribute to the deep nationalistic spirit of the Poles that their culture, traditions and cuisine survived the stormy centuries.

47

Today, the People's Republic of Poland, a part of the vast North European plain, is bounded by the USSR, Czechoslovakia, East Germany and the Baltic Sea. Its population is almost entirely Polish-speaking. Poland has not always had a Polish-speaking population because the boundaries have shrunk and expanded over the years to include parts of other countries. In fact, for decades in the eighteenth century Poland ceased to exist as a nation.

The Polish heritage is a rich and noble one. Ethnologically, the Poles are a branch of the western group of Slavs, closely related to the Czechs and Slovaks. The word Pole is derived from Polani, the name of a tribe that lived between the Oder and Vistula rivers and became powerful enough to overcome its neighbors. Records of the Polani's organized settlement date from 966 A.D.

The early Polish cuisine was in some respects quite similar to that of the Slavs who migrated and settled in Russia. There are common parallels in the basic dishes. The Poles, like the Slavs, had to grow grains that could withstand a fierce northern climate, and fortunately their soil was well suited for cereal crops. Poland means "field country," and on its vast expanses the people grew rye, wheat, millet, barley and buckwheat groats.

The Poles also developed a particular affinity for the nutty-flavored barley, which they used in interesting variations in their cookery. Barley is used in a nourishing soup, krupnik, and is a frequent ingredient in stuffings and baked dishes. A staple porridge called kasza has long been made with barley, although buckwheat groats or other cereals also may be used.

Grains and the foods prepared with them became all-important to the Poles, and were even revered as religious symbols. Pagan rites that were carried over into the Christian era exemplified this adulation. At Wigil, the treasured Christmas Eve sup , sheaves of grain, tied with colored ribbons, were placed in the four corners of the dining room. A prayer was said, to assure a good harvest in the coming year. The meal began with the breaking of a thin unleavened wafer, *Oplatek*, stamped with holy figures. It was called the bread of love.

Breads and rolls made of coarse-grained rye or refined wheat were a significant part of every meal, and even the crumbs were saved to be used later for cooking. Bread crumbs were important bindings, thickeners and garnishes, were used to line baking dishes, and became a basis for the famous sauce called Polonaise.

Fine flours were used inventively by Polish cooks for the creation of savory and sweet pancakes (nalesniki), a variety of dumplings, noodles, stuffed doughs, and a superb repertoire of baked goods, yeast-dough cakes, nut tortes, rich pastries, honey cakes, cookies and jelly-filled doughnuts (paczki), which became famous throughout Europe.

The Polish plain was ideal also for dairy and poultry farming, and many of the early dishes were created with an abundance of eggs, butter, cheese, milk and clabber, all of which are still significant ingredients in Polish cookery. Sour milk and cream became so popular that they were kept as kitchen staples and eaten simply with a sprinkling of sugar and cinnamon, or combined with other foods to make a hundred dishes, particularly piquant sauces. After the eighteenth century, when New World potatoes were introduced to Polish cookery, the potato, mixed with sour cream, became the mainstay of the country table.

The early Poles relied on their fertile earth to grow vegetables that would flourish during the short summer season and that could be preserved or stored for winter use. Cabbage in all its forms is one of the oldest traditional Polish foods. Stuffed cabbage leaves, golabki, made with a number of fillings, are a beloved Polish dish. Cabbage, both green and red, is eaten in salads, stews, baked dishes and stuffings. Soups are a particular Polish specialty, and one of the great favorites is kapusniak, a fresh cabbage or sauerkraut dish enriched with marrowbone, meat and dried mushrooms. Another is the ancient barszcz, often made with a meat base and similar to the Russian borshch, but more refined.

Although Polish vegetable cookery relies heavily on such tubers as carrots, turnips, celery root, kohlrabi, onions, beets and potatoes, the preparations are not monotonous. They are imaginative and should be more widely known and adapted.

A well-liked Polish dish is fish, and fortunately there has never been any problem in obtaining the highly prized carp, bream, pike, perch, salmon and trout from the inland rivers and lakes. Two common methods of cooking either whole or cut-up fish are poaching and baking. The local crayfish is a very popular food that is imaginatively prepared in soups or stews, or with sauces. The Baltic Sea provided such seafood as cod, sole, halibut and haddock, but the Poles have long been particularly partial to eel and herring, which they eat fresh, salted, smoked, pickled or combined with other foods.

Some of the most treasured foods of Poland came from the

forests. No food has been more highly regarded than the wide variety of wild mushrooms, which have appeared for centuries in abundance. At family mushroom gatherings, actually country social events, children have traditionally been taught by their parents how to identify various species. Great quantities of mushrooms were brought home to be freshly cooked or dried, and used in grzyby, or mushroom dishes. In Poland, no Christmas Eve supper or other important meal would be complete without mushroom soup. Dried Polish mushrooms, exported to Western Europe and America, are sought-after delicacies.

Another precious forest food was honey, and beekeeping early became an important occupation. Many kinds of honey were used extensively in the cookery, and Polish honey cakes and cookies were destined to become world famous. At the gay autumn harvest festival, a plate of honey and bread was the traditional offering of welcome by a host to his guests. One of the oldest known drinks in Poland is a honey mead, krupnik, mentioned affectionately throughout Polish literature as well as in folk tales and songs. Drunk in large quantities, the potent liquid has never been for weaklings. It is designed to fell even the strongest of men, and there is an ancient saying that "it goes to the legs."

Berries and fruits were also plentiful native foods and were used to make tart-flavored soups, jams, jellies, fillings, sauces and desserts. Poultry, meats and game flavored with fruits became common. Plums, apricots, pears, cherries and apples appear frequently in Polish cooking.

For meats, the Poles relied heavily on the superb game and wild birds found in the forests. Hunting was a national pastime, and the cooking of duck, venison, pheasant and quail, to name only some of the types of game, was an accomplished art. The wild pig, when domesticated and pampered in backyards or farms, became an important food. Even today Polish hams and sausages (kielbasi) are exported in considerable quantity and are rated among the world's best.

Polish cuisine has a superb collection of pork dishes, but some of the most interesting are those made with the less expensive cuts of pork. This was also the case with beef and veal, because peasant cooks learned to use all parts of the animals in cooking. They became devotees of innards, feet, knuckles, brains and particularly tripe.

For seasonings the Poles relied on all members of the onion family, as well as on such foods as anchovies, capers, lemons, horseradish and fermented juices and fruits to achieve the piquant flavorings preferred by the Slavs. Dill was the essential herb. Nuts and poppy seeds also came to be widely used, and in later years, spices introduced from the East, such as cinnamon, nutmeg, pepper, cloves and saffron, became symbols of wealth for those who could afford them.

Suffice it to say that the Poles, blessed with fertile farming lands, abundant lakes and rivers, and well-stocked forests, created for themselves an interesting and substantial but simple cuisine. The peaceful farmers were forced, however, into conflicts with their neighbors on all sides, which, during the hundreds of years of seemingly endless wars, had a great effect on the country, culture and cuisine.

An early Polish ruler, Mieszko I, embraced Christianity. His conversion provoked trouble with nearby pagan tribes, but it was to have long-lasting significance for the Poles. Thereafter, they were a devoutly religious people, guided by the doctrines of the Roman Catholic church. Consequently, Poles always felt more sympathy toward the countries of Western Europe than toward those of the East. Historians have pointed out that the deep-seated spiritual and national allegiance of the Poles became an important force of unification during perilous times. At any rate, the church established the traditions for religious ceremonies and festivals and for the family celebrations around which everyday life in Poland revolved. Traditional meals and dishes for holiday dining were given a tremendous amount of attention.

From medieval times until well into the nineteenth century, the cookery of Poland was also affected by the foreign royal houses and dignitaries who were continually making alliances with Polish rulers and guiding their government. Poland even had a number of kings and queens who were French, Saxon, Czech and Hungarian. Many of them were responsible for changes and refinements in the cuisine as well as in the culture.

In the fourteenth century Poland was united under the rule of Casimir III, whose reign was favorable to Jews expelled from Western Europe. Thus many Jewish dishes, a number of which are still very popular, became a part of the Polish cuisine. Under the Polish-Lithuanian royal merger headed by Wladislas IV in the late 1300s, Baltic dishes were interchanged, and it is still difficult to unravel the places of their specific origin. During this reign the expansion of Poland into a great empire began, and there were beginnings of a renaissance, influenced by close cultural ties with Western Europe. By the seventeenth century, Poland was one of eastern Europe's great powers, second only to Russia.

A Milanese princess, Bona Sforza, arrived in Poland to marry the future King Sigismund I. Her sizable entourage included not only cooks but also gardeners. At the royal court in Cracow the gardeners introduced such southern vegetables as tomatoes, eggplant, squash and greens. Thereafter, all green vegetables were called *wloszczyzna*, or "things Italian." The queen also introduced the Poles to pasta products and probably to ice creams, sherbets and rich pastries.

In the sixteenth century the influence in Poland of the French court was significant. As a result, Polish cooking became more complex, subtly flavored, elegant and refined. By then the Poles were living on vast feudal estates run by the nobility and worked by the peasants. The cookery of the upper class was French-inspired, whereas that of the poorer folk relied on the fields and forests. As in years past, the peasants' ingenuity for the art of cookery produced interesting culinary creations to augment the staple fare.

The lavishness of the aristocracy knew no bounds, and the Polish nobility was famous throughout Europe for its abundant tables, lengthy parties, lavish hunts and entertainments. The cookery of the upper class was a combination of continental-inspired delicacies and robust native dishes.

Eventually, and unfortunately, a succession of wars and political intrigues weakened Poland to the extent that it was no longer a significant power and was not strong enough to withstand three partitions (1772, 1793 and 1795) in which the country was divided among Prussia, Russia and Austria. In other words, Poland as a nation ceased to exist. During the succeeding years, until after World War I when Poland was resuscitated as a nation, there was considerable exchange of cooking lore between the Poles and their neighbors. Some Polish foods are the same as those of the Germans, Austrians and Russians, with slightly different names.

During the difficult and lengthy years of partition, however, Polish culture, cuisine and nationalism did not disappear. In fact, the country was strengthened in adversity. In Poland today church and family traditions are carried on as loyally as they were in the past. There is particular pride in home cooking, and favorite recipes are handed down from one generation to another.

Two of the most beloved Polish holiday meals are those eaten on Easter and Christmas Eve. Homemakers prepare in advance a fascinating array of traditional foods, and they are well rewarded for their efforts by the appreciative diners. The Easter feast is not served in courses, but a large amount of food is set up on a large table, with a centerpiece of a paschal lamb molded in butter or fashioned of pastry or white sugar, decorated with a Polish flag, and surrounded by brilliantly colored eggs. The meal contains a number of meats, such as suckling pig, roast veal, hams, and sausages; hard-cooked eggs, breads, sauces, cheese and fruit cakes; and a great many sweets, as well as the delicious Easter yeast cake, babka. Vodka enlivens the exchange of greetings, toasts and general conviviality.

The Christmas Eve supper, on the other hand, is a more somber occasion. It is a fast meal with no meat served. The Star of Bethlehem is the symbol of the observance, and supper begins when the waiting children can point to the first star of the evening. By tradition the meal must consist of an odd number of things to eat and an even number of people to enjoy them. Thus the courses usually number 7, 9 or 11. Soups are always three in number and must include barszcz. There are also three fish dishes, generally including carp or pike. Three accompaniments might be homemade noodles with poppy seeds, cheese filled pastries, and red cabbage with mushrooms. Of the three desserts one is a compote of twelve foods in memory of the twelve apostles. A favorite homemade specialty for the occasion is a delectable poppy seed filled roll.

Polish cookery reflects not only devotion to national tradition but also creative assimilation and adaptation of foreign influences. The following selection of traditional and representative recipes offers an introduction to a captivating cuisine that has great variety.

ZAKASKI

The Polish array of appetizers, unlimited in variety, is called zakaski. It is usually served in the living room on small plates, eaten with forks and accompanied by small glasses of vodka. The selection might include herring, marinated or in sour cream, red or black caviar, pickled mushrooms or other vegetables, sausages, cold meats or poultry, smoked fish, cheeses, chicken livers or salads. Included here are four typical specialties, which may be served accompanied by any of the above fare, together with dark bread and butter.

Fresh Mushrooms in Sour Cream

1 pound fresh mushrooms	1 tablespoon flour
½ cup sliced green onions, with tops	Salt, pepper to taste
2 tablespoons butter or margarine	1 cup sour cream at room temperature
1 tablespoon fresh lemon juice	2 tablespoons chopped fresh dill
	Small rounds of toast

Clean mushrooms by rinsing quickly under running water or wiping with wet paper toweling. Cut off any tough stem ends. Slice lengthwise through the stems. Sauté mushrooms and onions in butter and lemon juice for 4 minutes. Stir in flour and cook slowly, stirring, for 1 minute. Season with salt and pepper. Mix in sour cream and dill. Serve warm on small rounds of toast. Serves 4.

Purée of Anchovies

The Poles are very fond of anchovies, which are used creatively in their cookery in a number of inviting dishes. This is one easy-to-prepare appetizer.

Mince or pound 12 drained flat anchovy fillets. Moisten 3 slices of stale white bread with water to cover and squeeze dry. Break into bits or mince with a fork and add to the anchovies. Mix in enough sour cream or mayonnaise and vinegar to make a smooth tangy purée. Serve as a spread with dark bread rounds. Serves 4.

Pickled Herring

One of the most important zakaski dishes is herring, sledzie, which is served by itself or combined with other foods.

4 pickled herrings, drained
1 large onion, peeled and
   chopped
4 hard-cooked eggs, shelled
   and chopped

Salt, pepper to taste
1 cup (approximately) sour
   cream
2 tablespoons chopped fresh
   dill

Cut herring into small cubes. Mix with onion and eggs. Season with salt and pepper. Add sour cream, enough to bind the ingredients. Sprinkle with dill. Serve with dark bread. Serves 4.

Stuffed Eggs, Polish Style

8 hard-cooked eggs, shelled
¼ cup sour cream
2 tablespoons chopped
   chives or green onions

2 tablespoons minced fresh
   dill or parsley
Salt, pepper to taste
Paprika

Cut eggs into lengthwise halves. Remove yolks and mash. Mix with sour cream, chives or onions, dill, salt and pepper. Stuff egg halves with the mixture and sprinkle with paprika. Chill. Serves 8.

SOUPS

Polish Mushroom Soup

Zupa grzybowa, or mushroom soup, is one of the best-liked soups in the Polish soup repertoire. It is made in many variations. This is one of those that can be prepared with fresh cultured mushrooms, although the Poles prefer to use their flavorful dried wild mushrooms.

¾ pound fresh mushrooms
¼ cup butter or margarine
1 medium onion, peeled and
   chopped

6 green onions, with tops,
   chopped
1 tablespoon lemon juice
2 teaspoons paprika

2 tablespoons flour   1½ cups sour cream at
6 cups chicken broth or   room temperature
  vegetable stock   2 tablespoons chopped fresh
  Salt, pepper to taste   dill
2 egg yolks

Clean mushrooms by rinsing quickly or wiping with wet paper
toweling. Cut off any tough stem ends. Slice crosswise. Melt
butter in a saucepan and sauté onion and green onions in butter
until soft. Add mushrooms and lemon juice; sauté 4 minutes.
Stir in paprika and flour. Add chicken broth a little at a time.
Season with salt and pepper. Simmer, covered, for 30 minutes.
Meanwhile, stir egg yolks until light and creamy. Mix with sour
cream and dill. When broth is cooked, stir 2 or 3 tablespoons
of hot broth into sour cream mixture and mix well. Return
sour cream and broth to soup and leave over the low fire, stirring,
1 or 2 minutes, or until thickened. Serves 8 to 10.

Cold Cucumber-Beet Soup

A most interesting and popular Polish summer soup is called
chlodnik. It is made with a number of ingredients that can vary
considerably but that generally include beets, cucumbers, green
onions, radishes and sour cream. In regions where they are
readily available, some variations also include diced cooked veal
and crayfish. In America shrimp can be used as a good substitute.
Some recipes also include buttermilk. The soup should have a
tart flavor.

 1 small bunch of beets with   2 cups sour cream
   the leaves   1 dill pickle, minced
 6 cups water   (optional)
   Salt   3 tablespoons minced fresh
 1 medium cucumber, peeled   dill
   and diced   Pepper to taste
 6 red radishes, cleaned and   1 lemon, sliced
   sliced   2 hard-cooked eggs, shelled
 6 green onions, with tops,   and chopped
   sliced   12 cleaned cooked large
 2 tablespoons fresh lemon   shrimp, shelled and halved
   juice

Scrub beets and carefully wash the leaves. Leave whole and do not peel. Put in a kettle with water. Salt lightly. Bring to a boil. Lower heat and cook slowly, covered, until tender, for about 30 minutes or longer, depending on size of beets. Drain, reserving liquid. Peel and chop beets. Mince the leaves finely. Combine with reserved liquid, cucumber, radishes, green onions, lemon juice, sour cream, pickle and dill. Season with salt and pepper. Chill. Serve garnished with lemon slices, eggs and shrimp. Serves 6 to 8.

Barley-Vegetable Soup

A characteristic Polish soup called krupnik is made with various ingredients but always includes barley and, usually, dried mushrooms, potatoes and other vegetables. Krupnik has an interesting flavor and is very nutritious.

4 dried mushrooms, preferably Polish
1 soup bone with meat, about 1 pound
1 large carrot, scraped and chopped
1 large onion, peeled and diced
6 peppercorns, bruised
   Salt to taste

¼ cup pearl barley
3 tablespoons butter or margarine
3 medium potatoes, peeled and diced
1 cup sour cream at room temperature
3 tablespoons chopped fresh dill

Soak mushrooms in lukewarm water to cover for 20 minutes. Drain and slice, reserving liquid. Put soup bone and 8 cups water in a kettle. Bring to a boil and skim well. Add carrot, onion, peppercorns and salt; lower heat. Cook slowly, covered, for 1½ hours. Meanwhile, put barley and water to cover in a saucepan and cook slowly, covered, until barley is cooked, 1 hour or longer. Stir in butter. When soup has cooked the designated time, remove from heat and take out soup bone and meat. Cut meat from bone. Discard any gristle and dice meat. Return to kettle. Add sliced mushrooms, reserved liquid, and potatoes and put kettle back on stove. Continue to cook slowly, covered, until tender, about 25 minutes. Stir in cooked barley. Add sour cream and dill; mix well. Serves 6 to 8.

Barszcz Polski

Since earliest times a beet soup, barszcz, has been served in Poland for everyday and company meals. It is traditional for both Christmas and Easter dinners, and it is served cold for the harvest festival. There are innumerable varieties of barszcz, which can be made with vegetable or meat broth and can be either clear or include several ingredients. The foundation for the true barszcz, however, is a tart ferment called *kwas*, which is made from sour rye bread and beets. Kwas is not generally available in America. The following clear barszcz may contain cooked potatoes, sliced sausages, cooked meat or filled pastries, and, if desired, may be garnished with sour cream.

4 or 5 dried mushrooms	½ cup liquid from canned
4 large beets	pickled beets
1 quart stock or beef	1 teaspoon sugar
bouillon	Salt, pepper to taste

Soak mushrooms in lukewarm water to cover for 20 minutes. Squeeze dry and slice. Reserve liquid. Wash beets. Peel and chop finely. Put in a large saucepan with mushrooms, reserved liquid, and stock; bring to a boil. Lower heat and cook slowly, covered, until tender, about 35 minutes. Put through a sieve. Mix with pickled beet liquid, sugar, salt and pepper; heat. Serves 4. **Note:** For a more tart flavor, add wine vinegar or lemon juice, about 1 tablespoon, to the soup.

Cold Apple Soup

The Poles are partial to a number of cold soups that are made with fruits, sweetened with sugar, and flavored with spices, wine and either sweet or sour cream. This is one of them.

6 large apples, peeled, cored	1 cup sugar
and quartered	1 cup sour cream, at room
1 stick cinnamon	temperature
Grated rind of 1 lemon	Currant jelly (optional)
1 cup white wine	

In a saucepan, combine apples, cinnamon stick and lemon rind with 4 cups water. Cook slowly, stirring occasionally, until apples are soft. Strain through a sieve. Mix with wine and sugar and return to heat. Bring to a boil. Lower heat and stir in sour cream. Leave long enough to heat through. Remove from stove and chill. Serve topped with a little currant jelly, if desired. Serves 4 to 6.

GRAINS AND NOODLES

Barley-Mushroom Casserole

Barley, one of the world's oldest foods and a nutritious grain with an appealing nutty flavor, is widely used in Poland. The following barley dish can be served as an accompaniment to fish, meat or poultry. It is usually made with flavorful wild mushrooms, but cultivated ones are also good.

¼ cup butter or margarine	1 cup pearl barley
1 medium onion, peeled and chopped	2½ cups hot beef bouillon
½ pound fresh mushrooms, cleaned and sliced	Salt, pepper to taste

Melt butter in a heavy saucepan; sauté onion in butter until tender. Add mushrooms; sauté 4 minutes. Stir in barley and add hot bouillon. Season with salt and pepper. Mix well. Cook over low heat, tightly covered, until barley is tender and liquid is absorbed, about 1 hour. Serves 6.

Barley-stuffed Cabbage Leaves

Polish stuffed cabbage leaves or "birds," called golabki, can be filled with flavorful combinations made with barley or rice and mushrooms, or meat and rice. Very often golabki are served with a mushroom or sour cream sauce. This is an interesting variation that can also be prepared with pickled cabbage leaves if desired.

1 cup pearl barley
1 large head green cabbage
1 large onion, peeled and minced
3 tablespoons shortening or butter
½ cup fresh or canned mushrooms, diced
1 tablespoon fresh lemon juice

Paprika, salt, pepper to taste
⅓ cup chopped fresh parsley
1½ cups beef bouillon
2 tablespoons flour
1 cup sour cream (room temperature)
2 tablespoons fresh dill, chopped

Cook barley in water to cover for 1 hour or until tender, or according to package directions. Pull off and discard any wilted or coarse outer cabbage leaves. Cut out core to a depth of about 3 inches. Parboil cabbage in a large kettle of salted boiling water for about 15 minutes, or until leaves are soft enough to be pliable. Carefully cut out the tough part of the rib from each leaf. Sauté onion in shortening until soft. Add mushrooms and lemon juice; sauté 3 minutes. Season with paprika, salt and pepper. Add cooked barley and parsley and mix well. Spoon 1 or more large spoonfuls of stuffing onto each leaf, the exact amount depending on leaf's size. Roll up and fold in edges to securely enclose stuffing. Secure with toothpicks or tie with string. Place in a kettle. Cover with bouillon and cook slowly, covered, about 1½ hours, or until leaves are tender. Remove stuffed leaves and keep warm. Stir flour into drippings and cook, stirring, until smooth. Add sour cream and dill and heat through. Pour sauce over stuffed leaves. Serves 8 to 10.

Baked Noodles and Ham

The Poles are extremely fond of noodles, kluski, which housewives often prepare at home. Kluski are cooked with several foods such as poppy seeds and honey, cottage cheese and sugar, cottage cheese and sour cream, or fried bacon. This dish may be served as a luncheon or supper entrée.

½ pound wide noodles
1 cup cooked ham, minced
1 egg, beaten
2 tablespoons melted butter
¾ cup sour cream at room
  temperature

2 tablespoons fresh dill or
  parsley, chopped
Salt, pepper to taste
Fine dry bread crumbs

Cook noodles according to package directions until just tender. Drain. While noodles are still warm, combine with remaining ingredients, except for bread crumbs. Sprinkle the inner surfaces of a buttered shallow baking dish with bread crumbs; spoon the noodle-ham mixture into dish. Sprinkle top with bread crumbs. Bake in a preheated moderate oven (350°F.) for 40 minutes, or until mixture is cooked. Serves 4.

Mushroom-filled Pancakes

Some of the most inviting Polish creations are the delectable pancakes, or nalésniki. They can be filled with savory meat, cheese or mushroom combinations and eaten as entrées. Other pancakes are filled with sweet mixtures such as cheese, sour cream and sugar, jam or preserves, and eaten as desserts. These pancakes may be spread with any sweet filling, folded over and fried in butter, if desired.

Pancakes

1 cup milk
1 large egg
1 cup sifted all-purpose
  flour
¼ teaspoon salt

Butter or margarine for
frying
Mushroom Filling
(recipe below)
Sour cream at room
temperature

Combine milk and egg in a bowl; mix with a whisk or fork. Stir in flour and salt and mix again. Heat a lightly greased 7-inch or 8-inch skillet and spoon 3 tablespoons of batter into it. (Pour the batter all at once from a small glass). Tip pan quickly at once to spread batter evenly. Cook until underside is done and bubbles form on top. Turn over with a spatula and cook on the other side. Slip onto a warm plate and keep warm in a preheated 250°F. oven while cooking the other pancakes. When all pancakes are cooked, put a large spoonful of the Mushroom Filling lengthwise along each one; roll up. Serve at once topped with a spoonful of sour cream. Serves 10 to 12.

Mushroom filling

1 pound fresh mushrooms	1 tablespoon flour
6 green onions, minced	2 tablespoons fresh dill or
3 - 4 tablespoons butter or	parsley, chopped
margarine	Salt, pepper to taste
½ cup sour cream at room	
temperature	

Clean mushrooms by rinsing quickly or wiping with wet paper toweling. Sauté green onions in butter until tender. Add mushroom slices; sauté 4 minutes. Stir in remaining ingredients and leave on stove long enough to heat through.

ENTRÉES

Poached Pike with Horseradish Sauce

A favorite method of cooking readily available freshwater fish such as carp or pike is to poach the fish whole in a flavorful court bouillon. The most popular Polish fish sauce, made with horseradish and sour cream, accompanies it.

2 large carrots, scraped and diced	¼ cup chopped fresh parsley
1 large onion, peeled and chopped	1 bay leaf
	8 peppercorns
4 stalks celery, cleaned and chopped	Salt to taste
	1½ quarts water
1 leek, white part only, thinly sliced	1 whole pike, about 3 pounds, cleaned, head and tail left on
3 tablespoons butter or margarine	Horseradish sauce (recipe below)

1 large lemon, sliced   Chopped fresh dill

Sauté carrots, onion, celery and leek in butter in a saucepan for 5 minutes. Add parsley, bay leaf, peppercorns, salt and water. Bring to a boil. Lower heat and cook slowly, covered, for 10 minutes. Strain; reserve liquid. Wash pike and wipe dry. Sprinkle lightly with salt. Wrap in cheesecloth. Heat 4 cups of strained broth in a long baking dish. Lower fish into it. Simmer, covered, 10 minutes or longer, until fork-tender. Take out carefully and remove cheesecloth. Place fish on a warm platter. Cover with horseradish sauce. Garnish with lemon slices and chopped dill. Serves 4 to 6.

Horseradish sauce

1 cup sour cream	2 teaspoons lemon juice
⅓ cup freshly grated or pre-	Pinch of sugar
pared horseradish, drained	Salt to taste

Combine the ingredients and mix well. Chill.

Perch Fillets à la Polonaise

Another freshwater fish that is well-liked in Poland is perch, treasured for its firm white flesh and delicate flavor. A common way of cooking perch is in a flavorful wine sauce. Mushrooms may be added to the sauce if desired.

2 pounds perch fillets	2 tablespoons chopped fresh
2 cups dry white wine	dill or parsley
4 tablespoons butter or	Salt, pepper to taste
margarine	2 tablespoons flour
1 onion, peeled and sliced	2 egg yolks
	Lemon slices

Wash fillets and wipe dry. Put white wine, 2 tablespoons of butter, sliced onion, 1 tablespoon of dill, salt and pepper in a large skillet. Bring to a boil and cook briskly for 5 minutes. Reduce heat and add fillets. Cook slowly, covered, 6 to 10 minutes, until just fork-tender. Remove fish from dish and keep warm. Strain liquid and reserve. Melt 2 tablespoons of butter in a saucepan and blend in flour. Cook, stirring, 1 minute. Add strained liquid and cook slowly, stirring, until liquid is a thick and smooth sauce. Stir a little of the hot liquid into egg yolks and mix into sauce. Pour over poached fillets. Serve garnished with lemon slices and remaining 1 tablespoon of dill. Serves 4 to 6.

Chicken Livers in Madeira Sauce

Many Polish dishes are flavored with Madeira wine from the Portuguese island of the same name.

1 pound chicken livers	Flour
Milk	⅔ cup chicken broth
1 medium onion, peeled and	½ cup Madeira wine
minced	Salt, pepper to taste
2 tablespoons chicken fat or	
butter	

Cover chicken livers with milk; marinate 5 to 6 hours. Drain and set aside. Sauté onion in fat or butter. Dredge chicken livers with flour and brown both sides in drippings. Add broth, Madeira, salt and pepper. Cook slowly, covered, for about 10 minutes, or until tender. Serves 4.

Chicken in Dill Sauce

1 frying chicken (about 3	2 tablespoons flour
pounds), cut up	1 cup light cream
¼ cup butter or margarine	1 tablespoon lemon juice
Salt, pepper to taste	1 tablespoon fresh dill,
3 sprigs parsley	chopped

Sauté chicken pieces in butter in a heavy saucepan or kettle. Season with salt and pepper. Add parsley and enough water to cover chicken. Cook slowly, covered, about 30 minutes, or until chicken is tender. Remove chicken pieces to a warm plate and keep warm. Combine flour, cream, lemon juice and dill and add to drippings. Mix well and cook over low heat, stirring, until thickened. Correct seasoning. Spoon over chicken and serve with potatoes or rice. Serves 4.

Chicken Baked in Sour Cream

1 frying chicken, 2½ to 3 pounds, cut up	1 pint sour cream at room temperature
Salt, pepper to taste	¼ pound fresh mushrooms, cleaned and sliced
7 tablespoons butter or margarine	2 tablespoons fresh lemon juice
2 tablespoons flour	2 tablespoons chopped fresh dill or parsley
1 tablespoon paprika	

Wash chicken pieces and wipe dry. Season with salt and pepper. Melt 5 tablespoons butter in a large skillet and fry chicken pieces until golden on all sides. Remove to a greased baking dish. Sprinkle flour and paprika into pan juices and cook, stirring, for 1 minute. Stir in sour cream and mix well. Spoon over chicken pieces. Heat mushroom slices and lemon juice in remaining 2 tablespoons of butter for 1 minute; spoon over sour cream mixture. Sprinkle with dill or parsley. Bake, covered, in a preheated moderate oven (325°F.) about 30 minutes, or until chicken is tender. Serves 4.

Tripe and Vegetables, Warsaw Style

A favorite Polish meat is tripe, flaki, which is usually cooked with other foods to make flavorful creations.

2 pounds fresh tripe	1 celery root, peeled and diced; or 3 stalks celery, cleaned and chopped
1 pound soup bones	
Salt	
3 cups beef bouillon	1 leek, white part only, sliced
2 medium carrots, scraped and diced	3 sprigs parsley

2 tablespoons butter or margarine	½ teaspoon crumbled dried marjoram
2 tablespoons flour	Pepper to taste
¼ teaspoon ground nutmeg	¼ teaspoon ground ginger

Clean tripe very well and rinse several times. Put tripe in a kettle with soup bones; add cold water to cover. Season with salt. Bring to a boil. Lower heat and simmer, covered, 1½ to 2 hours, or until tender. Drain; cut into strips. Meanwhile, heat beef bouillon. Add carrots, celery root, leek and parsley; season with salt and pepper. Cook until vegetables are tender. Melt butter in a saucepan. Stir in flour to form a roux. Cook, stirring, for 1 minute. Add some of the hot vegetable liquid. Stir in nutmeg, ginger and marjoram. Season with salt and pepper. Cook slowly, stirring, until a smooth sauce. Add sauce with the cooked tripe to cooked vegetable mixture; leave on stove long enough to heat through. Serve with dumplings or boiled potatoes. Serves 8.
Note: Add ½ cup of light cream to sauce, if desired.

Hussar's Roast

An excellent Polish beef specialty is called pieczen huzarska. Vodka may be used instead of vinegar to blanch the meat, if desired. This is a good company entrée.

4 pounds boneless beef, rump or round	1 large onion, peeled and sliced
½ cup hot vinegar	1 cup fresh small bread cubes
Flour	
Salt, pepper to taste	1 large onion, peeled and grated or minced
6 tablespoons butter or margarine	1 egg, beaten slightly
½ cup hot beef bouillon or consommé	

Scald beef with hot vinegar and wipe dry. Dredge meat with flour seasoned with salt, pepper. Heat 4 tablespoons butter in large kettle; brown meat on both sides in butter. Add bouillon and sliced onion. Cook very slowly, tightly covered, about 2 hours.

Turn occasionally while cooking. Meanwhile, combine bread cubes, grated onion, egg and remaining 2 tablespoons of butter, melted. Season with salt and pepper. Take meat from kettle and cut into crosswise slices, about ¼ inch thick. Cut from the top to about 1 inch from the bottom so that the slices are apart but not separate. Place stuffing between slices. Skewer meat at each end; bind the roast with heavy thread. Carefully return roast to kettle. Sprinkle with a little flour and baste with drippings. Cook, covered, over low heat, 30 minutes. Remove to a warm platter. Remove thread and skewers. Thicken remaining liquid with flour to use as a gravy, if desired. Strain. Serve with boiled potatoes. Serves 8.

Hunter's Stew

Poland's national dish, a very old one, is called bigos. It is prepared with a large number of ingredients and is a marvelous party dish. Originally the stew was made with cabbage, onions, mushrooms and a variety of other vegetables, as well as with apples, prunes and an abundance of game and meats. The hearty dish supposedly evolved because it was a good way to use the ample supplies of game left over from lengthy banquets. Bigos became the staple food for hunters, particularly because it could be reheated and tastes even better that way. Served at many important Polish festivities, bigos is made today in several versions, but its basic characteristic is the same—a rich combination of hearty foods. Some of the stews are made in great quantity and take days to prepare. This is a simple but good variation.

2 ounces dried mushrooms, preferably Polish
¼ pound salt pork or bacon, diced
2 large onions, peeled and sliced
2 tart apples, cored, peeled and sliced
3 tomatoes, peeled and chopped

3 pounds mixed roasted or cooked meats, game or poultry
2 - 3 pounds sauerkraut, washed and drained
½ pound Polish sausage, kielbasi, cut into 1-inch rounds
Sugar, salt, pepper to taste
½ cup Madeira wine
Beef bouillon or water

Soak mushrooms in lukewarm water to cover for 20 minutes. Drain and squeeze dry, reserving liquid. Slice mushrooms. Fry salt pork in a large kettle. Add onions; sauté until tender. Add apples, tomatoes, meats, sauerkraut, sausage, sugar, salt and pepper. Mix in sliced mushrooms; add liquid, Madeira and bouillon to cover the ingredients. Cook slowly, covered, for 1 hour, or until ingredients are cooked. Serve with boiled potatoes. Serves 8 to 10.

VEGETABLES

Vegetables à la Polonaise

A Polish way of serving fresh vegetables in season is with a butter and bread crumb topping, known around the world as *à la Polonaise*. Sometimes other ingredients such as chopped chives, herbs, or hard-cooked eggs are added to the basic mixture. This is a good way of preparing asparagus, Brussels sprouts, cabbage or cauliflower. Cook vegetables until just tender. Drain. Season with salt and pepper. Melt 3 tablespoons butter in a small saucepan. Stir in 3 tablespoons fine dry bread crumbs. Pour over the warm vegetables and serve at once.

Potatoes in Sour Cream

The Poles consume great quantities of potatoes, which are prepared in interesting dishes. This is a typical one.

2 pounds (about 6 medium) potatoes, peeled	½ cup (approximately) sour cream at room temperature
2 medium onions, peeled and chopped	1 or 2 tablespoons chopped fresh dill
3 tablespoons butter or margarine	Salt, pepper to taste

Parboil potatoes for 5 minutes. Drain and slice. In a medium skillet, sauté onions in butter until tender. Add sliced potatoes, sour cream, dill, salt and pepper and cook slowly, covered, until tender, about 20 minutes. Serves 4 to 6.

Sweet-Sour Cabbage

Green, red and Savoy cabbage are used extensively in the Polish cuisine, and the cooks have devised innovative methods for cooking them. This is a characteristic preparation.

1 medium head green cabbage	1 tart apple, cored, peeled and chopped
Salt	3 tablespoons vinegar
1 medium onion, peeled and chopped	1 tablespoon sugar
	Pepper to taste

Remove any wilted outer leaves from cabbage. Cut out core and shred leaves. Put leaves in a bowl or colander and sprinkle with salt. Leave for 1 hour. Squeeze out all liquid. Put cabbage in a saucepan and add remaining ingredients. Cover with water and bring to a boil. Lower heat and cook slowly, covered, for 30 minutes, or until tender. Serves 4 to 6.
Note: The dish may be thickened with flour, if desired.

Baked Mushrooms

Another inviting preparation for the mushrooms that the Poles like so much.

1 pound fresh mushrooms	2 tablespoons flour
2 tablespoons lemon juice	¼ cup grated Parmesan cheese
¼ cup minced green onions, with tops	½ cup sour cream at room temperature
¼ cup butter or margarine	Fine dry bread crumbs
Salt, pepper to taste	

Clean mushrooms by rinsing quickly or wiping with wet paper toweling. Cut off any tough stem ends. Sauté with lemon juice and green onions in butter for 4 minutes. Season with salt and pepper. Stir in flour and cook, mixing, 1 minute. Spoon into a shallow baking dish. Combine Parmesan cheese and sour cream; pour over mushrooms. Sprinkle with bread crumbs and dot with butter. Bake in a hot oven (425°F.) for 10 minutes, or until bubbly and golden.

SALADS

Celery Root Salad

Celery root, or celeriac, is a greatly appreciated vegetable in Poland and is eaten both as a vegetable and as a salad. The gnarled and knobby brown root is not attractive in appearance, but it has an interesting celerylike flavor.

1 small celery root, or celeriac	4 tablespoons vegetable oil
2 tablespoons minced chives	2 tablespoons red vinegar
2 tablespoons chopped fresh dill	Pinch sugar
	Salt, pepper to taste

Wash and peel celery root. Cut into slices and cook in salted water to cover for about 15 minutes, or until just tender. Drain and cool. Put in a bowl and add remaining ingredients. Marinate 3 to 4 hours. Serves 4.

Cucumber Salad

Probably the most well-liked salad in Poland is made with cucumbers and is called salata mizerja. There are two ways of preparing it. One is to peel the cucumbers and slice them very thin. Sprinkle with salt and leave to drain for 30 minutes. Press to release all liquid and then put in a bowl. Cover with vegetable oil and red vinegar, using 2 parts oil to 1 part vinegar. Season with salt and pepper and sprinkle with chopped fresh dill. The second method is to add sour cream and vinegar to drained sliced cucumbers.

SAUCES

Bread Crumb and Butter Sauce

This sauce is internationally known as Sauce Polonaise.

6 tablespoons butter or margarine
1 cup fine white bread crumbs

2 teaspoons fresh lemon juice
2 tablespoons chopped fresh parsley
1 hard-cooked egg, shelled and chopped

Melt butter in a skillet. Add bread crumbs and cook until golden. Add lemon juice, parsley and chopped egg. Serve with vegetables such as asparagus, cauliflower or brussels sprouts. Makes about 1 cup.

Caper Sauce

¼ cup butter or margarine
3 tablespoons flour
1½ cups meat bouillon
⅓ cup light cream

2 tablespoons capers, drained
Salt, pepper to taste

Melt butter in a saucepan. Stir in flour to form a roux. Gradually add bouillon and cook, stirring, over medium heat until thickened. Add cream, capers, salt and pepper and cook 1 minute. Makes about 1¾ cups. Serve with veal or poultry.
Note: This sauce, if made with fish bouillon instead of meat bouillon, can be served with fish.

Madeira Sauce

1 medium onion, peeled and chopped
3 tablespoons butter or margarine
½ cup sliced mushrooms
2 tablespoons flour
1 cup beef bouillon
¼ cup Madeira wine
Salt, pepper to taste

Sauté onion in butter in a saucepan. Add mushrooms; sauté 4 minutes. Stir in flour. Slowly add beef bouillon and cook, stirring, until thickened. Add Madeira, salt and pepper; cook slowly 5 minutes. Makes about 1¾ cups. Serve with meats.

Horseradish Sauce

¼ cup butter or margarine
2 tablespoons flour
2 cups vegetable or meat broth
½ cup freshly grated or prepared horseradish, drained
2 tablespoons lemon juice
2 tablespoons fresh dill or parsley, minced
Salt, pepper to taste

Heat butter in a saucepan. Stir in flour. Slowly add broth and cook, stirring, until thickened. Add horseradish, lemon juice, dill, salt and pepper. Cook slowly, stirring often, about 10 minutes. Serve with roast meat or fish. Makes about 2 cups.

Fresh Mushroom Sauce

1 small onion or 3 green onions, peeled and minced
¼ cup butter or margarine
2 cups sliced fresh mushrooms
1 tablespoon lemon juice
Salt, pepper to taste
2 tablespoons flour
1 cup vegetable or beef bouillon
½ - 1 cup sour cream at room temperature
2 tablespoons minced dill or parsley

In a saucepan, sauté onion in butter until soft. Add mushrooms and lemon juice; sauté 4 minutes. Season with salt and pepper. Stir in flour and mix well. Slowly add bouillon and cook, stirring often, about 5 minutes, until thickened. Mix in sour cream and dill; leave on stove long enough to heat through. Makes about 2 cups. Serve with meat or fish.

Note: This sauce can also be made with dried mushrooms imported from Poland and sold in specialty food stores. Use 1½ ounces. Soak in lukewarm water to cover for 20 minutes. Drain and chop.

DESSERTS

Honey Cookies

One of Poland's finest products is its honey, which over the years has been used in making a large number of good dishes such as these flavorful cookies.

½ cup honey	½ teaspoon ground cinnamon
½ cup sugar	½ teaspoon ground nutmeg
2 large eggs	½ teaspoon ground ginger
3 cups (approximately) all-purpose flour	1 egg white
	Blanched almond halves
1 teaspoon baking soda	

Combine honey and sugar in a bowl; mix well. Add eggs; beat well. Sift flour, soda, cinnamon, nutmeg and ginger into mixture; stir well. Add enough flour to make a stiff dough. Shape into a ball and refrigerate for 2 hours. Roll out on a floured board to a ¼ inch thickness and cut with a round cookie cutter about 2½ inches in diameter. Brush top of each cookie with egg white and press an almond into center. Arrange on greased cookie sheets and bake in a preheated moderate oven (375°F.) for 12 to 15 minutes. Makes about 4 dozen.

Babka

The national cake of Poland is called babka. It is derived from the word for "old woman." This flavorful nut and raisin-studded yeast cake was probably so named because the fluted pan in which it is baked resembles the skirt of a woman. The cake, similar to the kulich of Russia, is traditional fare for Easter.

1 package active dry yeast; or 1 cake compressed yeast
¼ cup warm water
½ cup butter or margarine
½ cup sugar
5 egg yolks
1 teaspoon salt
1 tablespoon grated lemon rind

1 tablespoon grated orange rind
1 cup lukewarm milk
4 cups (approximately) sifted all-purpose flour
¼ cup chopped blanched almonds
1 cup golden raisins
Almond slivers

Sprinkle or crumble yeast into warm water. Use very warm water for dry yeast and lukewarm water for compressed yeast. After a minute or two, stir to dissolve. Cream butter in a large bowl. Add sugar. Beat 4 of the egg yolks with salt; add to butter mixture. Stir in yeast and lemon and orange rinds; mix well. Add milk and enough flour to make a soft dough; mix again. Stir in chopped almonds and raisins. Turn out on a floured board and knead until smooth and elastic. Form into a ball and place in a greased bowl. Turn over and place in a warm place, covered with a towel, to rise until doubled in bulk, about 2 hours. Arrange dough in a buttered fluted tube pan or a round pan. Let rise again, covered, until doubled in bulk. Mix remaining egg yolk with 2 tablespoons water and brush over top. Sprinkle top with almond slivers, pressing into dough (or omit almonds and spread with frosting when cooked and cooled). Bake in a preheated moderate oven (350°F.) about 40 minutes, or until cooked. Makes about 16 servings.

Baked Apples in Wine

The Poles are extremely fond of desserts, compotes or baked creations made with fruits such as apples, pears, peaches, or berries. Many such desserts are flavored with rum, brandy or wine.

6 large red apples
Cherry, raspberry or
strawberry preserves

⅓ to ½ cup sugar
1 cup sweet red wine

Remove cores from apples without making holes in the bottoms of them. Fill each apple with thick preserves. Place in a baking dish and sprinkle with sugar and wine. Bake, covered, in a pre-heated moderate oven (350°F.) for 1 hour. Serve hot or cold, with or without cream. Serves 6.

Mazurek

In the Polish cuisine there are several recipes for a type of cake that, because it is thin and chewy, is more like a cookie. One kind is made with ground nuts and another includes flour. The toppings or fillings might be nuts, cherries, apples, raisins, dates or candied fruits. This is one good example.

½ cup butter or margarine
4 ounces baking chocolate, melted
1 cup sugar
3 eggs
1 teaspoon vanilla

¼ teaspoon salt
2 tablespoons milk
2 cups sifted all-purpose flour
White frosting
Chopped nuts

Cream butter in a bowl. Add melted chocolate and sugar; mix well. Stir in eggs, one at a time; mix well. Stir in vanilla, salt and milk. Gradually add flour; mix well. Spread evenly in a greased shallow pan, 15 inches x 10 inches x 1 inch; bake in a preheated moderate oven (350°F.) about 20 minutes, or until cooked. Cut into pieces, each 2 x 2 inches, and decorate each piece with white frosting and chopped nuts. Makes about 25.

East German Cookery

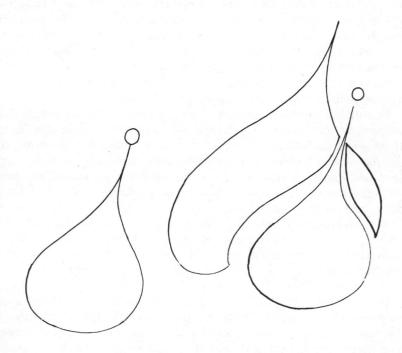

The East Germans enjoy rich and robust food that is quite similar to that of their countrymen on the other side of the political border. Yet East German cookery differs slightly because the East Germans have had long and close associations with their Slavic neighbors in Poland and Russia, who left an imprint on East German cuisine.

The German Democratic Republic was formed in 1945. Bordered by the Baltic Sea, Poland, Czechoslovakia and West Germany, it is but a fragment of a once vast empire. Except for a comparatively small southern area of rolling hills, the country lies within the great North European plain. Thus the cookery reflects the rigors of the cold flat lands, the closeness to the northern waters and, because of the nation's central location, the influences of surrounding cuisines.

Interesting regional contrasts exist within East Germany, which is now made up of the once independent provinces of Brandenburg, Mecklenburg, Pomerania, Saxony, Silesia and Thuringia, all of which have their own culinary and cultural heritages. The early tribes of this northern area were nomadic warriors and hunters who were dubbed Germans by ancient Romans. The earliest record about these people, *Germania*, was written in the 1st century A.D. by the Roman historian Tacitus, who remarked that these people subsisted primarily on simple fare with an emphasis on "fruits, nuts and sour milk."

Essentially, the Germans were hearty eaters who established a propensity for meats, which are still all-important to the diet. They were particularly fond of the wild boar, the ancestor of the pig, which has remained the supreme favorite over the years. Lard and bacon grease became the principal cooking fats, and the repertoire of German schwein, or pork creations, has long been one of the most imaginative and extensive in the world. Cooks created a seemingly endless number of substantial and inviting dishes to make use of every part of the pig—chops, loins, hocks, shins, ears, feet and knuckles. Many East German specialties are flavored with smoked bacon and with the world-famous German hams.

The early tribesmen also relied heavily on the great abundance of game readily available in the deep forests. The pleasures of the hunt became an established part of the German way of life, and hare, rabbit, venison, wild duck, geese, pheasant and small game birds such as quail and woodcock figured prominently in the cuisine. For centuries inventive cooks have practiced the techniques of transforming game into unusual and delectable gastronomic creations that were served in homes and restaurants. A typical method of marinating game, as well as some other meats, was to soak it in buttermilk, an effective tenderizer that also gave an interesting flavor to the flesh.

When the itinerant tribesmen settled down to converting the northern plain into cultivated fields, their task was not easy. A great deal of the sandy land was poorly suited to agriculture, and it became necessary to rely on such hardy grains as barley and rye to make gruels, porridges and breads. Barley was also vital for the everyday tipples, a strong honey-flavored mead and a crude brew of beer. Rye became the great favorite for making a wide variety of dark whole grain breads, which over the centuries have been standard in the family diet. Wheat did flourish in the more fertile Elbe River valley and enough was grown in later years to prepare the lighter white breads, dumplings, noodles and pancakes, all food beloved by Germans.

The eastern Germans also grew fond of dried lentils, beans and both yellow and green peas, which were used extensively in the rib-sticking, nourishing thick soups and stews such as the very typical Berlin specialty, erbsenpüree, yellow pea purée with bacon.

Also important for the everyday diet was the abundant supply of fish from the great rivers, northern seas and inland lakes. The fish provided the basis for many sustaining and imaginative dishes. By far the most cherished of the plentiful catches was the herring, long accorded noble treatment in the kitchen and on the table. Eaten for all meals, including breakfast, and in between meals as a snack, the herring, either fresh, smoked or pickled, has appeared in so many guises that one can only wonder if the Germans would have survived without it. Many German herring dishes were adapted from those of their northern neighbors in Scandinavia and other Baltic countries and reflect a fondness for tart flavors, particularly sour cream. Two other lasting culinary treasures from the sea, carp and eel, were also proffered in interesting variation on German tables.

An outstanding early characteristic of German cookery was an extraordinary predilection for fresh and dried fruits in a wide range of dishes. Such favorites as apples, cherries, pears and plums were used imaginatively in great quantity for cold soups, meat and vegetable creations, sauces, salads, stuffings, purées, jams, jellies, relishes, puddings, compotes and baked goods. Although very important as sweeteners, the fruits also were used as accompaniments for game, poultry and meats, as well as toppings for such popular dishes as dumplings and pancakes.

Perhaps this German reliance on fruits came about because their supply of vegetables was extremely limited to but a few kinds, such as the root varieties, turnips, beets and carrots, and particularly cabbage. No cooks have devised as many ways for preparing and serving fermented cabbage or sauerkraut, an acquisition from the Slavs. In fact the eating of this flavorful food is almost a way of life—it seems as if sauerkraut in some variation has appeared on just about every German plate for centuries. It still is flavored with caraway seeds, juniper berries, fruits, wine or beer, and is cooked with such foods as potatoes, beans, yellow peas, bacon, sausages and ham. Not only is sauerkraut a traditional ingredient in soups and stews, but it is also made into a number of salads.

Although the early German diet was limited in range it was adequate, relying on gifts of nature and on primitive agriculture. The cooks had an intuitive way of dealing with humble foods to make them not only nutritious but also innovative culinary creations. Thus the hefty soups, casseroles and stews had particular character and inventiveness. Even the roast haunches and lesser cuts of game and meat were imbued with distinction and appeal.

From the Romans, the Germans acquired not only their first primary culinary and cultural refinements but also Christianity. Emperor Charlemagne, who organized the European nations into an early empire, fostered a significant agricultural revival by dispensing advice about the planting of orchards and gardens, particularly those for vegetables and herbs. It was probably then that the Germans adopted parsley, dill and the members of the onion family as their traditional seasonings. Under the emperor's aegis the Germans also benefited from the great progress in the arts of brewing and baking that were mastered in the monasteries. The acceptance of Christianity was important, since the German year-round ritual of feast and fast days became synonymous with that of the Church.

It was most probably also from the Romans that the Germans learned the technique of making sausages—and certainly these savory foods became very important to the cuisine. The preparation of sausages was not only an important means of preserving meats, such as the prized pork, but it was also a way of using all parts of the animals. Just about every homeowner and farmer became an expert in the annual rite of making fresh and cured *wursts* and joined in the challenge of creating new varieties. Perhaps the Germans can be credited with originating as many as 300 kinds of sausage. At least the extraordinary variety displayed in butcher shops and grocery stores attests to the ingenuity of the many persons who have combined minced or ground meats with spices, and sometimes other foods, to fashion this traditional fare.

In medieval times German cookery was enhanced further by the introduction of other foods brought from many lands, but particularly from the Near and Far East. Capers, mustard and caraway seeds became characteristic flavorings for sauces, fish, meat and vegetable dishes, and such spices as anise, cardamom and ginger were freely used in a wide number of baked goods. Although the oldest and most famous of the German treasure trove of cakes and cookies were those flavored with honey, the pastry shops, or konditoreien, have long featured a wealth of other mouth-watering goodies made of spices, fruits and nuts. East Germans are devoted to such well-known creations as fruit-studded Dresden loaves, delicate bilberry buns, light Thuringer doughnuts, Berlin's jelly doughnuts (pfannkuchen) and fruit cake (napfkuchen). Coffee became the favorite German beverage and the pleasure of enjoying coffee and sweets with friends is an established way of life.

A New World gastronomic gift, however, had a particularly outstanding impact on German cookery. The potato or kartoffel, a name taken from the Latin for "little truffle," became the king of the German vegetables and one of the country's most important food products. The potato was not accepted as fit for human consumption until the late 1700s, and then only under the pressure of Frederick the Great of Prussia, who more or less forced the peasants to plant potatoes as an act of desperation during severe food shortages. Fortunately the South American import thrived in the northern soil, and the Germans became so fond of the potato that their cooks devised an incredible assortment of appealing potato dishes—salads, pancakes, dumplings and soups, among many others.

Until the nineteenth century eastern Germany was a conglomeration of small city states, principalities and provinces, ruled by princelings or other leaders who lived on large estates, each estate largely self-supporting. The agricultural lands that had been planted with many different crops yielded increasing bounty for a people who by then relished tables heavily laden with basic and robust food. Although the numerous German courts were influenced by the refinements of the French culture and cuisine that swept over Europe, the traditional food never became sophisticated. The eastern Germans reveled in robust conviviality with hearty and substantial meals, and they preferred beer to wine.

When Germany was a unified nation, from 1871 until after World War II, the regional cuisines were interchanged and

Germans enjoyed a wide range of native specialties. The cooking of East Germany still has much in common with that of the western nation. Yet East German cuisine has not become as modernized and remains more true to the traditional eating customs established long ago, as exemplified by this selection of recipes.

VORSPEISEN

In East Germany appetizers are called vorspeisen, before foods, and may consist of a few humble selections or a copious spread of sausages, smoked fish, pâtés, herring in sauces and marinades, pickles, stuffed eggs, filled pastries, canapes, salads, cold meat slices, cheeses, stuffed tomatoes, mushrooms or cold cooked seafoods. Some of the vorspeisen are purchased at delicatessens; others are prepared at home. Standard accompaniments are two or more kinds of white and dark bread, butter and mustard. The Germans generally drink Schnapps (strong spirits) or beer with the appetizers.

Mecklenburger Herring with Sour Cream

4 pickled herring, drained
1 cup sour cream
1 large dill pickle, chopped
2 tart apples, peeled, cored and chopped

2 large onions, peeled and chopped
Salt, pepper to taste
3 tablespoons chopped chives

Cut herring into 1-inch pieces. Combine with sour cream, pickle, apples and onions. Mix well. Season with salt and pepper. Serve garnished with chopped chives. Serves 4. This is traditionally eaten with small potatoes cooked in their jackets, light beer and Schnapps.

Rollmops of Berlin

This appetizer is popular throughout Germany.

4 salt herring in brine, cleaned	1¼ cups cider vinegar
Sharp prepared mustard	4 peppercorns, bruised
3 small sour pickles, chopped	1 tablespoon mustard seed
2 medium onions, peeled and sliced thinly	2 whole allspice
1 tablespoon capers	2 whole cloves
	1 bay leaf

Soak herring in cold water to cover for 24 hours, changing water several times. Drain well and rinse under running water. Cut into fillets, discarding heads and bones. Place, skin side down, on a board or table. Thinly spread each fillet with mustard. Top each one with pickles, onions and capers. Roll up and tie with string or secure with toothpicks. Put in a glass bowl or earthenware crock. Put any remaining onion slices among herring. Bring vinegar and ½ cup water to a boil. Cool and add to herring, with peppercorns, mustard seed, allspice, cloves and bay leaf. Leave 3 or 4 days, turning about now and then. Drain and serve on individual plates or serving dishes, garnished with parsley, if desired. Serves 4.

Beefsteak Tartar

Northern Germans are partial to a raw ground beef appetizer, usually served as a first course, which was brought to their country from Russia. Ground or chopped raw meat dishes eaten by the Asiatic Tartars gained great popularity in Germany, but, like this one, most of them were considerably embellished. The meat should be freshly ground and put through the grinder at least twice.

½ pound lean round or sirloin steak	2 raw egg yolks

Garnishes: Finely chopped onion, capers, caraway seeds, chopped anchovy fillets, chopped gherkins, grated fresh horseradish, chopped fresh parsley, minced chives

Accompaniments: Pepper, Worcestershire sauce, mustard, lemon juice

Meat should be as fresh as possible. Ask butcher to grind meat twice, and plan to buy it shortly before serving. Divide meat into two portions. Shape into 2 mounds and place each on a small serving plate. With back of a spoon, make a depression for egg yolks in the center of each mound of meat. Drop egg yolks into the depressions. Serve surrounded with separate dishes of any of the desired garnishes, or place small spoonfuls of the garnishes on the plate around the meat. Place the accompaniments on the table for each person to use as desired. The diner combines the meat and other ingredients as he wishes. Serves 2.

SOUPS

Berlin Pea Soup with Bacon

A specialty soup of Berlin is one made with yellow dried peas and bacon, to which sliced sausages, such as Bockwurst, are often added.

1 pound yellow dried peas	2 medium stalks celery,
2 tablespoons cooking fat	cleaned and sliced thinly
or oil	2½ quarts water
1 large carrot, scraped and	Salt, pepper to taste
diced	½ pound bacon in one piece
2 large onions, peeled and	2 tablespoons butter or
diced	margarine
2 leeks, white parts only,	¼ teaspoon dried thyme
cleaned and sliced thinly	¼ teaspoon dried marjoram

Rinse peas. Heat fat in a large kettle and add carrot, 1 onion, leeks and celery. Sauté 5 minutes. Add water and bring to a boil. Season with salt and pepper. Add peas and bacon; cook slowly, covered, for about 1 hour, or until peas are cooked. Meanwhile, sauté remaining onion in butter until tender. Add thyme and marjoram and mix into soup. To serve, take out bacon and chop or slice; return bacon to soup. Serves 6 to 8.

Cold Berry Soup

This is typical of the cold berry soups that are very much enjoyed by northern Germans.

1 quart elderberries (or blackberries)	½ cup sugar
2 tablespoons potato starch or cornstarch	Ground cloves or cinnamon

Cook berries in 6 cups water until tender. Press through a sieve. Dissolve potato starch or cornstarch in a little water and mix into berries. Bring to a boil. Add sugar (more, if a sweeter dish is desired) and remove from heat. Flavor with ground cloves or cinnamon. Chill. Serves 6.

ENTRÉES

Blue Trout

A favorite way of preparing trout (also fresh herring and carp) in several Eastern European countries, especially East Germany, is to briefly marinate or cook the fish in a vinegar solution, which turns the skin a vivid blue (*blau*). The flesh of fish prepared in this manner is particularly flavorful. For best results, however, the trout should be freshly caught.

4 trout, dressed	2 tablespoons chopped onion
1 cup vinegar	1 bay leaf
3 cups water	Salt, pepper to taste
2 sprigs parsley	

Wash trout under running water. If desired, form each fish into a ring by tying head to tail with a strong thread. Bring remaining ingredients to a boil in a kettle. Plunge in trout and simmer

4 to 6 minutes, just long enough to cook. Drain well. Serve garnished with parsley and lemon wedges, and with boiled potatoes covered with melted butter-parsley sauce or plain melted butter. Serves 4.

Pike with Sauerkraut

A very good and flavorful German baked dish is made with three staples—pike, sauerkraut and sour cream.

2 pounds pike or any other white firm-fleshed fish	2 tablespoons flour
	2 tablespoons chopped fresh dill or parsley
2 medium onions, peeled and chopped	½ cup sour cream at room temperature
1 large carrot, scraped and sliced	2 pounds (4 cups) sauerkraut, drained
Salt, pepper to taste	Fine dry bread crumbs
3 tablespoons (approximately) butter or margarine	

Have the fish dealer skin and bone fish and cut fillets into 2-inch lengths. Take home trimmings and bones as well as fillets. Prepare a court bouillon with trimmings, bones, 1 onion, carrot, salt, pepper and 4 cups water. Bring to a boil. Lower heat and cook slowly, covered, for 30 minutes. Strain and reserve the liquid.

Melt 3 tablespoons butter in a saucepan. Add remaining chopped onion and sauté until tender. Stir in flour to form a roux. Add 2 cups strained court bouillon, a little at a time; cook slowly, stirring, until mixture is a thick sauce. Add dill and sour cream; leave on the stove just long enough to heat through. Spoon a layer of sauerkraut into a greased shallow baking dish. Top with half the fish fillets and half the sauce. Sprinkle with bread crumbs. Repeat layers, topping with bread crumbs. Dot with butter. Cook in a preheated moderate oven (375°F.) about 30 minutes, or until fish is tender and top is golden. Serves 6.

Braised Duck with Red Cabbage

Two characteristic and superb foods of East Germany—duck,

ente, and red cabbage, rotkohl—are combined in this creation to make one of the country's best dishes. Traditionally, the dish is prepared with wild duck.

1 duckling, about 5 pounds, cut up	1 large onion, peeled and chopped
Salt, pepper to taste	1 tablespoon flour
1 medium head red cabbage	½ cup (about) red wine
⅓ cup lemon juice	1 teaspoon sugar
¼ pound salt pork, diced	

Wash duckling and pat dry. Season with salt and pepper. Place in a shallow pan and roast in a preheated moderate oven (375°F.) for 30 minutes. Meanwhile, blanch cabbage in boiling water for 5 minutes. Drain and sprinkle with lemon juice. Fry salt pork in a large saucepan or kettle. Add onion and sauté until tender. Mix in flour. Add cabbage, red wine and sugar. Season with salt and pepper. Cook slowly, covered, for 30 minutes. Put the partially cooked duck pieces and some of the drippings from the pan over cabbage. Continue to simmer, covered, for 1 hour, or until duck is cooked. Add more red wine while cooking, if needed. Serves 4.

Hasenpfeffer

This well-known German specialty, literally "pepper hare," is typical of the jugged game dishes made with sweet-sour marinades. Hare is not available in America, but rabbit is a good substitute.

2 fresh or frozen rabbits (2½ to 3 pounds), cut into serving pieces	4 whole cloves
	2 tablespoons sugar
	6 peppercorns, bruised
Equal parts of wine vinegar and water to cover the rabbit pieces	Salt
	Flour
	Pepper
2 medium onions, peeled and sliced	Butter or margarine
	½ cup sour cream at room temperature
2 medium bay leaves	
4 juniper berries	

Put rabbit pieces in a large crock or kettle; add vinegar and water, onions, bay leaves, juniper berries, cloves, sugar, peppercorns and salt. Let stand, covered, in a cool place for 2 days. Turn rabbit pieces over 1 or 2 times daily. When marinating is finished, take out rabbit. Strain and reserve marinade. Wipe rabbit dry; dust with flour seasoned with salt and pepper. Fry in butter until golden on all sides. Add some strained marinade and cook very slowly, covered, until rabbit is tender, about 1 hour. Add more marinade as needed while cooking. Mix in sour cream and remove dish from stove. Serves 6 to 8.

Fried Liver with Apples and Onions

This is one of the great specialties of Berlin. Serve with boiled potatoes sprinkled with chopped parsley.

1 pound calf or beef liver, thinly sliced
Flour
Salt, pepper to taste
2 large onions, peeled and sliced

2 large apples, peeled, cored and sliced crosswise
⅓ cup (approximately) butter or shortening
Chopped fresh parsley

Dredge liver slices in flour seasoned with salt and pepper; set aside. In a small skillet, sauté onions and apples in ¼ cup butter until tender. Keep warm. In another skillet, sauté liver slices in remaining butter to brown on both sides and until tender, 5 minutes or more. Serve at once topped with onion and apple slices. Sprinkle with chopped parsley. Serves 3 or 4.

Bratwurst in Beer, Berlin Style

The small whitish sausages called Bratwurst originated in Nürnberg but are used in Berlin in this specialty.

12 Bratwurst (or pork sausage)
2 tablespoons butter or margarine

2 medium onions, peeled and sliced
2 bay leaves

1¼ cups (approximately) beer   3 tablespoons chopped
     Salt, pepper to taste   parsley
1 tablespoon flour

Place Bratwurst in a saucepan and cover with boiling water.
Cook 3 minutes; drain. Melt butter in a skillet; add Bratwurst
to brown. Remove to a warm plate. Pour off all except 2 tablespoons fat. Add onions; sauté until tender. Return sausages to
skillet. Add bay leaves, beer, salt and pepper. Cook slowly for
15 minutes. Add more beer during cooking, if needed. Remove
Bratwurst to a warm platter. Mix flour with a little cold water;
stir into hot liquid. Cook, stirring, until liquid is a thick sauce;
remove bay leaves. Add parsley; pour over sausage. Serve with
mashed potatoes and red cabbage. Serves 4.

Meatballs in Caper Sauce

A great German specialty, Königsberger Klopse, originated in the
eastern port city of Königsberg, which was once an important
fortress of Prussia. Now the city is a part of the Soviet Union
and its name has been changed to Kaliningrad. The meatballs
are traditionally made with ground pork and another meat, either
veal or beef, and are particularly appealing because of the piquant
flavor derived from capers and lemon juice.

1½ cups stale bread cubes   3 flat anchovy fillets, drained
     Milk   and minced
2 pounds ground lean meat   Salt, pepper to taste
     (a mixture of pork and veal   4 cups beef bouillon
     or beef)   3 tablespoons butter or
1 large onion, peeled and   margarine
     minced   3 tablespoons flour
2 eggs, beaten   Juice of 1 large lemon
                                      3 tablespoons drained capers

Soak bread cubes in milk to cover. When soft, squeeze dry and
put in a large bowl. Add ground meat and mix well. Stir in
onion, eggs, anchovy fillets, salt and pepper; work mixture with
hands until well combined. Form into 2-inch balls. Bring bouillon
to a boil in a large saucepan; drop in meatballs. Cook over

medium heat until meatballs rise to the top, about 15 minutes. Remove from liquid with a slotted spoon and keep warm. Strain and reserve liquid. Melt butter in a saucepan. Stir in flour and blend well. Cook 1 minute. Gradually add 3 cups strained liquid; cook slowly, stirring constantly, until liquid is thickened and smooth. Add lemon juice and the capers. Season with salt and pepper. Add meatballs and heat through. Serves 6 to 8.

DUMPLINGS

The East Germans are devotees of dumplings, or knödel, which they make in seemingly endless variety. Some knödel are prepared with a yeast dough; others are made of flour or potatoes, and include such ingredients as bread cubes, cheese, meats, fish, semolina and fruits. Knödel may be either savory or sweet and are served in soups or stews, as accompaniments to meats, game, poultry or fish and as desserts. Following are four typical kinds.

Meat Dumplings

½ pound ground meat
(veal, pork or beef)
2 eggs, well beaten
2 tablespoons melted
shortening
1 tablespoon chopped chives

2 tablespoons chopped
parsley
Salt, pepper to taste
⅔ cup fine dry bread crumbs

Combine all ingredients and mix well. Shape into walnut-sized dumplings. Drop into a kettle of boiling salted water and cook, uncovered, until dumplings rise to the top. Makes about 22.

Bread Dumplings

3 cups ½ inch white bread
cubes
½ cup milk

3 slices bacon, finely
chopped
1 small onion, peeled and
minced

2 eggs, beaten
2 tablespoons chopped
   parsley

1¾ cups (approximately) sifted
   all-purpose flour

Place bread cubes in a large bowl and cover with milk. Fry bacon
and pour off all except 1 tablespoon fat. Add onion; sauté until
tender. Add bacon, onion, eggs and parsley to bread cubes;
mix well. Stir in enough flour to make a stiff dough; beat well.
With floured hands, shape dough into six balls. Drop into a
large kettle of boiling salted water. Boil, uncovered, until dumplings rise to the top. Cover and cook 10 to 15 minutes, or until
done. Test by tearing one dumpling apart with two forks. Remove
with a slotted spoon and drain. Makes 6.

Steamed Yeast Dumplings

1 package active dry yeast;
   or 1 cake compressed yeast
¼ cup lukewarm water
¾ cup butter or margarine
¾ cup milk

¼ cup sugar
¼ teaspoon salt
2 eggs, beaten
2½ to 3 cups sifted all-purpose
   flour

Sprinkle or crumble yeast into a large bowl. Add water. Use slightly
warmer water for dry yeast. After a minute or two, stir to dissolve.
Heat ¼ cup of butter and ¼ cup of milk in a saucepan. Remove
from stove and leave until butter melts. Add sugar, salt and
eggs; add to the yeast. Mix well. Gradually stir in enough flour
to make a stiff dough; beat well. Knead on a floured board until
smooth and elastic. Form into a ball and put in a greased bowl.
Turn over once. Cover with a cloth and let rise in a warm place
until doubled in bulk, about 1½ hours. Punch down and turn
out on a floured board. Cut off small pieces and shape with
floured hands into balls about 2 inches in diameter. Arrange
on a large plate and cover. Let rise until doubled in bulk. Melt
remaining ½ cup of butter in a large skillet or heavy casserole.
Add remaining ½ cup of milk; heat. Arrange dumplings, one
next to another, in the dish. Cook over low heat, covered, until
all liquid has evaporated and butter crackles, about 30 minutes.
The dumplings should have a crisp golden crust. Serve with
stewed fruit or a sweet sauce. Makes about 12.

Miniature Dumplings

One of the most popular German forms of pasta is the tiny Spätzle, which means literally "tiny sparrows." It is considered both a dumpling and a noodle. Although native to Swabia in West Germany, Spätzle are also favorites in the eastern regions. Spätzle are served in soups and as accompaniments to meats, poultry, game or stews. This basic recipe may be flavored with minced cooked ham, spinach or cheese, if desired.

2½ cups sifted flour	2 eggs
½ teaspoon salt	¾ cup (about) water

Combine ingredients, adding enough water to form a stiff dough. Beat several times. On a wet chopping board, smooth out ½ of dough until very thin. Cut off small pieces of dough with a wet knife. Drop into a kettle of salted boiling water; cook until noodles rise to the top, about 5 minutes. Remove with a slotted spoon; drain. Proceed with remaining portion of dough. Serve at once or sauté in melted butter before serving. Serves 4 to 6.

VEGETABLES

Potato Pancakes

Kartoffelpuffer, potato pancakes, are favorite fare throughout Germany but in the north they are served traditionally *mit Apfelmus* (with applesauce).

2 pounds (6 medium) potatoes	1 small onion, peeled and grated
2 small eggs	Salt, pepper to taste
⅓ cup (approximately) flour	Fat or butter for frying
	Applesauce

Wash and peel potatoes. Put potatoes in cold water while peeling the others. Grate potatoes very finely; squeeze out moisture. Mix with eggs, flour, onion, salt and pepper, adding enough flour to make a fairly firm mixture. Drop by tablespoons into hot fat in a skillet; fry until crisp and golden on both sides. Take out with a spatula and drain on absorbent paper. Serve with applesauce sprinkled with salt. Serves 6.

Potato Salad

The Germans have devised many appealing preparations for their favorite Kartoffelsalat, potato salad, which is eaten either hot or cold and may be adorned with a number of flavorful dressings. This is one of the most widely eaten potato salads.

6 medium potatoes	3 tablespoons chopped fresh parsley
2 medium onions, peeled and chopped	Salt, pepper to taste
3 tablespoons chopped fresh dill	3 tablespoons salad oil
	3 tablespoons vinegar
	1 teaspoon sugar

Peel, cook and drain potatoes. Cut into thick slices. Combine with onions, dill and parsley. Season with salt and pepper. Heat oil, vinegar and sugar. Pour over potato mixture. Serves 4 to 6. If desired, this salad may be garnished with cucumber slices and pieces of pickled herring.

Leipziger Vegetable Platter

This dish is an attractive way of serving an assortment of vegetables for a company meal. The vegetables are cooked separately and then arranged decoratively on a platter. On occasion they are served with a sauce.

Individually cook any desired amount of asparagus tips, green peas, small whole carrots, cauliflower flowerets, whole or sliced mushrooms, and kohlrabi pieces. Immediately after the vegetables are drained, flavor each variety with butter, a little sugar, salt and pepper. Arrange on a platter and serve with a sauce made with butter, flour, the vegetable broth, salt and pepper.

Sauerkraut with Apples

This is usually served with pork or game.

1 medium onion, peeled and chopped	2 tart apples, pared, cored and chopped
2 tablespoons lard or bacon fat	1 teaspoon sugar
1 pound sauerkraut, drained	½ teaspoon caraway seeds
½ cup beef bouillon or consommé	1 medium raw potato, peeled and grated
	Salt, pepper to taste

In a saucepan, sauté onion in fat until tender. Add sauerkraut; sauté 1 minute. Add remaining ingredients. Cook slowly, covered, for 30 minutes. Serves 4.

Creamed Kohlrabi

A favorite vegetable in East Germany, as well as in Poland and Hungary, is kohlrabi, or the "cabbage turnip," which is prepared similarly in the various cuisines. Its thick skin should be cut off completely before cooking. The vegetable is an excellent accompaniment to roast pork. If the leaves are tender, they may also be cooked.

2 small kohlrabi	Salt, pepper, nutmeg to taste
7 tablespoons butter or margarine	¼ cup flour
¼ cup light cream	⅓ cup chopped parsley

Cut kohlrabi leaves and cook them in salted water about 20 minutes, until tender. Drain and chop. Add 3 tablespoons butter and cream. Season with salt, pepper and nutmeg. Keep warm.

Meanwhile, trim kohlrabi roots; peel and slice. Cook slices in 2 cups boiling salted water for about 25 minutes, or until tender. Drain, reserving liquid. Melt remaining butter in a saucepan and stir in flour to blend well. Season with salt, pepper and nutmeg. Add reserved vegetable liquid; cook slowly, stirring, until liquid is a thick smooth sauce. Add cooked kohlrabi slices and parsley; heat. Serve surrounded by the cooked leaves. Serves 4.

Beet Salad

Germans are fond of vegetable salads that have sweet-sour dressings, such as this one.

1 large onion, peeled and sliced	1 bay leaf
¾ cup wine vinegar	2 teaspoons sugar
½ teaspoon caraway seeds	2 cups sliced cooked beets

Combine all ingredients except beets. Bring to a boil. Add beets; remove from heat. Marinate 24 hours. Discard bay leaf. Serve cold with grated horseradish, if desired. Serves 4 to 6.

SAUCES

Horseradish Sauce

½ cup heavy cream	1 teaspoon sugar
2 tablespoons freshly grated or prepared horseradish, drained	½ teaspoon vinegar
	Pinch salt

Whip cream until thick. Stir in remaining ingredients. Mix well. Serve cold with cold cooked meat or fish. Makes about 1 cup.

Anchovy Sauce

2 tablespoons butter or margarine	1 tablespoon lemon juice
1 small onion, peeled and minced	1 can (2 ounces) anchovy fillets, minced
1 tablespoon flour	Salt, pepper to taste
1 cup meat bouillon	1 egg yolk

Melt the butter in a saucepan. Add the onion and sauté until tender. Stir in the flour. Gradually add the bouillon and cook 1 minute. Add the lemon juice, minced anchovies, salt and pepper and simmer, stirring frequently, for 10 minutes or until cooked. Pour a little of the hot sauce to mix with the egg yolk. Stir well and return to the sauce. Remove from the heat. Makes about 1¼ cups. Serve with fish.

DESSERTS

Wine Cream

A favorite German dessert, particularly for luncheon, is a chilled Weincreme. The same mixture may be used to spoon over sponge cake.

2 cups dry white wine	1 teaspoon grated lemon
½ cup sugar	rind
4 eggs	1 teaspoon grated orange
	rind

Combine all of ingredients in top of a double boiler. Cook, beating with a whisk or fork, until frothy and thickened. Pour into serving dishes and chill. Serve with whipped cream, if desired. Serves 4.

Apple Pancakes

Favorite East German desserts are sweetened pancakes embellished with such fruits as apples, plums or cherries and sometimes with whipped cream. Apfelpfannkuchen is one of the best.

6 tablespoons butter or margarine	1 teaspoon ground cinnamon
4 tart apples, peeled and sliced thinly	1 cup sifted all-purpose flour
2 teaspoons grated lemon rind	¼ teaspoon salt
½ - ¾ cup sugar	1 cup milk
	2 eggs, beaten
	Confectioners' sugar

Melt 4 tablespoons butter in a skillet; add apple slices. Cook slowly until tender. Add lemon rind, sugar to taste and cinnamon. Mix well. Leave in skillet. Combine flour, salt, milk and eggs in a bowl;

stir with a fork or whisk until smooth. Add remaining 2 tablespoons of butter, melted, and mix again. Heat a 7- or 8-inch skillet, lightly greased, and add 3 tablespoons of batter. Tilt pan at once to spread batter evenly. Cook over medium heat until underside of pancake is golden. Turn over with a spatula and cook on other side. Turn out onto a warm plate; keep warm in a preheated 250° F. oven. Continue cooking other pancakes. Spread ½ of each pancake with a thin layer of warm apple mixture. Fold over and sprinkle with confectioners' sugar. Serve at once. Serves 8.

Fruit Kuchen

In German Kuchen means cake. This kind of Kuchen is generally made with a slightly sweetened batter covered with various toppings, which may be simply cinnamon and sugar, ground nuts and honey, or such fruits as apples, peaches, berries or plums. It is an excellent cake to serve with coffee.

⅓ cup softened butter or margarine	1 cup sifted all-purpose flour
⅓ cup sugar	2 tablespoons milk
½ teaspoon vanilla	2 cups fresh fruit slices
2 eggs	(peaches, apricots,
1 teaspoon baking powder	strawberries)
	Whipped cream

Cream butter in a large bowl and mix in sugar. Beat until light and fluffy. Add vanilla and eggs, one at a time, beating well after each addition. Sift baking powder with flour. Add, alternately with milk, to creamed mixture. Mix well. Spoon into a 9-inch x 1¼-inch round cake pan lined with wax paper; spread evenly. Bake in a preheated moderate oven (350° F.) for 30 minutes, or until done. Cool for 5 minutes. Turn out on a rack and take off paper. Cool. Arrange fruit slices, sweetened with sugar if desired, over cake. Serve decorated with whipped cream. Serves 6.

Berliner Pfannkuchen

These well-known fruit-filled yeast doughnuts, a famous specialty of Berlin, are essential for the convivial celebration of the New Year.

1 package active dry yeast;   1 teaspoon salt
   or 1 cake compressed yeast   4½ cups (about) sifted
1 cup lukewarm milk   all-purpose flour
¼ cup butter or margarine,   Plum or apricot preserves
   melted   1 egg white beaten
½ cup sugar   Fat or oil for deep frying
3 large eggs   Confectioners' sugar
1 teaspoon grated lemon
   rind

Sprinkle or crumble yeast into a large bowl. Add ¼ cup lukewarm
milk. Use very warm milk for active yeast and lukewarm for
compressed yeast. After a minute or two, stir to dissolve. Add
melted butter, sugar, eggs (one at a time, beating after each
addition), lemon rind and salt. Gradually add enough flour to make
a soft dough; beat well after each addition. Form into a ball and
put in a greased bowl. Turn over so top of dough is greased. Place
in a warm place and let rise, covered, until doubled in bulk. Turn
out on a floured board and knead well. Roll out to a ¼-inch
thickness; cut into rounds with a 3-inch cookie cutter or glass.
Place a small amount of plum or apricot preserves in center of
half of the rounds. Moisten edges with egg white or water; top
with other rounds of dough. Press firmly together to completely
enclose preserves. Arrange on a large cookie sheet; put in a warm
place, covered, until large and light. Drop into a kettle of hot deep
fat (370° on a frying thermometer) and cook until golden brown on
both sides, only a few minutes. Remove with a slotted spoon and
drain. Serve warm, sprinkled with confectioners' sugar. Makes
about 30.

Czechoslovakian Cookery

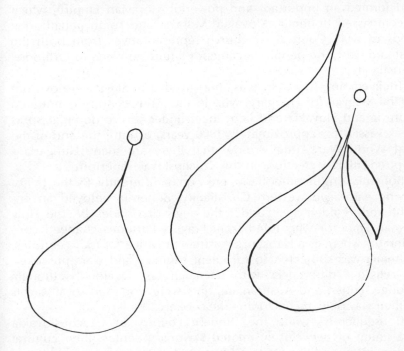

Czechoslovakia is comparatively new as a nation, having come into existence only after World War I. The present socialist republic was founded in 1948. The three provinces that comprise this small, boot-shaped and land-locked country, however—Slovakia in the east, central Moravia and Bohemia in the west—have a long and checkered history. Their fertile lands, located on vital trade and travel routes, made them subject to alien invasion, conquest and demands for allegiance. Despite adversity, however, the people developed a cookery that, while bearing evidence of foreign influences, shows marked ingenuity and originality.

Occupied in ancient times by Celtic tribes, some of the lands that now comprise Czechoslovakia were colonized by the Romans, who planted vines in the southeastern locales. In Slovakia grapes are still grown, and the wine-drinking heritage continues. Germanic tribes overcame and drove out the Romans, but by about 500 A.D. the tribes were replaced by waves of Slavs from the north and east who settled in these regions. By the ninth century the Slavs had formed an important and powerful Moravian Empire, which encompassed Bohemia, Slovakia, Moravia and some neighboring lands as well. Courted by church representatives from both the east and west, the people became for a time converts to Orthodox Christianity.

Their empire, however, was short-lived. The Slavs were overrun by the Magyars of Hungary, who in the tenth century conquered Moravia and Slovakia and kept them under severe domination as weak vassals for approximately 1000 years, or until the end of the First World War. Little wonder that there are many Hungarian-inspired culinary creations in the Czechoslovak repertoire.

Bohemia, on the other hand, grew quite differently. By the 1300s, having embraced western Christianity, Bohemia enjoyed an en-lightened "golden age" under the aegis of Charles IV, the Holy Roman Emperor who ruled from Prague. Fortunes changed con-siderably when, as a Habsburg Austrian province for four centuries, Bohemia was subjected to turbulent troubles and wars provoked by religious differences with its neighbors. Decidedly, though, strong German and Austrian imprints were imparted to all facets of their way of living, including the cookery.

Consequently, while the modern country of Czechoslovakia is a union of two closely related Slavonic peoples, their cultural and culinary traditions were different. The Czechs, long a part of the Austrian Empire, were oriented toward Vienna, while the Slovaks, attached for centuries to the Kingdom of Hungary, toward Budapest.

Despite their centuries of travail, the Czechoslovaks were always fortunate in having game-rich forests and productive farm lands to provide them with ample food. And, possibly because of their adversities, the cooks became most adept at fashioning the native fare into innovative and nourishing dishes.

The superb soil was particularly suited for growing exceptional crops of grain. Wheat, barley and rye were used to make some of the greatest national dishes. Czechoslovakian cooks became celebrated all over Europe for their baked goods made with native flour, prized for its high quality. The appealing variety of light and dark breads, made in fascinating forms and with a number of types of dough, have long been outstanding.

The cornerstone of Czechoslovakian cookery became the beloved dumplings, knedlíky, which were made not only with flour but also with such other ingredients as bread crumbs or cubes, potatoes, semolina or cottage cheese. Ever present on the table and indispensable to the menu, the dumplings can be light or firm, filled or unfilled, round, oval or sliced. Some are minuscule; others are as large as grapefruit. They are served in soups, as side or main dishes, and for dessert.

Probably the most famous of the notable collection are the bread dumplings, houskove knedlíky, made with bread cubes and flour in the shape of a thick roll, which is boiled in water. When cooked, the dumplings are sliced with a taut piece of thread, since the Czechoslovaks believe they should never be touched by a knife. Not to be overlooked are the sweet dumplings made by wrapping squares of dough around juicy plums, apricots or cherries. These dumplings are eaten either as supper entrées or for dessert, with toppings of melted butter, sugar, ground nuts, poppy seeds or cinnamon.

Although all Czechoslovakian cooks developed an enviable artistry in the preparation of their famous pastries, sweet yeast doughs and other baked goods, the Bohemians became the acknowledged masters. Many of them are aware that the prizes of the distinguished Viennese pastry shops were originally created in Bohemian kitchens and adapted later by the Austrians. The reputation of Bohemian cooks still excels for the preparation of delicate cookies, crumbly streusel cake, braided raisin and fruit-studded doughs, filled thin pancakes, mouth-watering strudels, simple sponge cakes, elaborate cakes made with creams, nuts and frostings, and such filled doughs as the famous koláčky—plump yeast buns embellished with thick plum jam or other sweet fillings.

In considering the numerous accomplishments of Czechoslovakian cookery, it is most interesting to note how humble the basic ingredients that they used to make appealing dishes were. This is particularly true of the soups. Although the national favorite and traditional first course is beef bouillon with liver dumplings, the repertoire also includes soups made simply with such flavorings as garlic and rye bread or caraway seeds. It has often been said that these people have a talent for preparing soup with anything. Perhaps so. Other good soups are made with potatoes, dried beans, mushrooms, barley and tripe, lentils and sausages, or one or more vegetables. Sometimes enriched with small dumplings, noodles or slices of thin pancakes, the soups are standard fare for dinner first courses or for one-dish meals.

It may also be observed that Czechoslovakian cooks developed a particular knack for dealing with pork, one of the great national favorites. Many families still raise their own pigs, and slaughtering them is a traditional ritual. Every part of the pig is used to make a favorite dish. Pork, fresh or cured, is the mainstay of the country's cookery. Although the crisp caraway-flavored roast pork is generally conceded to be the national dish, many pork products rank high on the daily menu. Revered by all Czechoslovaks are smoked bacon, the world-famous Prague ham, and a vast array of sausages that is the pride of every butcher shop. Throughout the day and night, workers and shoppers gain sustenance or simply pleasure from stopping by any of the ubiquitous stands or shops for their favorite *parky*, similar to frankfurters but sold in pairs.

Czechoslovaks are also partial to beef, generally well-cooked and served with thick gravy; a number of good veal dishes, particularly their version of Wiener schnitzel; and a selection of variety meats, prepared in novel ways. Typical also and standard fare for many meals are flavorful stews and goulashes, many of which came from Hungary and are spiced with paprika.

The people of this country have long relied on the wealth of their forests for game birds, hare and such highly prized meats as wild boar and venison. These meats are served with rich sauces, on beds of sauerkraut, or in rich stews. But for holiday fare they traditionally choose goose, or perhaps duck. Many Czechoslovaks raise and tend their own geese and practice the custom of forced feeding to enlarge the livers. Thus they can relish both gastronomic treats—the flavorful flesh and the liver.

Although the Czechoslovaks have been able to draw ample supplies of fish from their well-stocked lakes, rivers and streams, seafood is not primary in the cookery. There are, however, a number of interesting dishes featuring trout and carp in several variations is traditionally served on Christmas Eve. Among the classic ways to prepare carp is with a black sauce of such diverse ingredients as beer, prunes, nuts, raisins, sugar and vinegar.

For accompaniments, the Czechoslovaks prefer dumplings and potatoes, but noodles are also served with some stews and goulashes. Tart stewed fruits appear frequently, as do members of the cabbage family, particularly spicy red cabbage and sauerkraut flavored with caraway seeds.

In fact, it can be said that these aromatic seeds seem to appear in just about all of the native dishes. But there also is a fondness for sour cream as a flavoring, particularly to enrich sauces or dressings for a typical salad such as thinly sliced cucumbers. As in other Central European cuisines, both fresh and dried mushrooms are highly prized, and appear in a great many characteristic dishes.

Czechoslovaks also have developed a penchant for pickles, especially the tiny dill-flavored kind that are named after the Moravian town of Znojmo. Although they are used to flavor some dishes, these pickles are also relished as accompaniments for meats, particularly ham and sausages. But perhaps they are most beloved as a snack food, enjoyed in a tavern or beer hall and eaten with a thick slab of whole-grained bread, a square of the Carpathian mountain sheep-milk cheese, bryndza, and a slice of cold smoked meat. For although Czechoslovaks produce good red and white wines, and drink plum brandy, slivovice, their favorite drink is their famous beer, prepared with good native hops. Among the best known is the light and flavorful kind brewed in Plzen or Pilsen of Bohemia. Drinking foamed glasses of beer is a cherished way of life.

Given below is a selection of the best of the Czechoslovakian traditional dishes.

APPETIZERS

Bohemian Stuffed Tomatoes

Nadívaná rajska jablíčka, stuffed tomatoes, may be served as an appetizer or first course.

6	medium-sized tomatoes Salt	½	(approximately) cup fine dry bread crumbs
1	medium onion, peeled and minced	½	cup ground or minced cooked ham
2	tablespoons butter or margarine Salt, pepper, paprika to taste	¼ 2	cup chopped fresh parsley flat anchovy fillets, minced

Cut tops from tomatoes. Scoop out pulp and reserve. Sprinkle insides with salt; invert tomatoes to drain. Sauté onion in butter until tender. Add tomato pulp and mash finely. Season with salt, pepper and paprika. Cook 1 minute. Stir in bread crumbs, ham, parsley and anchovies. Mix well and remove from heat. Spoon mixture into tomato shells. Bake in a preheated moderate oven (375° F.) for about 30 minutes, or until tender. Serve warm or cold. Serves 6.

Beef Spread

This cold beef spread may be sliced and put on small rounds of bread or served whole in a mound.

1 small onion, peeled and minced	½ pound ground beef
1 garlic clove, crushed	⅛ teaspoon dried thyme
1 medium carrot, scraped and minced	Salt, pepper, paprika to taste
3 tablespoons butter or margarine	½ cup tomato juice
	2 slices stale white bread
	2 eggs, beaten

Sauté onion, garlic and carrot in butter until onion is tender. Add beef and cook, separating with a fork, until all redness disappears. Mix in thyme, salt, pepper and paprika. Add tomato juice; cook slowly, uncovered, for 10 minutes. Soften bread in cold water and squeeze dry. Mash with a fork; add with eggs to meat mixture. Mix thoroughly and spoon into a greased round baking dish. Cook in a preheated very hot oven (450° F.) 10 to 15 minutes, or until done. Cool and remove from dish. Serves 6 to 8.

SOUPS

Potato Soup

The Czechs are very fond of potato soup, bramborová polévka, which is made in many versions. One of the most popular also includes mushrooms.

1 medium onion, peeled and chopped
1 medium carrot, scraped and diced
1 cup diced celery
2 tablespoons fresh parsley, chopped
Salt, pepper to taste
5 medium potatoes, peeled and cubed
½ cup chopped mushrooms
¼ teaspoon dried marjoram
2 tablespoons flour
3 tablespoons butter or margarine

Put onion, carrot, celery and parsley with 4 cups water in a large kettle. Bring to a boil. Season with salt and pepper. Lower heat; cook slowly, covered, for 15 minutes. Add potatoes, mushrooms and marjoram; continue to cook until potatoes are tender, 30 minutes or longer. Combine flour and butter; stir into the soup. Cook, stirring, 5 minutes. Serves 4.

Cauliflower Soup with Bread Dumplings

The Czechs created several interesting dishes with cauliflower, karfiol. This soup is simple but flavorful. The dumplings are actually small balls of bread crumbs.

1 medium head cauliflower
1 tablespoon fresh lemon juice
3 tablespoons butter or margarine
2 tablespoons flour
¼ teaspoon powdered mace
Salt, pepper to taste
6 tablespoons (approximately) fine dry bread crumbs
1 egg, beaten
2 tablespoons chopped parsley

Wash cauliflower and trim off stem and leaves. Put in a kettle with 2 cups lightly salted water and lemon juice. Cook, uncovered, 5 minutes. Cover and cook another 15 minutes. Drain, reserving liquid. Cut cauliflower into small pieces. Melt 2 tablespoons of butter in a large kettle; mix in flour. Gradually add cauliflower liquid; cook slowly, stirring, until a thick sauce. Add 4 cups water, cauliflower pieces and mace. Season with salt and pepper. Cook slowly, covered, for 25 minutes or longer, until cauliflower is mushy. While soup is cooking, make dumplings. Cream rest of butter in a small dish. Stir in bread crumbs, egg and parsley. Season with salt and pepper. The mixture should be quite firm. Form into tiny marble-sized balls and leave at room temperature while soup cooks. When soup is done drop dumplings into the soup; leave soup on heat until dumplings rise to the top. Serves 6 to 8.

Beef Bouillon with Liver Dumplings

One of the most typical of the Czech soups is this soup with liver dumplings, called polévka s jatennimè knedlíky. It is a favorite luncheon or dinner first course.

1 pound chuck beef or soup meat, cubed	1 leek, white part only, cleaned and sliced
1 small carrot, scraped	(optional)
1 small onion, peeled and chopped	2 tablespoons chopped celery leaves
4 sprigs parsley	Salt, pepper to taste

Put all ingredients with 6 cups of water in a kettle. Bring to a boil. Skim well. Lower heat and cook slowly, covered, for 2 hours. Skim again. Strain bouillon. Correct seasoning. Reheat bouillon and drop in Liver Dumplings (recipe below). Cover and cook until dumplings rise to the surface, about 10 minutes. Spoon dumplings into large soup bowls and pour broth over them. Serves 6.

Liver dumplings

½ pound beef liver	Salt to taste
2 tablespoons butter or margarine, softened	Dash pepper, marjoram and allspice
1 small garlic clove, crushed	2 small eggs, slightly beaten
½ teaspoon grated lemon rind	1¼ cups (approximately) fine dry bread crumbs

Grind liver or cut finely. Mix with butter, garlic, lemon rind, salt, pepper, marjoram, allspice. Mix in eggs. Stir well. Add bread crumbs, enough to make a stiff mixture. Form into small balls. Leave at room temperature for 1 hour. If not stiff enough, add more bread crumbs.

ENTRÉES

Pike Fillets with Horseradish Sauce

This is a Czechoslovakian way to prepare pike, or stika, which is also served with an anchovy and caper cream sauce. Any firm-fleshed white fish may be used as a substitute for the pike.

2 pounds pike fillets
   Salt, pepper, cayenne to
   taste
   Flour
   Fat for frying
¼ cup freshly grated or
   prepared horseradish,
   drained

2-3 teaspoons prepared
   mustard
2 tablespoons flour
1 cup (approximately) water
   Chopped fresh dill or
   parsley

Season fillets with salt, pepper and cayenne. Dredge in flour; fry in hot fat for 3 to 5 minutes on each side. Remove to a warm platter and keep warm. Add horseradish, mustard and flour to pan drippings; mix well. Add water and cook slowly, stirring, until a thick and smooth sauce. Pour over fish and serve. Garnish with dill or parsley. Serves 6 to 8.

Carp in Black Sauce

Kapr na černo is a traditional Christmas Eve dish in Czechoslovakia, and the purchase of the live carp is an important holiday errand, for most homemakers prefer that the fish be kept alive until the time of preparation. To non-Czechs the ingredients of this sweet-sour black sauce seem strange, but the good flavor is surprising.

1 medium carrot, scraped
   and diced
1 medium onion, peeled
   and sliced

1 small celery root, peeled
   and diced or 3 stalks
   celery, diced
2 bay leaves

5 whole peppercorns	1 cup red wine vinegar
¼ teaspoon thyme	1 quart water
¼ teaspoon ground allspice	1 4-pound carp, cleaned and
2 teaspoons chopped parsley	cut into serving portions
5 whole cloves	

In a large saucepan combine all ingredients except carp; bring to a boil. Lower heat and cook slowly, covered, for 30 minutes. Add fish pieces and cook another 20 minutes, or until fish is just tender. Remove fish pieces to a warm platter. Strain liquid and reserve. In a saucepan, combine 1 cup of reserved liquid with Black Sauce (recipe below); bring to a boil. Pour over fish and serve. Serves 4 to 6.

Black sauce

½ pound pitted dried prunes	1 cup diced rye or
1 cup light beer	pumpernickel bread
1 tablespoon lemon rind	¼ cup grated gingersnaps
2 tablespoons sugar	¼ cup seedless raisins
2 teaspoons butter	2 tablespoons chopped
	blanched almonds

Cook prunes in water to cover until tender. Drain, reserving liquid. Chop prunes and return to a saucepan. Add reserved liquid, beer, lemon rind, sugar, butter and diced bread. Bring to a boil. Lower heat and cook slowly, covered, 10 minutes. Put through a sieve or whirl in a blender. Add raisins and almonds; mix well.

Roast Goose with Sauerkraut

The traditional Christmas dinner bird in Czechoslovakia is the goose, which is roasted only with caraway seeds or a flavorful sauerkraut for stuffing. Since the goose is the fattest of all poultry, it is necessary to drain off the accumulated fat during the cooking. The fat is reserved to be used as a spread for bread, for cooking, or for combining with other ingredients. Some stuffings also include chopped apples. Pečená husa se zelim, roast goose with sauerkraut, is an inviting entrée for any occasion.

1 young goose, 8 to 10 pounds	Salt, pepper to taste
	½ lemon

1 large onion, peeled and
 chopped

6 cups sauerkraut, drained
 and washed in cold water
2 teaspoons caraway seeds

Wash and wipe goose dry. Remove any fat from cavity and reserve. Rub goose inside and outside with salt and pepper. Prick skin in several places and rub with cut lemon half. Sauté onion in 2 tablespoons of reserved goose fat until tender. Add sauerkraut; sauté 1 minute. Add caraway seeds; season with salt and pepper. Cook slowly, covered, for 10 minutes. Stuff lightly into goose. Close cavity by sewing. Place goose breast side up, in a roasting pan; roast in a preheated slow oven (325° F.) for 2 to 2½ hours, or until tender. Spoon off fat as it accumulates in pan. Serve with dumplings. Serves 6 to 8.

Rabbit with Cream Sauce

In Czechoslovakia this dish is made with hare, a cousin of the rabbit, larger and sometimes less tender. In America it can be made with fresh or frozen rabbit.

3 slices lean bacon, chopped
2 tablespoons butter or
 margarine
1 rabbit, about 3 pounds,
 cut up
1 medium carrot, scraped
 and chopped
1 medium onion, peeled and
 chopped

1 bay leaf
¼ teaspoon ground allspice
¼ teaspoon dried thyme
2 tablespoons flour
1 pint sour cream at room
 temperature
1 teaspoon grated lemon
 rind

Fry chopped bacon in a heavy casserole or kettle until crisp. Drain off all except 3 tablespoons fat. Add butter and rabbit pieces; fry until golden brown. Remove to a plate. Stir chopped carrot and onion into drippings; sauté until onion is soft. Return rabbit pieces to dish. Add bay leaf, allspice and thyme; cook slowly, covered, about 40 minutes, or until meat is tender. If rabbit pieces stick to the pan, add a little water during cooking. Remove rabbit to a warm platter and keep warm. Stir flour into drippings; cook for 1 minute. Add sour cream and lemon rind; mix well. Strain sauce and serve with cooked rabbit. Serve with dumplings. Serves 4.

Pork Roast with Caraway

This Czech national dish, called vepřová pečené, is usually served with sauerkraut and dumplings. It is easy to prepare and has an appealing caraway flavor. Some cooks put a slice of onion on top of the roast.

1 pork loin roast, about	Salt
5 pounds	2 - 3 teaspoons caraway seed

Score any fat on the top of roast to make small squares. Rub roast well with salt; place in a shallow baking pan or dish. Sprinkle caraway seeds over top of roast. Add some water to pan, about ½ inch deep. Roast in a preheated slow oven (325° F.) for about 2½ hours or longer, allowing 35 to 40 minutes per pound, basting occasionally. Add more water while cooking, if needed. The skin should be golden and crisp. Serve with dumplings and sauerkraut. Serves 6 to 8.

Beef in Sour Cream Sauce

This meat dish, commonly called Svíčková, has an appealing sweet-sour flavor.

1 boneless beef roast (tenderloin, sirloin tip or eye of round), about 4 pounds	1 cup chopped celery
	8 peppercorns
	4 whole allspice
2 thin slices bacon, cut into narrow strips	2 small bay leaves
	¼ teaspoon dried thyme
2 large onions, peeled and chopped	1 teaspoon salt
	Red wine vinegar
1 large carrot, scraped and diced	2 tablespoons flour
	2 cups sour cream

Cut gashes in meat. With a larding needle, insert strips of bacon into gashes. Tie meat with string and place in a crock or kettle. Add next 8 ingredients; cover with equal parts of red wine vinegar and water. Leave to marinate for 24 hours. Turn over 1 or 2 times during the marinating. Spoon vegetables, seasonings and liquid into a shallow baking dish; place meat on top of them. Roast, uncovered, in a preheated moderate oven (325° F.), allowing 35 to 40 minutes per pound, to desired degree of doneness. When finished cooking, remove from oven. Take meat from the pan. Keep warm. Strain drippings and liquid. Put strained liquid into a saucepan; stir in flour. Cook slowly, stirring with a whisk or fork, until thickened. Add sour cream; leave on stove long enough to heat. Slice meat and serve covered with sauce. Serves 8.

Steak with Caper Sauce

2 pounds round steak, ½ inch thick
Salt, pepper to taste
Flour
4 tablespoons butter or margarine

2 medium onions, peeled and chopped
¼ cup capers, drained
2-3 tablespoons sharp prepared mustard
1 cup sour cream at room temperature

Pound steak with a mallet to make as thin as possible. Season with salt and pepper. Dredge in flour. Melt 2 tablespoons butter in a large skillet. Add steak; brown on both sides. Remove to a plate. Add remaining butter to drippings; fry the onions. Add capers, mustard, 1 cup water and steak. Cook very slowly, covered, 30 minutes, adding more water if necessary. Remove steak to a warm platter and keep warm. Stir gravy in pan; add sour cream. Leave on stove long enough to heat through. Spoon over the steak. Serves 4.

Lemon-Flavored Veal Stew

The Czechs are fond of piquant meat dishes, and those that are cooked by stewing them slowly are similar to a goulash. This is an interesting variation.

2 pounds boneless lean veal, cut into 1½-inch cubes

Salt, pepper to taste
Flour

1 small carrot, scraped and diced	3 tablespoons butter or margarine
1 medium onion, peeled and chopped	1 tablespoon grated lemon rind
½ cup diced celery root (optional)	Juice of 2 lemons
	Pinch of mace

Season veal cubes with salt and pepper. Dredge in flour. In a large saucepan, sauté carrot, onion and diced celery root in butter for 5 minutes. Push aside and add floured meat cubes to brown on all sides. Add water to cover; cook slowly, covered, for about 1 hour, or until meat is tender. Add lemon rind, lemon juice and mace; continue to cook another 10 minutes. Serves 4 to 6.

VEGETABLES

Slovakian Rutabaga

1 medium rutabaga, washed pared and cubed	1 tablespoon lard or bacon fat
1 cup beef consommé	1 tablespoon flour
1 teaspoon sugar	Pinch of ground ginger
	Salt, pepper to taste

Cook the rutabaga cubes in the consommé with the sugar, covered, for about 25 minutes or until just tender. Drain, reserving the liquid. Melt the lard in a saucepan. Stir in the flour to blend well. Slowly add the rutabaga liquid and cook, stirring, until a smooth and thick sauce. Add the ginger, salt, pepper and cooked rutabaga. Heat through. Serves 4 to 6.

Mushroom Goulash

3 tablespoons shortening or bacon fat	1 tablespoon paprika
1 large onion, peeled and chopped	1 large green pepper, cut into strips

3 large tomatoes, peeled
  and chopped

1 pound fresh mushrooms,
  cleaned and sliced thickly
  Salt, pepper to taste

Heat shortening in a saucepan; fry onion in shortening until tender. Add paprika; cook 1 minute. Stir in green pepper and tomatoes; cook slowly for 10 minutes. Add mushrooms, salt, and pepper; cook slowly for 5 minutes. Serves 4.

DUMPLINGS

Bohemian Potato Dumplings

One of the best-liked kinds of Czech dumplings are those made with potatoes, called bramborové knedlíky. They can be prepared with ½ cup semolina or farina and ½ cup flour, as well as with flour.

2 cups cooked potatoes,
  cooled and riced
2 medium eggs
1 teaspoon salt

1 cup (approximately)
  all-purpose flour
Melted butter
Fine dry bread crumbs

Combine potatoes, eggs and salt in a bowl; beat with a wooden spoon to combine thoroughly. Add flour, enough to make a stiff dough; mix well. With floured hands, shape dough into balls about 1½ inches in diameter. Drop into a large kettle of boiling water; bring water to a slow boil again. Cook about 12 minutes, or until dumplings rise to the top. Test by tearing one dumpling apart with two forks. Remove with a slotted spoon and drain. Serve with melted butter and a sprinkling of bread crumbs, if desired. Makes about 18.

Bread Dumplings

1 cup stale 1-inch white
  bread cubes

¼ cup butter or margarine
2 eggs, beaten

½ cup milk   2 cups (approximately) sifted
¾ teaspoon salt   all-purpose flour

Sauté bread cubes in butter until golden and crisp. Remove to a
large bowl. Add eggs, milk and salt; mix well. Stir in enough flour
to make a soft dough. Mix vigorously to combine well. With
floured hands, shape dough into 6 dumplings. Drop into a large
kettle of boiling salted water. Boil, uncovered, until dumplings rise
to the top. Cover and cook 10 to 15 minutes, or until done. Test
by tearing one dumpling apart with two forks. Remove with a
slotted spoon and drain. Serves 6.

SALADS

Potato-Sauerkraut Salad

4 medium-sized potatoes   2 tablespoons vinegar
2 cups drained sauerkraut   ½ teaspoon caraway seeds
1 medium onion, peeled and   2 teaspoons sugar
  chopped   Salt, pepper to taste
¼ cup salad oil

Peel and cook potatoes until just tender. While still warm, slice
and mix with sauerkraut. Add remaining ingredients; mix well.
Serves 4.

Moravian Lettuce Salad with Bacon

The Czechs are fond of salads made with raw or cooked vegetables
and piquant dressings. Toss washed and dried lettuce leaves with a
dressing prepared of vinegar diluted with water, a pinch of sugar
and salt. Garnish with hard-cooked egg slices and crisply cooked
bacon.

SAUCES

Plum Sauce

    2 cups pitted canned   ¼ to ⅓ cup sugar
       prune-plums   ¼ cup rum

Drain plums, reserving liquid. Put through a sieve or whirl in a
blender. Add sugar to taste, rum and ½ cup of reserved liquid.
Bring to a boil. Serve with dumplings, pancakes or puddings. Makes
about 2½ cups.

Apple-Horseradish Sauce

    ¼ cup freshly grated   1 cup apple sauce
       horseradish or prepared   1 teaspoon lemon juice
       horseradish, drained   Salt to taste

Combine ingredients and chill. Serve with boiled beef. Makes
about 1¼ cups.

Berry Sauce

    4 teaspoons cornstarch   ½ cup sugar
    2 cups milk   2 tablespoons butter or
    2 cups bilberries or   margarine
       blueberries, washed

Combine cornstarch and milk in a small saucepan; mix until smooth.
Add berries and sugar; bring to a boil. Cook slowly, stirring
constantly, for 1 minute, or until thickened. Remove from heat;
add butter. Serve with pancakes, dumplings or puddings. Makes
about 3 cups.

DESSERTS

Plum Dumplings

Of all the Czech dumpling creations, those made with plums, called svestkove knedlíky, are the favorites for dessert.

4 tablespoons butter or margarine	2 cups (approximately) sifted all-purpose flour
2 eggs, beaten	14 to 16 sugar cubes
1 teaspoon salt	14 to 16 small blue plums, pitted
2 cups cooked potatoes, riced and chilled	Ground cinnamon
	⅔ cup fine dry bread crumbs

Cream 2 tablespoons butter in a bowl; add eggs. Mix well. Stir in salt, potatoes and enough flour to make a stiff dough. Mix well. Roll out ¼-inch thick on a floured board; cut into 3-inch squares. Put a sugar cube in center of each plum; sprinkle sugar with cinnamon. Place each stuffed plum in center of each square of dough. Fold dough around plum to enclose it completely. Press edges to close firmly. With floured hands, roll each dumpling into a small round ball. Drop gently into a large kettle of boiling salted water; simmer, covered, about 12 minutes, or until cooked. Test dumplings by tearing one apart with two forks. Remove with a slotted spoon and keep warm. Melt remaining 2 tablespoons of butter in a skillet; fry bread crumbs in butter until golden. Spoon over cooked dumplings. Makes 14 to 16 dumplings.

Note: These dumplings may be made also with apricots, peaches or cherries.

Meringue Kisses

These delicate tiny "cookies" are very popular in Czechoslovakia. They may be made in various sizes.

6 egg whites	1 teaspoon grated lemon or
½ teaspoon salt	orange rind
1½ cups sugar	

Beat egg whites until stiff. Add salt and beat again. Beat in sugar gradually; add grated rind. When well mixed, spoon into a pastry bag with a star-shaped tip. Squeeze out onto a greased and floured cookie sheet. Bake in a slow oven (250° F.) about 45 minutes, or until dry and a little golden. The number will depend on size of cookie.

Ground Nut Cake

These cakes are made only with a large number of eggs, sugar and ground nuts, generally hazelnuts or walnuts. The delicate creations are covered with whipped cream or icing, and may be decorated with nuts or candied fruit.

8 eggs, separated	1 cup heavy cream, whipped
1 cup sugar	and sweetened
2 cups chopped shelled	1 tablespoon light rum
walnuts, ground	

Beat egg yolks with sugar, preferably with an electric mixer, until light and creamy. Add ground nuts; mix well. Beat egg whites until stiff; fold into egg and nut mixture. Spoon into 2 greased 9-inch cake pans. Bake in a preheated moderate oven (325° F.) for 45 minutes, or until cakes are cooked. Cool and remove from pans. Combine whipped cream and rum; spread over both cakes. Put together. Decorate with candied fruit, if desired. Serves 8 to 10.

Note: If desired, this cake may be filled and frosted with a coffee frosting.

Koláčky

This very well known yeast-raised bun may be filled with apples, apricots, plums, peaches, nuts, a cottage cheese mixture, poppy seeds or jam. Native to Bohemia, koláčky are beloved throughout Czechoslovakia.

1 package active dry yeast; or 1 cake compressed yeast	1 teaspoon grated lemon rind
2 tablespoons lukewarm water	4 cups sifted all-purpose flour
⅔ cup butter	1 cup (approximately) light cream or milk
3 egg yolks	
¼ cup sugar	Plum or apricot jam
1 teaspoon salt	Confectioners' sugar

Sprinkle or crumble yeast into a small dish. Add water, very warm for dry yeast and lukewarm for compressed yeast. After a minute or two, stir to dissolve. Cream butter in a large bowl. Add egg yolks, sugar, salt and lemon rind, beating after each addition. Stir in yeast; mix again. Add 2 cups of flour. Then alternately add remaining flour and cream; mix well to make a soft dough. Form into a ball and put in a greased bowl. Turn over. Put in a warm place, covered with a towel, to rise until doubled in bulk. Turn out on a floured board; roll to a thickness of ¼ inch. Cut into 2-inch rounds. Arrange on ungreased cookie sheets; let rise, covered, in a warm place until doubled in bulk. Make a depression in the center of each round; put in an adequate amount of jam. Bake in a preheated moderate oven (375° F.) about 12 minutes, or until cooked. Sprinkle with confectioners' sugar. Makes about 4 dozen.

Hungarian Cookery

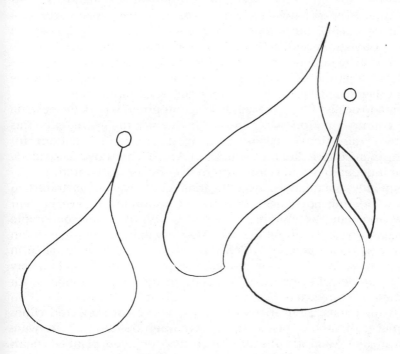

The Hungarians have a creative cuisine that developed out of nomadic Asiatic traditions into one of the most appealing and original in Eastern Europe. The vibrant people have a natural gift for cooking and are renowned for their devotion to the pleasures of the table.

A flat, landlocked country of the great European plain, the Hungarian People's Republic, formed in 1949, has always been noted for its agricultural wealth. The country still has a high proportion of its land devoted to farming, viniculture, grazing and the growing of fruit. From their abundant native bounty, Hungarian cooks evolved an exotic cuisine that reflects both eastern and western influences, derived from succeeding waves of invaders.

Among the earliest arrivals were the Romans, who by the first century had planted grapevines, grains and fruit trees in the fertile lands, thus bequeathing to the inhabitants a liking for foods made from these crops. Succeeding barbaric Asiatic tribes, more interested in fighting than in farming, ravaged the plains. One of these tribes, however, the Magyars, gave the present-day Hungarians their heritage. Nomadic horsemen from the Ural mountain regions of southern Russia, the Magyars gradually drove out the Slavic and Hun population, and by 1000 A.D., they had settled permanently on the plains around the Danube River. Their direct descendants still call themselves Magyars and speak the Magyars' distinctive Finno-Ugric language, one that is unique in Eastern Europe.

Paradoxically, the first Magyar king, Stephen, who later became the country's patron saint, chose Christianity for his people. This eastern ruler thus established a western-oriented pattern for Hungarian culture. But the heritage of Asiatic ancestors, particularly their independent and carefree spirit, was never obliterated.

Similarly, foundations of Hungarian cookery can be traced to the wandering horsemen, who at first continued to live in their new homeland as they had in Asia. Relying primarily on simple products from their herds, the Magyars had a diet based on milk and meat, both of which are still of utmost importance in the cuisine. The Hungarian devotion to sour cream, used in a very wide number of dishes, can be traced to the Magyar fondness for fermented mare's milk.

As for meats, Hungarians are still devotees of skewered cubes or pieces of lamb or beef, cooked over open outdoor fires, as were the ancient Magyars. The herdsmen also enjoyed planked meats served on round slabs of wood cut from fallen trees, with special indentations for the drippings. According to legend, this was the origin of a Hungarian specialty called fatangyeros, a marvelous mixed grill comprised of pork chops, bacon, beef and veal fillets and fried potatoes, garnished with salad and pickles. Other inviting creations with intriguing names reminiscent of the past are bandit's roast (zsiványpecsenye), robbers' meat (rablóhus) and gypsies' roast (cigánypecsenye).

The Magyar horsemen developed a knack for preparing rich and flavorful stews comprised primarily of dried meats, which they heated in liquids. The world-famous Hungarian goulash dates back to those early days, and, in fact, the name literally means "herdsmen's stew." Although no longer made with dried meat as in the past, gulyás is often still prepared in a large copper cauldron called a bogrács, but it is not necessarily cooked over an open outdoor fire.

Over the years gulyás changed considerably from a basic shepherd dish to a rich paprika-flavored stew of innumerable variations. Although gulyás is the best-known of all the great Hungarian stews, the cuisine actually has four categories of paprika-flavored dishes: gulyás, pörkölt, tokány and paprikás. Traditionally a gulyás is made with cubed beef, onions, paprika and diced potatoes, to which other ingredients such as garlic, caraway seeds, tomatoes or tomato paste, green peppers and noodles are often added. Pörkölt, which means singed, can be prepared with any kind of meat or game and includes more onions and a thicker gravy than a gulyás. To make a tokány, the beef or veal is cut lengthwise and cooked with such foods as mushrooms or other vegetables and sour cream. One of the most elaborate versions is called Seven Chieftains' Tokány, named for the seven Magyars who according to legend led their people to their present homeland. It is made with a variety of meats, vegetables and sour cream. A paprikás is usually prepared with large pieces of chicken or veal and has a rich sour cream gravy.

In addition to milk and meat dishes, the Asiatic horsemen had an important staple called tarhonya, made by kneading flour and eggs into a dough, which was broken into tiny pellets and dried in the sun until very hard. Called egg barley because of its resemblance to that grain, the tarhonya could be easily carried and then boiled in water and eaten with sun-dried meat or cooked in stews. These dough pellets are still common in Hungary, where they are boiled in water, cooked in soups or stews, or fried in lard with onions and paprika and served as accompaniments to richly sauced meats.

Although the early Hungarian cuisine developed from Magyar traditions, the food was considerably enhanced by a wide number of other influences from many different directions. During Hungary's golden age, late in the fifteenth century, the Italian princess Beatrice, wife of the enlightened King Matthias Corvinus, brought many Renaissance refinements to the royal court. She introduced the art of pastry-making, for which the Hungarians became famous, and probably also the caramel gild or adornment characteristic of many Hungarian cakes. Like the Italians, the Hungarians became fond of dishes made with a base of sautéed onions and sometimes garlic. Hungarian cooks, however, used lard instead of oil.

From other royal marriages came additional gifts. Hungarians adopted foreign dishes and then revised them to their own taste. Quite understandably, they came to share many culinary preferences with their neighbors—the Russians, Romanians, Yugoslavs, Austrians and Czechoslovaks. For example, they acquired the Slavic preference for sour foods, particularly sauerkraut. In Hungary flavorful pork-stuffed cabbage rolls (töltött káposzta), cooked with sauerkraut, became traditional. Fermented cabbage is also an important ingredient in the Transylvanian goulash called szekely, as well as in a hearty pork casserole. When cooked with such seasonings as dill, sour cream and paprika, sauerkraut is served as an accompaniment to pork and other meats.

The Hungarians also share with their neighbors a fondness for dough products made with their exceptional wheat flour, very rich and glutenous. The cooks devised an inviting repertoire of fragrant breads, light dumplings, pancakes and, in particular, noodles, which are glorified in the Hungarian cuisine. Experts in handling and cooking doughs, Hungarian cooks cut their noodles, or metelt, into widths or squares of varying size. Csipetke, however, are pinched into little bits, and galuska are a special soft variation. In both sweet and savory dishes, noodles appear frequently in the cookery. Very treasured are those combined with sweet sauces, nuts or poppy seeds, or those filled with fruit and served as supper entrées or for dessert. An excellent baked dish is made simply with noodles, cottage cheese, sour cream and crumbled crisp bacon.

During the lengthy occupation by the Turks, lasting, after the conquest of Hungary in 1526, for more than 150 years, the country acquired a number of most important foods that effected vital changes in the cookery. Under Turkish influence the Hungarians became devotees of coffee, enjoying it with a galaxy of desserts and pastries that their cooks created. With the paper-thin leaves of dough brought by the Turks and used in the Near East to make baklava, the Hungarians invented their flaky and delectable rétes. Because these specialties were later adopted and named strudels by the Austrians, controversies still exist as to who originated them. But there is no doubt about the Hungarian expertise in preparing them. In their home kitchens, girls learn the secrets of making and stretching the challenging thin dough and the formulas for the traditional flavorful fillings based on apples, cherries, plums, nuts, poppyseeds, cottage cheese and cabbage.

Hungarians became adept at making such other toothsome

delights as flaky cookies, coffee and tea cakes, cream-embellished tortes, fragrant yeast buns, sweet dumplings and two very special treats, Dobos Torta (a many-layered spongecake with chocolate fillings and a caramel glaze) and Rigó Jancsi (a chocolate-filled and frosted chocolate cake).

Also highly prized for desserts were very thin pancakes called palacsinta, filled variously but particularly with a preserve made with luscious apricots. Brought also by the Turks, the apricot flourished in the rich Hungarian soil and became a national favorite. Enjoyed both raw and cooked, it also became the basis for the country's two most popular drinks, a brandy named barackpalinka and a liqueur called baracklikor.

Paprika, the Hungarian word for red pepper, has now become so widely associated with the country's cuisine that many persons assume the spice was always native to Hungary. But astounding as it may seem, it was probably also during the Turkish occupation that the all-important spice was introduced. In fact, the place of origin of the sweet red pepper from which the dried powder derives is still a matter of conjecture. Some persons believe it was native to India, while others point out that it probably came, like other members of the *Capsicum* or pepper family, from Central and South America.

Regardless of its origin, paprika was cultivated most successfully in Hungary, and acres of colorful fields are still devoted to its growth. Centered around the southern city of Szeged, the country's paprika capital, the farms yield annual harvests of bright red peppers that, when ground, provide the Hungarians with the finest kind of this spice in the world. Although there are many varieties of paprika, the best is mild and sweet, imparting an appealing flavor to food. Over the years paprika has become indispensable to Hungarian cookery, and no kitchen is without this national spice.

After the defeat of the Turks in 1683, the Hungarians fell under the domination of another strong country and neighbor, Austria. Eventually the powerful dual monarchy formed by the courts of Austria and Hungary became such an influential empire that it lasted over 250 years, until the end of World War I. Although both the Austrians and Hungarians had national cuisines, their culinary specialties became so intermingled that it is difficult to differentiate between them. They still share a fondness for breaded and deep-fried and braised poultry specialties, rich game creations and goose, including the liver as well as the flesh and fat. Salad and vegetable preparations are very similar, as are also the previously mentioned desserts and pastries. Unlike the Austrians, however, the Hungarians never retained the influence of the French culture and cuisine that, through other royal courts, became so powerful throughout Europe. Admittedly, the nobility in Budapest did imitate many of the fashions of Vienna inspired by the French. The Hungarian nobles adapted rich French soups and sauces and wine-flavored braised foods and preferred sweet instead of sour cream and butter rather than lard. But despite the leanings of royalty to a more sophisticated cookery, the Hungarian cuisine retained its national characteristics and dishes that had been carefully and creatively evolved in home kitchens.

Given below are some of the great Hungarian specialties that are still enjoyed with great pleasure by a people who enjoy eating well.

APPETIZERS

Liptói Cheese Spread

In Hungary a favorite spread is made with Liptói cheese, a soft cheese made from sheep's milk and a number of flavorings. The cheese is named after a province where it originated, but is confused with similar cheeses of Czechoslovakia and Romania, which are called by different names. The spread has also been popularized in Austria, where it is called Liptauer. Although cottage cheese does not have the same flavor, it can be used as a good substitute. Other names for Liptói are brynza, brinza and bryndza.

½ pound cottage cheese	1 teaspoon caraway seeds
¼ pound butter, softened	1 teaspoon minced capers
1 tablespoon Hungarian paprika	1 tablespoon grated onion
1 teaspoon prepared mustard	¼ cup (approximately) sour cream

Sieve cottage cheese; mix with butter to blend well. Add remaining ingredients; mix well again. Put in refrigerator 3 hours or longer to become firm. Serve as a mound with dark bread and beer. Makes almost 2 cups.

Goose Liver

The king of Hungarian delicacies, goose liver, is world renowned, especially when made into a delectable pâté de foie gras. A particular reason for its appealing flavor is the Hungarian tradition of each household having a prized gaggle, carefully fed on such foods as corn, buttermilk and walnuts. Hungarian goose liver is eaten in many ways. As an appetizer, it is served cold, sprinkled with paprika, on small rounds of bread, while as a pâté or spread it may be mixed with other ingredients.

Since goose liver is not always readily available, some Hungarian cooks make an excellent appetizer with leftover goose fat and chicken livers. To prepare, sauté whole chicken livers in quite a lot of goose fat, until just tender. Grate livers and mix with minced onions, chopped hard-cooked egg, softened goose fat, salt and pepper. Shape into a mound. Garnish with pickles and hard-cooked egg slices. Serve with black bread.

Lescó

This Hungarian vegetable dish sometimes includes sliced smoked sausages and can be made more spicy by adding red peppers. It is usually enjoyed as an appetizer with black bread and beer; or it can be served as an accompaniment for meats.

4 slices thin bacon, chopped
2 tablespoons lard
3 medium onions, peeled and chopped
1 tablespoon Hungarian paprika

3 large green peppers, cleaned and cut in strips
3 large tomatoes, peeled and chopped
Salt, pepper to taste

Fry bacon in a skillet; pour off all except 2 tablespoons fat. Add lard and onions; cook until tender. Add paprika; cook 1 minute. Mix in remaining ingredients; cook slowly, covered, for 20 minutes, or until vegetables are cooked. Serves 4.

SOUPS

Budapest Bean Soup with Pinched Noodles

This Hungarian soup, called Bableves Csipetkével, is a favorite everyday dish for family meals.

2 cups dried white beans	3 tablespoons butter or
1 large carrot, scraped and diced	margarine
	2 tablespoons flour
2 tablespoons chopped fresh parsley	1 cup sour cream at room temperature
1 teaspoon salt	Pinched Noodles (recipe
1 large onion, peeled and chopped	below)
	2 tablespoons fresh dill, chopped

Cover beans with water; bring to a boil. Boil for 2 minutes. Remove from heat. Let stand, covered, for 1 hour. Drain. Put beans with 6 cups fresh water, carrot, parsley and salt in a large kettle. Bring to a boil. Lower heat; simmer, covered, until beans are cooked, about 2 hours. Sauté onion in butter. Stir in flour to blend well. Pour in 1 cup of hot bean broth; mix well. Return to soup. Cook 1 or 2 minutes, stirring. Stir in sour cream. Add Pinched Noodles; cook until they rise to the surface. Spoon into soup plates. Garnish with chopped dill. Serves 8.

Pinched noodles
  1 cup all-purpose flour
  ½ teaspoon salt
  1 large egg

Sift flour and salt into a bowl. Make a well in center and break egg into it. Add a little water, enough to make a soft dough. Mix well. Knead to make smooth. Roll out to ⅛-inch thickness. Pinch off little pieces of dough with fingers and add to soup. Cook until noodles rise to surface.

Sauerkraut Soup

Hungarians sincerely believe that this flavorful soup will alleviate the aftereffects of imbibing too liberally. Thus, the very popular dish is called "hangover soup" or "tipplers' soup."

1 large onion, peeled and chopped	½ pound smoked sausage, sliced
¼ cup bacon fat or shortening	Salt, pepper to taste
1 tablespoon Hungarian paprika	1 tablespoon flour
	3 tablespoons chopped dill
3 cups finely chopped sauerkraut, drained	1 cup sour cream at room temperature
1 garlic clove, crushed	

Sauté onion in fat until just tender. Take off stove; stir in paprika. Return to heat; add sauerkraut. Sauté, mixing with a fork, for 1 minute. Add garlic and sausage. Season with salt and pepper. Pour in 6 cups water. Cook slowly, covered, for 30 minutes. Stir flour and dill into sour cream. Add to soup; cook slowly, stirring, until thickened and smooth. Correct seasoning. Serves 6.

Caraway Seed Soup

The medicinal properties of caraway seeds have been highly praised since ancient times, particularly by Slavic peoples. Hungarians greatly appreciate the small seed's gastronomic value and use it in many dishes. They recommend this soup, called Köménymagos leves, as excellent for the stomach.

3 tablespoons bacon fat or shortening	2 tablespoons flour
	1 tablespoon caraway seeds

1 tablespoon paprika   2 tablespoons butter
1 garlic clove, crushed   Croutons
Salt, white pepper to taste

Melt fat in a saucepan. Stir in flour to blend well. Add caraway
seeds; cook 1 minute. Remove from heat; stir in paprika, garlic,
salt and pepper. Mix well. Return to heat; add butter. Cook,
stirring, until butter melts. Add 6 cups boiling hot water; cook
slowly, covered, for 10 minutes. Strain and serve with croutons
on top. Serves 6.

Goulash Soup

In Hungary this soup, gulyásleves, which sometimes includes
small pinched noodles as well as potatoes, is a meal in itself.
It is thick and flavorful.

2 medium onions, peeled   1 large carrot, scraped and
  and chopped   diced
3 tablespoons fat   Salt, pepper to taste
2 tablespoons Hungarian   1 large tomato, peeled and
  paprika   chopped
1½ pounds boneless beef   2 medium potatoes, peeled
  chuck, cut into 1½-inch   and cubed
  cubes

In a large saucepan, sauté onions in fat until limp. Remove from
fire; add paprika. Mix well and return to heat. Add meat cubes;
brown. Add carrot, salt, pepper and 4 cups water. Simmer, covered,
for 1 hour. Add more water while cooking, if needed or desired.
Add tomato and potatoes; cook another 30 minutes. Serves 4 to 6.

ENTRÉES

Danube Carp-Paprika Stew

The Hungarians are very fond of carp, particularly those that
come from the Danube River. They use carp to make many
inviting dishes, including this flavorful stew.

1 pound onions, peeled and chopped	3 green peppers, cleaned and chopped
3 tablespoons lard or fat	Salt, to taste
2-3 tablespoons Hungarian paprika	1 carp (or other freshwater fish), about 3 pounds, cut into large pieces
3 large tomatoes, peeled and chopped	

Sauté onions in lard until soft. Add paprika; cook 1 minute. Stir in tomatoes and green peppers; cook about 5 minutes, until soft. Season with salt. Arrange fish pieces in a saucepan or kettle and top with vegetables. Add just a little water. Cook slowly, covered, about 30 minutes, or until fork-tender, adding a little more water, if necessary. The gravy, however, should be thick. Serves 6.

Baked Fish and Potatoes

This casserole can be easily made with any white-fleshed fish.

4 medium-sized potatoes, cooked and thinly sliced	⅔ cup dry white wine
2 tablespoons butter or margarine	Salt, pepper to taste
1 cup sour cream at room temperature	2 pounds white-fleshed fish fillets, cut into serving pieces
½ pound mushrooms, cleaned and sliced	2 tablespoons chopped fresh dill or parsley

Arrange potato slices in a buttered baking dish. Dot with butter. Spread with ½ cup sour cream. Put mushroom slices in a layer. Sprinkle with wine, salt and pepper. Arrange fish pieces over ingredients. Top with remaining ½ cup sour cream. Sprinkle with dill or parsley. Bake in a preheated moderate oven (350°F.) for about 30 minutes, or until fish is cooked. Serves 4 to 6.

Szeged Halászlé

One of the greatest Hungarian fish dishes is a flavorful soup-stew called halászlé. Unfortunately, halászlé is not easy to duplicate outside the country, because it is made with several local fresh-water fish such as *fogas*, sterlet, carp, catfish, pike or perch. One version is that of Lake Balaton, where the ingredients are cooked in layers in a large kettle. The following version is named for the ancient city of Szeged, on the banks of the Tisza River, where the fishermen's soup, preferably prepared by them, is eaten to the accompaniment of lyrical gypsy music. Traditionally, halászlé is cooked in a large kettle over an open fire.

4 large onions, peeled and sliced	4 pounds mixed fresh fish (catfish, carp, pike, perch), cleaned and cut into large cubes
3 tablespoons lard or fat	
2 to 3 tablespoons Hungarian paprika	Salt, pepper to taste

In a large kettle, sauté onion slices in lard until tender. Stir in paprika; cook 1 minute. Carefully place fish over onions; season with salt and pepper. Add water to cover. Cook very slowly until fish is tender; the time will be longer if fish is cooked over an open fire. Serves 8.

Chicken Paprika

One of the glories of the Hungarian cuisine is the well-known csirke paprikás, which is made in many variations. The most typical kind is prepared only with chicken, flavorings and sour cream. Tomatoes and green peppers are optional additions.

2 frying chickens (about 3 pounds each), cut up	2 to 3 tablespoons Hungarian paprika
4 tablespoons (approximately) lard, butter or margarine	1½ cups (approximately) chicken broth
	Salt, pepper to taste
2 medium onions, peeled and chopped	2 tablespoons flour
1 or 2 garlic cloves, crushed	2 cups sour cream at room temperature

Wash chickens and wipe dry. Heat lard in a large skillet; fry chicken pieces on both sides until golden. Remove as cooked and keep warm. When all pieces are cooked, pour off almost all fat; add onions and garlic. Sauté until tender. Stir in paprika; cook 1 minute. Mix in chicken broth; bring to a boil. Season with salt and pepper; return chicken pieces to skillet. Cook slowly, covered, until chicken is tender. Add more broth during cooking, if needed. Remove to a warm platter. Combine flour and sour cream; mix into the skillet. Cook slowly, stirring, until thickened and smooth. Return chicken pieces to sauce; leave on stove long enough to heat through. Serves 8.

Goulash

Hungary's national dish, gulyás, eaten in one form or another around the world, means shepherd's or herdsmen's stew. It is thought that gulyás was invented by shepherds, who cooked it on an outdoor fire. Traditionally, it is prepared in a large kettle called *bogrács*. There are so many versions of goulash served in other countries that it is difficult to identify the truly Hungarian dish. However, the stew is a thick one made with cubes of beef, preferably a little fatty, onions and paprika. Sometimes the stew is also flavored with garlic or caraway seeds, and some versions include tomatoes or tomato purée and green peppers. Diced potatoes or small noodles may be cooked with or added to the goulash. The stew is properly thickened, not with flour, but by long, slow cooking. Hungarians point out that in order to make a really good goulash, one must use their highly prized sweet paprika.

2 pounds boneless beef chuck or stew meat	2 to 3 tablespoons Hungarian paprika
2 tablespoons (approximately) lard or other fat	Salt, pepper to taste
2 large onions, peeled and chopped	2 medium tomatoes, peeled and chopped (optional)
	1 pound (3 medium) potatoes, peeled and diced

Wipe meat dry and brown in lard on all sides in a kettle. Push meat aside; add onions and more lard, if needed. Sauté until tender. Stir in paprika and cook 1 minute. Add enough water to cover; cook very slowly, tightly covered, for 1 hour. Add tomatoes and potatoes; continue to cook another 30 minutes, or until beef and potatoes are tender. It may be necessary to add a little more water during cooking, but final gravy should be thick. Serves 4 to 6.

Veal Pörkölt

A Hungarian paprika-flavored stew, pörkölt is most commonly prepared with veal, but it may also be made with other meats, poultry or fish. Pörkölt has a generous number of onions and a rich thick sauce.

2 pounds boneless veal stew meat (or shoulder), cut into 1½-inch cubes	1-2 tablespoons Hungarian paprika
3 tablespoons lard or fat	Salt, pepper to taste
4 large onions, peeled and sliced	3 tablespoons tomato paste
	1 medium green pepper, cleaned and sliced

Wipe veal dry and brown in hot fat in a large saucepan or kettle. Push meat aside; add onions. Sauté until tender. Add paprika; cook 1 minute. Add just enough water to cover ingredients; cook very slowly, covered, for 45 minutes, adding more water if necessary. Add tomato paste and green pepper slices; continue to cook another 20 minutes, or until meat is tender. It may be necessary to add a little more water, but finished dish should have a thick, rich gravy. Do not stir while cooking, but dish can be shaken now and then. Keep tightly covered throughout cooking. Serve with noodles or dumplings. Serves 4 to 6.

Pork Tokány

Another paprika stew, tokány, differs from others in that the meat can be cut into strips and because it contains a number of vegetables.

2 pounds lean boneless pork, cut into 3 strips 3 x 1 inches	¼ cup lard or shortening
	Salt, pepper to taste

1 tablespoon Hungarian
paprika
1 large onion, peeled and
chopped
1 large carrot, scraped and
thinly sliced
1 large green pepper,
cleaned and sliced

2 medium tomatoes, peeled
and chopped
2 cups sliced mushrooms
1 tablespoon flour
1 cup sour cream at
room temperature

Wipe pork dry and brown in lard in a large saucepan. Season with salt and pepper. Add paprika and onion; cook until onion is tender. Cook slowly, covered, for 30 minutes. Add carrot, pepper and tomatoes; cook another 30 minutes, or until done. Stir in mushrooms 10 minutes before cooking is finished. Add flour and sour cream; cook over low heat, stirring, until thickened and smooth, about 5 minutes. Serves 4 to 6.

Székely Gulyás

The people of the mountainous region of Transylvania are called Székely, and this dish is named for them. This gulyás differs from others in that it is made with only pork or a combination of meats and includes sauerkraut and sour cream. It is generally flavored with garlic, caraway seed and dill.

2 pounds boneless shoulder
pork, cut into 1½-inch
cubes
3 tablespoons lard or fat
2 medium onions, peeled
and chopped
1½ teaspoons caraway seeds
1 small garlic clove, crushed

2 tablespoons Hungarian
paprika
Salt, pepper to taste
2 pounds sauerkraut, drained
1 cup sour cream at
room temperature
2 tablespoons chopped fresh
dill

Wipe pork cubes dry and brown in lard or fat. Push cubes aside; add onions. Sauté until tender. Stir in caraway seeds, garlic and paprika; cook 1 minute. Season with salt and pepper. Add enough water to cover ingredients; cook slowly, covered, for 1 hour. Add more water during cooking, if needed. Add sauerkraut; continue to cook about 30 minutes longer, or until meat is tender. Mix in sour cream and dill; leave on stove until heated through. Serves 6.

Noodle-Cheese Casserole

This Hungarian baked dish, Turós Csusza, may be served as an accompaniment to meats or poultry or enjoyed as a supper dish.

¼ pound sliced bacon	1¼ cups sour cream at room temperature
1 package (8 ounces) wide noodles, cooked and drained	1 cup cottage cheese
	⅓ cup minced onion
	Salt, pepper to taste

Cook bacon until crisp. Drain, reserving 3 tablespoons of fat; crumble. Set aside. Mix reserved fat with cooked noodles, sour cream, cottage cheese and onion. Season with salt and pepper. Spoon into a buttered casserole. Sprinkle with crumbled bacon. Bake in a preheated moderate oven (350°F.) for about 30 minutes. Serves 8.

VEGETABLES

Egg-Potato Casserole

Rakott Krumpli is a good accompaniment for meats and poultry; or, it can be eaten alone as a supper dish.

6 medium potatoes	1 cup sour cream at room temperature
¼ pound thin bacon slices	
6 hard-cooked eggs, shelled and sliced	Fine dry bread crumbs
Salt, pepper to taste	Butter or margarine

Peel and cook potatoes in salted water until just tender. Drain and slice. Fry bacon slices until crisp; drain. Arrange potatoes, hard-cooked egg slices and bacon in layers, sprinkling each with salt and pepper, in a greased 1½-quart casserole. Pour sour cream over ingredients. Sprinkle top with bread crumbs and dot with butter. Bake in a preheated moderate oven (350°F.) about 20 minutes, until bubbly. Serves 4 to 6.

Paprika Potatoes

Paprikás burgonya can be prepared as in this recipe or with the addition of tomatoes and green peppers or sliced smoked sausages.

2 medium onions, peeled and chopped	Salt, pepper to taste
2 garlic cloves, crushed	6 medium potatoes, peeled and cubed
3 tablespoons lard or fat	1 cup sour cream at
¼ teaspoon caraway seeds	room temperature
1 to 2 tablespoons Hungarian paprika	

In a saucepan, sauté onions and garlic in hot lard until tender. Stir in caraway seeds, paprika, salt and pepper; cook 1 minute. Add potatoes and enough water to barely cover. Cook slowly, covered, for 20 minutes, or until potatoes are cooked. Stir in sour cream; leave on low heat until hot. Serves 6.

Squash in Sour Cream

This flavorful vegetable creation, called tökfäzelék, is made with a light green summer squash cut into narrow strips with a special slicer. Zucchini or summer squash can be used as a substitute.

3 medium zucchini; or 1 summer squash	Pepper to taste
Salt	2 tablespoons flour
2 tablespoons butter or margarine	1 cup sour cream at room temperature
1 medium onion, peeled and chopped	2 tablespoons chopped fresh dill
1 garlic clove, crushed	2 tablespoons vinegar

Peel and cut zucchini or squash into narrow strips. Sprinkle with salt; let stand for 15 minutes. Drain off moisture. Melt butter in a saucepan; sauté onion and garlic in butter until tender. Add the zucchini and sauté until just tender. Season with salt and pepper. Combine flour and sour cream; spoon over zucchini. Leave over very low heat for 5 minutes. Mix in dill and vinegar. Serves 4 to 6.

Green Pepper Salad

This paprika saláta is one way of serving the green peppers that are used so frequently in Hungarian cookery.

4 large green peppers	3 tablespoons chopped fresh
¼ cup vegetable oil	parsley
2 to 3 tablespoons vinegar	Salt, pepper to taste
1 medium onion, peeled and	
minced	

Clean green peppers and cut into strips. Sauté in oil until just tender. Remove with a slotted spoon to a small bowl. Strain oil; add with other ingredients to peppers. Chill for 24 hours. Serves 4.

SAUCES

Dill Sauce

2 tablespoons butter or	2 cups hot chicken bouillon
margarine	Juice of ½ lemon
1 medium onion, peeled	½ cup sour cream at
and minced	room temperature
2 tablespoons flour	2 tablespoons chopped fresh
Salt, pepper to taste	dill

Melt butter in a saucepan. Add onion; sauté until tender. Blend in flour; cook 1 minute, stirring constantly. Season with salt and pepper. Add hot bouillon; cook, slowly, stirring occasionally, until thickened. Add lemon juice, sour cream and dill. Leave on stove just long enough to heat through. Serve with cold meat, vegetables or fish. Makes about 3 cups.

Sour Cream Salad Dressing

1 cup sour cream	1 teaspoon sugar
¼ cup wine vinegar	Salt, white pepper to taste
3 tablespoons chopped dill	

Combine ingredients. Chill. Serve with cucumbers, leaving to marinate for about 3 hours, or over lettuce leaves. Makes about 1 cup.

DESSERTS

Pancakes with Chocolate Sauce

Mouth-watering Hungarian desserts are the palacsinta, thin pancakes that are eaten either folded or rolled around fruit fillings. Or, fillings can be made with ground nuts, chocolate or sweetened cottage cheese.

2 eggs, beaten	Butter for frying
1½ cups milk	Apricot, strawberry or
1 tablespoon sugar	raspberry jam
¼ teaspoon salt	1 cup prepared chocolate
1 cup sifted all-purpose	sauce
flour	2 tablespoons light rum

Combine eggs, milk, sugar, salt and flour in a bowl; mix until smooth. Heat a lightly greased 7- or 8-inch skillet. Add 3 tablespoons of batter all at once; quickly tilt pan to spread evenly. Cook over medium heat until underside is golden. Turn over with a spatula and cook on other side. Turn out on a warm plate and keep warm in a preheated slow oven (250°F.). Continue to cook other pancakes. Spread each with a thin layer of jam, and roll or fold over. Serve at once with chocolate sauce and rum, heated together. Sprinkle with chopped nuts, if desired. Serves 10 to 12.

Witches' Froth

This unusual light dessert is called boszorkány hab.

Whites of 2 eggs
2 cups chilled apple purée
(or applesauce)
2-4 tablespoons sugar

1 teaspoon grated lemon rind
1 tablespoon apricot brandy (optional)
Grated sweet chocolate

Whip egg whites until stiff. Combine with apple purée, sugar, lemon rind and brandy, folding carefully. Spoon into serving dishes and garnish with grated chocolate. Serve cold. Serves 4.

Baked Sweet Noodles

In Hungary interesting desserts are made with sweetened home-made noodles, which may be baked or fried.

1 package (8 ounces) wide noodles
¼ cup butter or margarine
½ cup chopped nuts

⅓ - ½ cup sugar
3 tablespoons apricot jam
1 cup light cream
Confectioners' sugar

Cook and drain noodles. Combine, while still warm, with butter, nuts, sugar and jam. Spoon into a buttered shallow baking dish. Pour cream over ingredients. Sprinkle with confectioners' sugar. Bake in a preheated moderate oven (350°F.) for 30 minutes. Serves 4 to 6.

Deep-Fried Cherries

Fresh fruit, coated with batter and deep-fried, is a favorite dessert in several Eastern European countries. Plums, apples or currants are prepared in the same manner. In Hungary this dessert is called Cseresznye Kisütve.

1 pound fresh ripe red cherries	⅓ cup dry white wine
1 cup all-purpose flour	3 eggs
¼ cup sugar	Fat for frying
⅓ cup milk	Confectioners' sugar
	Cinnamon

Wash cherries and wipe dry. Do not remove stems. Tie with thread to form clusters of 4 cherries. Combine flour, sugar, milk, wine and eggs in a bowl. Mix to make a smooth batter. Dip each cluster of cherries into batter, coating well; and drop into a kettle of hot deep fat (375°F. on a frying thermometer). When golden, remove with a slotted spoon and drain. Serve at once with confectioners sugar and cinnamon. Serves 6.

Filled Layered Pancakes

Stacked or layered pancakes called rakott palacsinta, which are spread with appealing sweet mixtures, make an elegant company dessert. This one has a meringue topping and resembles a handsome cake in appearance.

1 cup milk	2 teaspoons vanilla
2 eggs	⅔ cup currants or chopped seedless raisins
½ cup sifted all-purpose flour	½ cup apricot jam or orange marmalade
¼ teaspoon salt	
1 tablespoon sugar	
Butter for frying	2 tablespoons light rum or orange juice
1 cup finely chopped walnuts	2 egg whites
⅓ cup confectioners' sugar	¼ cup sugar

Combine milk, eggs, flour, salt and sugar in a bowl; mix until smooth. Heat a lightly greased 7- or 8-inch skillet; add all at once 3 tablespoons of batter. Quickly tilt pan to spread evenly. Cook over medium heat until underside is golden. Turn over with a spatula to cook on other side. Slip onto a warm plate and keep warm in a preheated 250°F. oven. Continue to cook other pancakes. Combine chopped nuts, confectioners' sugar and 1 teaspoon of vanilla in a bowl. Combine the currants and jam and rum in another bowl. Place one pancake in a buttered shallow baking dish. Spread with a thin layer of walnut mixture. Top with another pancake; spread with a thin layer of currant combination. Repeat layers to use all pancakes and filling, leaving top pancake without anything on it. Beat egg whites until stiff. Add sugar and remaining teaspoon of vanilla; beat again. Spread egg whites over top pancake. Bake in a slow oven (325°F.) about 15 minutes, until egg white mixture is lightly browned. To serve, cut into wedges while still warm. Serves 10 to 12.

Romanian Cookery

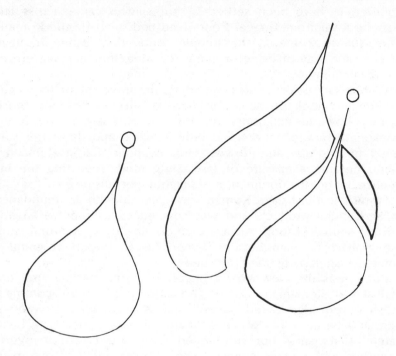

An outpost of Rome some two thousand years ago, whence came its name, Romania has a Latin language and is the only Eastern European country linked culturally with the Latin world. The nation has not been without its share of conquerors, however: the Greeks, Goths, Tartars, Bulgars, Magyars, Turks and Russians have all left their imprints. Romanian cuisine bears interesting resemblances to Slavic, Hungarian and Turkish dishes, but the Romanian touch is deftly added.

A comparatively small country noted for its rugged beauty, sparkling seacoast and wondrous Danube River delta, the modern People's Republic of Romania, formed in 1948, is comprised of the two former Danubian principalities of Moldavia and Wallachia, plus Transylvania, once a part of the Austro-Hungarian Empire.

The history of Romania, its people and cuisine is at once complex and fascinating. Originally called Dacia, the land is believed to have been settled by tribes who came across the Danube River from Thrace. Conquered and ruled by the Romans from 106 to 271 A.D., the people acquired a lasting heritage of the Latin way of living, a liking for wine and the pleasure of convivial dining.

With a succession of foreign rulers, the three major provinces of Romania took on separate characteristics, particularly those of their powerful neighbors, the Hungarians, Russians and Turks. Romania achieved nationhood only in 1877, and thereafter survived further ups and downs. Little wonder that a Romanian menu became a mixture of fascinating foods reflecting the influence but not the domination of neighboring cuisines.

From its earliest days, Romania was blessed with an abundance of agricultural products and was coveted by its foes as an important source of food. Always a predominantly agricultural land, the Wallachian plain became famous as an important granary, where wheat in particular flourished.

But it was the New World maize, or corn, that became the mainstay of Romanian cookery. An all-purpose staple, cornmeal mush or porridge called mamaliga, was introduced by way of Italy and became the Romanian national dish. It has long been eaten for all meals—hot with melted butter, sour cream or yogurt; garnished with cottage cheese, eggs or preserved fish; or served with sauces as an accompaniment to meats or poultry. Allowed to become cold and firm, mamaliga can be fried until crisp and golden or layered with other foods in a casserole and baked. Traditionally mamaliga is cooked in a large pot and stirred with a wooden spoon. To cut the cooled pudding into slices, a heavy string is preferable to a knife.

Romania has also been fortunate in having an inviting Black Sea coastline and the large Danube River flowing the length of the land into the sea. From these waters, particularly the enormous and rich Danube delta, fishermen took a plethora of superb fish—carp, pike, bream, tuna, sterlet and perch, but above all the treasured enormous sturgeon, which still yields some of the world's finest caviar. Fish has been very important to Romanian cookery. It is served in interesting variety. Favorite appetizers, or meze, the adopted Turkish word, are a carp roe paste called icre and portions of flavorful marinated cold fish. Fish is prepared in superlative soups and stews, rich with favorite Romanian seasonings of onions, peppers and tomatoes; stuffed with seasonings or vegetables; or baked on beds of mixed vegetables.

It was in the rich repertoire of soups, or ciorbas, that the Slavic fondness for tart flavors became most prominent. Soups featuring beans, onions, potatoes, tripe, fish, meatballs, tomatoes or other foods are traditionally flavored with such souring agents as fermented grains or fruits, beer or vinegar. Several kinds of soup made with cabbage and sauerkraut are related to the borshchs of Russia. Romanians became devotees of fermented cabbage and evolved a national favorite, sarmale, meat-stuffed cabbage leaves that are sometimes served with another Slavic favorite, sour cream.

Other vegetables have also long thrived in the Romanian soil and are served extensively and creatively. Raw radishes, cucumbers, onions, tomatoes and peppers may be simply nibbled as appetizers or combined with other foods to make handsome salads displaying their richness of color and flavor. Two particular favorites, mushrooms and eggplants, appear in a number of guises, all good and interesting. From the Turks the Romanians acquired a fondness for *dolmas*, squash, peppers, tomatoes or eggplants, stuffed with rice or ground meat. The glory of all the creations, however, is the beloved ghiveciu, a handsome baked medley of perhaps a dozen vegetables, and sometimes meat, with a topping of green grapes.

Romanians, like the Bulgarians and Yugoslavs, are addicted to peppers in their cookery and have devised many ways for using them in a wide number of dishes. Also frequently used are such seasonings as olive oil, onions, leeks, olives, dill, tarragon and wine.

On the Romanian menu can be found a number of inviting creations that are culinary legacies from the Hungarians. Among the best are the tocanas, richly flavored stews akin to goulashes, which feature such combinations as beef, potatoes and peppers; pork, sauerkraut and sour cream; chicken, onions and paprika; and fish, vegetables and seasonings.

From earliest days the Romanians had a fondness for fowl, both domesticated and wild, and it is always well and uniquely prepared. Fowl may be, for example, stewed with fruits or vegetables, braised with black or green olives and wine, sauced with sour cream and dill, or stewed with red or green cabbage. As for meats, the Romanians have a predilection for pork, and one of the most widely eaten foods is pastrama, smoked highly spiced meat, generally pork but also lamb or mutton. The national favorite, however, is mititei, cylinder-shaped garlic flavored beef sausages. Eaten as commonly as hamburgers are in our country, mititei, which means "very small," are popular appetizers, snacks or entrées and are generally accompanied by hot peppers.

Everyday Romanian foods are traditionally simple but nourishing and flavorful, relying heavily on such foods as olives, beans, fresh and pickled vegetables (particularly peppers), rye or other dark breads, and two sheep or goat milk cheeses, soft white brynza and firm yellow kashkaval. Fruit is also important, and the Romanians have a rich harvest of apples, cherries, apricots, berries, peaches and plums, among others, which are eaten fresh in season and used to make a characteristic year-round sweet confiture, dulceata. The Romanians adopted the Turkish custom, popular throughout the Balkans, of serving a very sweet fruit preserve with water as a gesture of welcome to guests. This and the drinking of Turkish coffee constitute an established way of life.

Fruits have also been important in making such desserts as the Austro-Hungarian-inspired filled yeast doughs, tortes, cakes, pastries and strudels, some of which are also prepared with nuts and poppy seeds. The Romanian dessert array truly reflects the numerous neighboring influences on the cuisine. It is a fascinating medley that includes the rich honey and nut Turkish sweets such as baklava; thin pancakes called clătite, filled or spread with both savory and sweet mixtures; noodles sauced with nuts or jam; cheese cakes; deep-fried doughs and cookies.

Perhaps the fun-loving Romanians enjoy their plums and grapes most of all in liquid form. Tuica, a potent brandy and national drink, is the traditional appetizer beverage, but fine and varied wines, both red and white, sweet and dry, flow before, during and after meals. The colorful and gay Romanian folk festivals and holiday get-togethers have long been enlivened with spirited singing and dancing as well as with food specialties and ample drinking. Romanians share with Hungarians a fondness for lyrical gypsy music, and many outdoor celebrations are enhanced by the talents of itinerant entertainers who roam the countryside in caravans.

The following recipes include some of the best Romanian specialties.

MEZELICURI

Pickled Leeks and Mushrooms

Romanians favor a variety of cold vegetables in oil-vinegar or lemon juice and herb marinades as a part of their mezelicuri, or appetizers.

6 leeks, white parts only, cleaned and cut into 1½-inch pieces	¼ teaspoon dried thyme
	1 teaspoon fennel seeds
24 medium fresh mushrooms	1 bay leaf
24 ripe olives	Salt, pepper to taste
½ cup olive oil	3 tablespoons chopped fresh parsley
1 lemon, sliced	

Wash leeks well to remove any sand between leaves. Cook in a little salted boiling water until tender, about 15 minutes. Drain well and cool. Clean mushrooms by rinsing quickly or wiping with wet paper toweling. Snip off any tough stem ends. Boil in salted water to cover for 5 minutes. Drain and cool. Combine leeks, mushrooms and olives with remaining ingredients except parsley; leave, stirring occasionally, for 2 days. To serve, discard lemon slices and bay leaf. Sprinkle with parsley. Serves 6.

Eggplant Caviar

A popular Romanian appetizer is made with eggplant and a number of different ingredients. The most common combination is eggplant with chopped tomatoes, garlic, onion, lemon juice and olive—also a favorite Bulgarian dish. This is another good way of preparing vinete, or eggplant.

1 large eggplant	2 garlic cloves, crushed
6 green onions, with tops, minced	2 tablespoons lemon juice

| 3 tablespoons chopped fresh dill | Freshly ground pepper |
| 1 teaspoon salt | ⅓ cup (approximately) sour cream |

Put eggplant in a kettle of boiling water and cook until tender, about 20 minutes. Drain and cool. Cut off stem and peel off skin. Mince finely and drain off any water. Mix with onions, garlic, lemon juice, dill, salt and pepper. Chop until ingredients are well mixed. Add enough sour cream to make a thick mixture. Chill. Serve with buttered black bread. Serves 6 to 8.

Grilled Sausages

Among the most popular Romanian appetizers and snacks are the spice- and garlic-flavored skinless sausages called mititei. The name means "very, very small." Throughout the country these sausages are grilled over charcoal or cooked on stoves and sold by street vendors, and served at informal cafes and in first rate restaurants. Their aroma permeates the air wherever mititei are being cooked and served.

2 pounds ground beef in- cluding some suet, or a mixture of beef, pork and lamb	½ teaspoon summer savory
	½ teaspoon ground allspice
	Salt, freshly ground pepper to taste
3 to 4 garlic cloves	Vegetable oil
½ cup beef broth or bouillon	

Mix sausages the day before they will be served so the flavors will blend together. Grind meat once or twice to make it very fine. Add remaining ingredients except oil; mix well. When ready to cook, shape sausages with wet hands into cylinders about 3 inches long and 1 inch thick. Brush broiler rack with oil; cook sausages on both sides about 3 inches from the heat until done, about 7 minutes. Makes about 16. Serve with peppers in oil and dill pickles.

SOUPS

Bean Soup

Ciorbă de fasole is one of the most well-liked of the many Romanian soups. It has a typical tart flavoring.

2 cups dried white beans, washed and drained
2 quarts water
1 medium carrot, scraped and diced
2 medium tomatoes, peeled and chopped
Salt, pepper to taste

2 tablespoons minced onion
2 tablespoons butter or margarine
1 tablespoon flour
1 medium egg
1 tablespoon sour cream
2 tablespoons vinegar

Put beans and water in a large kettle; bring to a boil. Boil for 2 minutes. Remove from heat and let stand for 1 hour. Put back on stove and bring to a boil again. Add carrot, tomatoes, salt and pepper; lower heat. Simmer, covered, for 1¼ hours, or until beans are tender. Meanwhile, sauté onion in butter until tender. Stir in flour. Mix into soup; then add egg, sour cream and vinegar, mixed together. Cook over low heat, stirring, for about 5 minutes or until smooth and thickened. Serves 8 to 10.

Onion Soup

This Romanian supá de ciapá, onion soup, has a tart flavor that makes an interesting dish.

5 large onions, peeled and chopped
⅓ cup (approximately) butter or margarine
5 cups beef bouillon

Salt, pepper to taste
3 tablespoons vinegar
3 tablespoons chopped leeks
1 large potato, peeled and diced

2 teaspoons sugar	1 cup sour cream at room
2 tablespoons chopped fresh	temperature
parsley	

Sauté chopped onions in butter in a large saucepan. Add bouillon, leeks and potato. Season with salt and pepper. Cook slowly, covered, until onions and potato are tender, about 40 minutes, or longer. Put through a sieve. Return to kettle; add vinegar and sugar; bring to a boil. Stir in parsley and sour cream; leave on stove long enough to heat through. Serves 6.

ENTRÉES

Olive-Stuffed Carp

The Romanians have an interesting variety of fish that come primarily from the Danube River. Among their favorites are the highly esteemed carp, sturgeon and sterlet. Generally the fish are made into flavorful soups and stews or baked with other ingredients such as seasonings and vegetables. Given below are two characteristic fish dishes.

1 3-4 pound fish (carp, stur-	¼ cup chopped fresh parsley
geon, hake, cod), cleaned	2 large onions, peeled and
1 cup chopped green olives	sliced
1 garlic clove, crushed	1 lemon, sliced
2 tablespoons lemon juice	Salt, pepper to taste
5 tablespoons olive oil	Fine dry bread crumbs

Wash fish and wipe dry. Sprinkle inside and out with salt. Combine olives, garlic, lemon juice, 1 tablespoon olive oil and parsley; spoon into fish cavity. Arrange onions and lemon slices evenly in a buttered shallow baking dish. Place fish over them. Sprinkle with salt, pepper and bread crumbs. Add remaining 4 tablespoons olive oil and ¼ cup hot water. Bake in a preheated hot oven (400°F.), allowing 10 minutes per pound, until fork-tender. Serves 4 to 6.

Baked Fish with Vegetables

2 pounds white-fleshed fish
  fillets (carp, cod, pike,
  perch, flounder)
2 medium onions, peeled
  and sliced
2 garlic cloves, crushed
2 leeks, white parts only,
  cleaned and sliced
½ cup olive or vegetable oil
½ cup diced carrots

½ cup sliced green beans
3 medium tomatoes, peeled
  and chopped
3 tablespoons chopped fresh
  dill
⅓ cup chopped fresh parsley
  Salt, pepper to taste
¼ cup seedless raisins
2 tablespoons fresh lemon
  juice

Arrange fish fillets in a greased shallow baking dish. In a skillet, sauté onions, garlic and leeks in hot oil until soft. Add carrots, green beans and tomatoes; sauté 5 minutes. Stir in remaining ingredients and mix well. Spoon over fish fillets, spreading evenly. Bake, covered, in a preheated moderate oven (350°F.) for about 25 minutes, or until tender. Serves 4 to 6.

Chicken Tocană

This well-seasoned chicken stew is typical of Romanian poultry dishes, which are cooked slowly to combine the flavorings.

2 frying chickens, about
  2½ pounds each, cut-up
  Salt, pepper to taste
2 medium onions, peeled
  and thinly sliced
1-2 garlic cloves, crushed
⅓ cup (approximately) olive
  or salad oil

2 cups dry white wine
1 cup sliced pitted black
  olives
½ cup chopped fresh parsley
½ cup sour cream at
  room temperature

Wash chicken pieces and wipe dry. Season with salt and pepper. Sauté onions and garlic in olive oil in a large kettle. Add chicken pieces; brown on both sides. Add wine; mix well. Cook slowly, covered, for 1 hour. Add olives, parsley and sour cream; cook another 5 minutes, or until chicken is tender. Correct seasoning. Serves 6 to 8.

Tongue with Olive Sauce

1 fresh veal or beef tongue,
  cleaned
2 medium onions, peeled
  and chopped
4 whole cloves
2 bay leaves
1 large carrot, scraped and
  diced
  Salt, pepper to taste
2 tablespoons butter or
  margarine

2 tablespoons flour
3 tablespoons tomato paste
1 cup dry white wine
¾ cup sliced pitted black
  olives
2 tablespoons chopped fresh
  dill
2 tablespoons chopped fresh
  parsley

Place tongue in a kettle and cover with cold water. Add 1 chopped onion, cloves, bay leaves, diced carrot, salt and pepper. Bring to a boil. Lower heat and cook slowly, allowing about 1 hour per pound, until fork-tender. Remove from liquid. Strain liquid and reserve. Cut off any bone and gristle; peel off skin. Cut into slices.

Sauté remaining chopped onion in butter. Mix in flour to form a roux. Cook 1 minute. Add tomato paste, reserved liquid, white wine and olives. Season with salt and pepper. Cook, stirring, about 10 minutes, until ingredients are well blended. Add tongue slices, dill and parsley; leave on stove long enough to heat through. Serves 4 to 6.

Sarmale

This Romanian favorite, brined cabbage leaves with a ground meat stuffing, can be prepared in several variations and eaten as an appetizer or as a main dish with cornmeal, mamaliga. Sarmale is enjoyed in Romania on every festive occasion and is truly a great cabbage dish. It can be prepared with fermented or parboiled fresh cabbage leaves. To ferment leaves, put a large head of cabbage in medium-salted water to cover in a crock or kettle. Leave to soak 5 or 6 days. Drain and separate the leaves.

⅓ cup uncooked long grain
  rice

1 medium onion, peeled and
  minced

2 teaspoons oil or lard
1½ pounds lean ground pork
½ teaspoon dried oregano
  Salt, pepper to taste
1 large head green cabbage,
  fermented or fresh

2 pounds sauerkraut, drained
  and rinsed
½ pound unsliced bacon
1 can (6 ounces) tomato
  paste
2 small bay leaves

Add rice to 1 cup boiling water; cook slowly, covered, for 10 minutes. In a skillet, sauté onion in oil until just tender. Mix in a bowl with rice, pork, oregano, salt and pepper; combine thoroughly. If fermented leaves are used, trim any tough rib ends from them and cut the large ones into halves. If a fresh cabbage is used, wash and put in a large kettle of salted boiling water to cover. Cook over fairly high heat for 10 minutes. Remove and take off all leaves that are soft. Return to water; keep boiling and removing leaves until all are soft. Drain. Trim off any rib ends from leaves and put aside. Place a small ball of stuffing— 1 tablespoon or more for larger leaves—on each leaf and roll up. Tuck in ends to completely enclose stuffing. Attach with toothpicks. Put ⅓ of the sauerkraut in a large pot. Arrange some of the cabbage rolls in circles over it, leaving a hole in the center for bacon. In layers add remaining sauerkraut and rolls. Put bacon in center. Thin tomato paste with 1 cup water; pour into pot. Add bay leaves; season with salt and pepper. Bring to a slow boil. Lower heat and cook slowly, covered, for 30 minutes. Then put in a preheated moderate oven (350°F.) for 30 minutes, or until cooked. Serve with mamaliga and sour cream, if desired. Serves 8 to 10.

Transylvanian Pancake "Casserole"

This is an interesting main dish made with stacked pancakes spread with ground beef and spinach mixtures. It is believed to have originated in the northern mountainous region of Transylvania.

1 large onion, peeled and
  chopped
2 tablespoons lard or fat
1 pound ground beef

1 teaspoon paprika
¼ cup chopped fresh parsley
  Salt, pepper to taste
1½ cups chopped cooked
  spinach

1½	cups tomatoes, chopped	½	teaspoon salt
	and peeled	1	cup milk
1	cup grated Parmesan cheese	2	eggs, beaten
1	cup all-purpose flour		Butter

Sauté chopped onion in shortening until tender. Add ground beef; cook, separating with a fork, until redness disappears. Stir in paprika, parsley, salt and pepper. Cook 1 minute. Spoon into a bowl. Season spinach with salt and pepper; spoon into a bowl. Place the two bowlfuls, tomatoes and grated cheese next to each other in a working area where the pancakes will be assembled.

Sift flour and salt into a bowl. Add milk and eggs; mix until smooth. Heat a lightly greased 7- or 8-inch skillet; pour 3 tablespoons of batter into it all at once. Tilt pan quickly to spread batter evenly. Cook until underside is golden. Turn over with a spatula; cook on other side. Remove to a plate and keep warm in a preheated 250°F. oven. Continue to cook other pancakes.

To assemble, place one pancake in a buttered casserole. Spread with a layer of meat mixture topped with spinach, tomatoes and grated cheese. Repeat layers to use all pancakes and filling. Leave top pancake without anything on it. Spread generously with butter. Bake in a preheated moderate oven (350°F.) for 30 minutes. To serve, cut into wedges. Serves 4.

Sauerkraut with Pork

Varzá cu porc is a flavorful baked dish made with two favorite Romanian foods, sauerkraut and pork.

1	large onion, peeled and	2	cups beef bouillon
	sliced	1	teaspoon sugar
2	leeks, white parts only,	1	tablespoon lemon juice
	cleaned and sliced	2	tablespoons fresh dill
3	tablespoons bacon fat or		or parsley, chopped
	shortening		Salt, pepper to taste
2	pounds sauerkraut, drained	2	pounds smoked pork or
2	tablespoons flour		ham, cut up into 2-inch
¼	cup tomato paste		pieces

In a kettle, sauté onion and leeks in hot fat until onions are tender. Remove with a slotted spoon to a large bowl; mix with sauerkraut. Set aside. Stir flour into fat drippings; mix to blend well. Add tomato paste and then bouillon, sugar, lemon juice, dill or parsley, salt and pepper. Cook slowly, uncovered, for 10 minutes. Arrange meat and sauerkraut mixture in layers in a greased casserole. Pour tomato sauce over ingredients. Bake in a preheated slow oven (250°F.) for 1 hour. Serves 4 to 6. Serve with sour cream.

Ghiveciu

A most attractive and delectable Romanian baked dish is a flavored vegetable stew that may or may not include meat, generally veal or pork. Its name is taken from the Turkish *güvec*, for the earthenware pot in which the ingredients are cooked. Ghiveciu closely resembles a Bulgarian dish called *ghivetch*. The Romanians have a beautiful variety of vegetables, and sometimes as many as twelve or more will be used in preparing ghiveciu. There is no particular recipe for the stew, since every Romanian cook seems to be guided by instinct or family tradition. In addition to the vegetables listed below the stew might include: cauliflower, celery root, green peas, cabbage, leeks, squash and turnips. Green grapes are used by some cooks as a colorful topping. Although the dish could be cooked on the top of the stove, it is customarily baked. It will be more flavorful if all of the vegetables are sautéed individually in oil beforehand, but some cooks do not do this.

2 medium onions, peeled and sliced

1½ cups (approximately) olive or salad oil

2 medium potatoes, peeled and sliced

1 medium unpeeled eggplant

1 large green pepper, cleaned and cubed

2 large carrots, scraped and sliced

1 cup fresh or frozen green beans

1 cup hot vegetable bouillon

2 garlic cloves, crushed

¾ cup chopped fresh parsley

¼ cup mixed fresh herbs
Salt, pepper to taste

4 medium tomatoes, peeled and sliced

¼ pound seedless green grapes, washed

In a large frying pan, sauté onion slices in 1/3 cup oil until tender. Spoon out and set aside. Add potato slices; sauté until just tender. Spoon out and set aside. Slice eggplant; sauté also, adding more oil if necessary, until tender. Take out and set aside. Sauté green pepper and carrots. Arrange sautéed vegetables and green beans in an extra-large shallow round or oblong baking dish. Combine bouillon, garlic, parsley and herbs; pour over ingredients. Also add any oil drippings in pan. Season with salt and pepper. Bake, covered, in a preheated moderate oven (350° F.) about 30 minutes, or until the vegetables are cooked. Add tomatoes and grapes during last 15 minutes of cooking. The dish may be eaten warm or cold. Serves 8 to 10.

GRAINS

Cornmeal Porridge

Cornmeal, or mamaliga, the most beloved food in Romania, is as popular as bread or potatoes are in America. Mamaliga is cooked and enjoyed in various ways. As a thick cornmeal mush, for example, it is eaten by itself or with a gravy or sauce, vegetables and meats. A favorite Romanian meal includes mamaliga with meat-stuffed cabbage leaves (sarmale).

To cook mamaliga, bring 2½ cups salted water to a boil. Slowly add 1 cup yellow cornmeal; stir vigorously with a wooden spoon until mixture is thick and smooth. The water should continue to boil. Cover and leave over low heat for about 12 minutes, until meal takes shape of pan. Run a knife around its edges and invert on a plate. Serve hot, plain, with sour cream, grated cheese, melted butter, gravy or topped with fried eggs. Serves 4.

Cornmeal Pudding

Bring 3 cups salted water to a boil. Slowly add 1 cup yellow cornmeal; stir strongly until mixture is thick and smooth but is softer than the above mamaliga. Spoon a layer into a buttered baking dish. Cover with a layer of crumbled white cheese (brynza, farmer's or dry cottage) and grated Parmesan cheese, mixed together. Repeat layers until cornmeal is used up. Dot with butter; sprinkle with fine dry bread crumbs. Bake in a preheated moderate oven (350° F.) for 15 minutes or until golden brown on top. Excellent with sauerkraut. Serves 4 to 6.

Fried Mamaliga

Cool cooked mamaliga (recipe above) and cut into slices. Dip each slice in beaten egg. Sprinkle generously on each side with grated yellow cheese. Fry in hot butter on both sides until golden. Serve with sour cream or yogurt. Serves 4 to 6.

Farina Dumplings

2 eggs, beaten	1 cup farina or cream of
2 tablespoons melted butter or margarine	wheat
¼ teaspoon salt	⅓ cup (approximately) milk

Combine eggs, butter, salt and farina in a bowl; mix well. Add milk, enough to make a stiff dough. Drop by the spoonful into a kettle of boiling salted water. Cover and cook about 10 minutes, or until tender. Test by tearing one dumpling apart with two forks. Makes 8. Serve with melted butter or sour cream or yogurt, if desired.

Baked Eggplant-Rice Casserole

Rice (orez) is grown in Romania in the fertile Danube River delta area and is used in making stuffings and baked dishes. Given below are two good rice creations.

5 tablespoons butter or margarine	3 medium tomatoes, peeled and chopped

4 cups chicken bouillon   Olive or salad oil for frying
2 cups uncooked rice   3 tablespoons chopped
Salt and pepper to taste   parsley
2 medium eggplants

Melt butter in a saucepan; sauté tomatoes in butter for 1 to 2 minutes, until mushy. Add bouillon; bring to a boil. Stir in rice. Season with salt and pepper. Lower heat and cook slowly, covered, about 25 minutes, or until rice is tender and liquid is absorbed.

Cut unpeeled eggplants lengthwise into ⅛- to ¼-inch thick slices. Fry in hot oil until golden on both sides and fork-tender. Drain on absorbent paper. Arrange eggplant slices on bottom and sides of a casserole, overlapping slices for contrast in color. Arrange so close together that slices completely cover surfaces of dish. Spoon cooked rice into dish, spreading it evenly. Press lightly with a spoon. Sprinkle with parsley. Bake in a preheated moderate oven (350° F.) for about 25 minutes. Invert carefully onto a warm platter and serve at once. Serves 8.

Rice with Mushrooms

1 medium onion, peeled   ½ pound fresh mushrooms
and chopped   3 tablespoons butter or
3 slices bacon, diced   margarine
2 cups chicken broth   2 tablespoons lemon juice
1 cup uncooked rice   2 tablespoons chopped
Salt, pepper, paprika to   chives
taste

Sauté onion with diced bacon in a saucepan until onion is tender. Drain off all except 2 tablespoons fat. Add chicken broth; bring to a boil. Stir in rice. Season with salt, pepper and paprika. Lower heat and cook slowly, covered, about 25 minutes, or until rice is tender and liquid is absorbed. Wipe dry or wash mushrooms. Slice crosswise; sauté in butter for 4 minutes. Add lemon juice and chives. Stir into cooked rice while rice is still warm. Mix well and serve. Serves 4 to 6.

VEGETABLES

Peppers in Oil

For each person cut one cleaned large green pepper into quarters. Put under broiler to roast until darkened and skin breaks. Remove to a bowl; cover with vinegar and olive or vegetable oil, using 1 part vinegar to 3 parts oil. Sprinkle with salt and pepper; leave to marinate, covered, 1 or 2 days. Serve with black olives, cubes of white cheese and green onions. These peppers are a traditional accompaniment to mititei.

Braised Cabbage

Other vegetables may be prepared in the same manner as this cabbage, varzá.

1 medium onion, peeled and chopped	Salt, pepper to taste
3 tablespoons lard, butter or vegetable oil	2 tablespoons vinegar
1 medium head green cabbage, cored and shredded	¼ cup sour cream at room temperature

Sauté onion in lard in a large saucepan. Add shredded cabbage; sauté 2 or 3 minutes. Season with salt and pepper. Add just a little bit of water; simmer, tightly covered, about 15 minutes or longer, until tender. Mix in vinegar and sour cream; leave on stove long enough to heat. Serves 4 to 6.

Sour Cream-Potato Salad

4 cups diced cooked potatoes	1 large onion, peeled and chopped

1 large green pepper, chopped	1 tablespoon lemon juice
¾ cup sliced fresh mushrooms	1 cup (approximately) sour cream
3 tablespoons chopped dill or parsley	Salt, pepper, paprika to taste

Combine all ingredients and mix well. Chill. Serves 6.

DESSERTS

Cheese-filled Pancakes

Romanians are very fond of their pancakes, clătite, which are usually filled with cottage cheese or jam and folded over or rolled up. They may also be sauced with liqueurs and flamed. This is an interesting baked dish.

2 eggs, beaten	1½ cups dry cottage cheese
2 tablespoons melted butter or margarine	½ teaspoon vanilla
1 cup milk	½ cup sugar
¼ teaspoon salt	1½ cups sour cream at room temperature
1 cup all-purpose flour	Confectioners' sugar

Combine eggs, melted butter, milk, salt and flour in a bowl; mix well to combine ingredients. Heat a lightly greased 7- or 8-inch skillet; add 3 tablespoons of batter all at once. Tilt pan at once to spread batter evenly. Cook over medium heat until underside of pancake is golden. Turn over with a spatula; cook on the other side. Slide onto a warm plate and keep warm in a preheated 250° F. oven. Continue cooking other pancakes. Combine cottage cheese, drained of all liquid, vanilla and sugar. Spread each pancake evenly with cheese mixture; roll up each one, folding in sides to enclose filling. Arrange, side by side, in a shallow baking dish. Cover with sour cream and sprinkle with confectioners' sugar. Bake, covered with foil, in a preheated moderate (350° F.) oven for 20 minutes. Serves about 10.

Sweet Omelet with Fruit Sauce

2 cups fruit purée	2 teaspoons grated lemon
2 tablespoons cornstarch	or orange rind
2 tablespoons light rum	¼ cup cold water
6 eggs	Butter for frying
Pinch salt	Confectioners' sugar
3 tablespoons sugar	

Put fruit purée in a saucepan. Mix cornstarch with a little cold water until blended. Add to fruit. Cook, stirring, over low heat until mixture thickens a little. Stir in rum and keep warm. Break eggs into a bowl; beat to blend. Add salt, sugar, lemon rind and water. Beat until smooth and creamy. Pour into a buttered omelet pan or skillet; cook over moderate heat until mixture is set. Sprinkle the top with confectioners' sugar; remove omelet with a spatula to a warm platter. Fold over from the two sides toward the middle; serve at once with warm fruit sauce. Serves 6.

Bulgarian Cookery

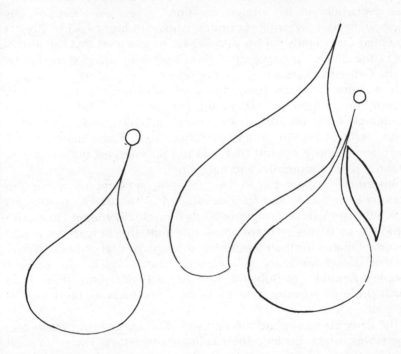

The cookery of Bulgaria is distinctive in that it has a Slavic heritage with pronounced Turkish overtones, yet has remained a nationalistic cuisine. The Bulgarians have one of the most healthy diets in Eastern Europe. They rely heavily on grains, vegetables, fruits, nuts and yogurt to make their rich repertoire of creative dishes. Little wonder that they have long been internationally known for their vigorous longevity.

The history of this ancient land that lies in the southeastern corner of Europe dates back to the time of the early Greeks and Romans. The country endured a turbulent past that left its imprint on the culture and cookery. The Bulgars, a Finno-Tartar race from the Asiatic steppes, were comparatively latecomers to the area, but they managed to overcome their foes. By about 800 A.D. the Bulgars had settled down to the pursuit of agriculture. After mingling with the Slavic population they adopted its language.

161

An early and important east-west crossroads for trade caravans, Bulgaria also suffered the passage of various armies as the country was overwhelmed by foreign invasions. Their own empire was crushed by the Byzantines, under whose influence King Boris I accepted Christianity for his people. Yet he decreed that the liturgy be in the Slavic language, and thereafter Bulgarians were linked to the Orthodox Russians.

It was the Ottoman Turks, however, who left the most lasting imprint on Bulgaria. After being conquered in 1392, Bulgaria unwillingly endured Turkish rule for about 500 years. It is to the great credit of the Bulgarians that they created and maintained a basic and inviting cuisine that was not submerged but enhanced by those of its conquerors and neighbors.

Bulgarian cookery began in the early settlements along the Danube River valley and later developed in the Balkan mountains where the nomads first migrated. *Bulgar* originally meant "man with a plow," so it was perhaps inevitable that the Bulgarians would become famous for their gardening and agricultural prowess. These ancient occupations are still expertly continued in the present People's Republic of Bulgaria, formed in 1946, where there is as much pride in growing delectable food products as there was in the past.

The early Bulgars found the rich soil ideal for growing grains and vegetables, which became their culinary mainstays. The cultivation of wheat and barley, and later, rice and corn, has long been important. These foods, along with vitamin-rich dried legumes such as lentils, peas and beans, played dominant roles in the everyday diet. Bulgarians have been particular devotees of dried white beans, often called the national vegetable. The beans are consumed in great quantity in soups, stews and casseroles. Cold beans flavored with oil, carrots and mint was an early household staple.

The Bulgarians became most partial to their fresh vegetables, which flourished for centuries and are still displayed handsomely at open markets throughout the country. Because the flavor of these vegetables was so superb, early cooks devised a number of colorful mixed salads featuring them with appropriate seasonings. Other praiseworthy dishes were relishes, spreads and a variety of pickles for winter use. Bulgarian cooked main dishes included such vegetables as leeks, onions, tomatoes, eggplant, squash, spinach and okra. In fact, one of their greatest creations is ghivetch, which is similar to Romania's *ghiveciu* and is made with a mixture of vegetables and seasonings, with or without meat. Also indispensable to the cookery were peppers, grown in great variety and kept year-round in the kitchens as staples. They were fashioned into a number of creative dishes and used also as seasonings.

Another product of Bulgaria's fertile lands were high quality nuts grown in extensive hillside groves. Over the years both green and ripe walnuts and, to a lesser extent, almonds and hazelnuts, have been inventively added to soups, salads, sauces, stuffings and desserts. Abundant crops of sunflowers became important not only for their seeds but also for their oil, which is still preferred for cooking to olive oil, butter or lard.

For flavor and attractiveness, probably none of Bulgaria's food products can match the fruits, which have been carefully tended for centuries in the gardens, orchards and vineyards. Apples, plums, cherries, melons, pears, figs, apricots and peaches are still enjoyed fresh or used for making jams, jellies, compotes and other desserts. The highly prized plums are also vital for making the national drink, a brandy called slivova. Although most vineyards produce grapes for palatable red and white wines, Bulgaria has long been noted for the quality of its large and flavorful dessert grapes which are exported in considerable quantity.

From the fields the housewives gathered aromatic wild herbs, which they learned to cultivate. They developed expertise in using herbs in cooking. They understood well which particular herb was best suited to flavor a particular food or dish. Mint, dill, savory, thyme and a type of native tarragon are used extensively. Although Bulgarians have used many spices in their cookery, their principal concern has been to preserve the natural flavor of foods as much as possible; therefore, Bulgarian dishes are more lightly seasoned than many persons assume.

With fish from the Danube River and the Black Sea, the cooks created flavorful stews and baked dishes, many of them rich with vegetables and herbs. Carp stuffed with rice, nuts and onions became a cherished holiday specialty.

For meats, the Bulgarians have traditionally preferred lamb and mutton to veal and pork. Typical dishes were created to use all parts of the animals in stews. Other characteristic dishes were kebabs, meatballs, stuffed roast whole lambs or pigs, and mixed grills. Perhaps the Bulgarians have been most successful in the cookery of game, and their repertoire of dishes for quail, wild duck, partridge, pheasant, hare and venison is particularly imaginative, effectively making use of such foods as olives, nuts, wine, vegetables, rice and onions.

Slavic influences on Bulgarian cooking were less pronounced than in neighboring countries. Tart flavors were characteristic of some soups, sauces and dishes, but the tartness was usually achieved with lemon juice rather than with vinegar. Bulgarians adapted sauerkraut as a favorite food and used it in some stews as well as in sarma, stuffed cabbage or sauerkraut leaves.

Sour cream was never as favored as yogurt in Bulgaria. Bulgarians literally became addicts of the tangy semisolid cultured milk, which they consumed in considerable quantities with their meals or as a snack, and which they used in various aspects of cooking. When this so-called "milk of eternal life" was comparatively unknown in Western Europe, a French bacteriologist, Ilya Metchnikoff, traveled to Bulgaria to learn why the hard-working farmers lived such healthy long lives. Later he noted in his book, *The Prolongation of Life*, that "the good health and long life of the Bulgarians was due to the custardy fermented milk that they consumed in great quantity. . . ."

Like a great many Bulgarian dishes, some of the yogurt creations have a Turkish or Near Eastern heritage. For example, the Bulgarians enjoy an array of appetizers called meze, as do the Turks, and include similar foods such as a spicy dry sausage, pasterma; fresh white goat's cheese, sirene; and cured yellow cheese, kashkaval.

The Bulgarians also adapted the Turkish kebabs, pilafs and musaka (a casserole of potatoes or eggplant with ground meat). From the Turks they also learned to drink small cups of thick dark coffee and to eat rice and milk puddings, rich honey and nut pastries, cakes and puddings, including one made with sweetened pumpkin. Banitsa, a well-known Bulgarian dish, is made with paper-thin dough in various forms, especially as small and large pies, with fillings of cheese, spinach or pumpkin.

Perhaps the most significant gift of the Turks to the Bulgarians was the lovely fragrant and oil-rich roses planted in the Kazanlak basin in the 1600s. Each year the miles and miles of beautiful flowers in the famed "valley of roses" are used to make the important attar of roses. Although some is used by the Bulgarians to make preserves, most of it is shipped to Turkey and other countries where rosewater has a traditional place in the cookery.

This selection of recipes is representative of Bulgarian cookery, which has sturdily maintained its national character despite the pressures of foreign conquest and influence.

APPETIZERS

Eggplant-Pepper Appetizer

This very typical Bulgarian dish, Zelen haviar, is a popular appetizer that in America can be served as a dip with crusty bread or crackers. It may be made even better with the addition of more garlic and peppers.

1 large eggplant	⅓ cup olive oil
2 medium green peppers, cleaned and minced	3 tablespoons fresh lemon juice or red wine vinegar
2 medium tomatoes, peeled, seeded and minced	3 tablespoons chopped fresh parsley
2 to 3 garlic cloves, crushed	Salt, freshly ground pepper
1 small hot red or green pepper, seeded and minced (optional)	to taste

Prick eggplant in several places and put on a cookie sheet. Cook in a preheated hot oven (400° F.) until soft, about 50 minutes. Peel off and discard skin. Put pulp in a bowl; chop with a knife. Then beat with a wooden spoon to purée. Add remaining ingredients and mix well, beating as adding. Chill. Serve in mound on a plate, garnished with strips of tomato or green pepper, if desired. Serves 4 to 6.

White Beans in Olive Oil

Fasoul iahnia, a cold bean dish, is a traditional Bulgarian appetizer. It also can be served as an accompaniment to kebabs or other meats.

1 pound dried white beans
4 garlic cloves, crushed
2 medium onions, peeled
   and chopped
2 medium carrots, scraped
   and diced
1 cup olive oil

1 teaspoon salt
2 tablespoons wine vinegar
   or fresh lemon juice
2 teaspoons sugar
3 tablespoons chopped fresh
   parsley

Cover beans with water. Bring to a boil; boil 2 minutes. Remove from heat. Let stand, covered, for 1 hour. Return to stove; simmer, covered, until partially cooked, about 45 minutes. Add a little more water while cooking, if needed. Add garlic, onions, carrots, olive oil and salt. Continue to cook slowly, covered, until beans are tender, about 45 minutes. Stir in vinegar or lemon juice and sugar. Cook another 5 minutes. Serve cold in a large bowl; garnish with parsley. Serves 8 to 10.

Black Sea Raw Vegetable Relish

Such is the goodness and variety of the Bulgarian vegetables that they are eaten generously at all meals. This is a good spread for dark bread.

2 medium onions, peeled
   and minced
4 large tomatoes, peeled
   and chopped
2 green peppers, seeded
   and chopped

3 tablespoons pine nuts
3 tablespoons chopped
   fresh parsley
⅓ cup olive oil
2 tablespoons vinegar
   Salt, pepper to taste

Combine all ingredients and mix well. Chill. Serves 6 to 8.

SOUPS

Tarator

This chilled yogurt-cucumber soup, flavored with garlic and walnuts, is served in Bulgaria in summer.

2 medium cucumbers,
  peeled, seeded and diced
  Salt
4 cups plain yogurt
2 garlic cloves, crushed
½ cup finely chopped
  walnuts
1 tablespoon red wine
  vinegar

2 tablespoons sunflower or
  olive oil
1 tablespoon minced fresh
  mint
1 tablespoon minced fresh
  dill
  White pepper to taste

Put diced cucumbers in a colander or bowl; sprinkle with salt. Leave to drain for 30 minutes. Mix in a large bowl with remaining ingredients and chill. Serve in individual soup dishes or bowls with 3 or 4 ice cubes in each. Serves 6 to 8.

Rice and Meatball Soup

The Bulgarians, like the Romanians, flavor their soups with tart flavorings, but the Bulgarians prefer lemon juice to vinegar.

¾ pound ground beef
1 small onion, peeled
  and minced
1 tablespoon chopped fresh
  dill
2 eggs, beaten
1 garlic clove, crushed
  Salt, pepper to taste

  Flour
6 cups beef bouillon
⅓ cup uncooked rice
  Juice of ½ lemon
2 tablespoons chopped
  fresh parsley
1 cup plain yogurt (optional)

Combine ground beef, onion, dill, 1 egg, garlic, salt and pepper. Mix until ingredients are well blended. With hands shape into small balls, about 1 inch in diameter. Dredge in flour. Set aside. Heat beef bouillon to boiling. Drop in meatballs and rice. Lower heat; cook slowly, covered, until rice is tender and meatballs are cooked, about 30 minutes. Mix together lemon juice and remaining egg. Stir in parsley. Add some of the hot broth to lemon mixture beating constantly while adding. Return to soup and mix well. When well blended, remove from heat. Serve with a spoonful of yogurt put on top of each serving, if desired. Serves 6 to 8.

Hot Yogurt-Chicken Soup

This is an appealing light soup that can be served as a first course for luncheon or dinner.

6 cups chicken broth
  Salt, pepper to taste
2 cups plain yogurt
1 tablespoon flour
2 egg yolks, well beaten

2 tablespoons butter or
  margarine
2 tablespoons chopped mint
  or parsley

Bring broth to a boil in a saucepan. Season with salt and pepper. Lower heat. Combine yogurt, flour and beaten egg yolks; stir about 3 tablespoons of hot broth into mixture. Mix well; return to broth. Cook over low heat, stirring, 1 or 2 minutes. Add butter and mint and serve. Serves 6 to 8.

ENTRÉES

Rice-Nut Stuffed Fish

A common Bulgarian method of preparing freshwater fish from the Danube River is to stuff and bake it.

1 medium onion, peeled
  and chopped
3 tablespoons olive or
  vegetable oil
⅓ cup chopped pine nuts
½ cup uncooked rice
1 cup chicken broth or water
¼ cup currants

¼ teaspoon cinnamon
3 tablespoons chopped fresh
  parsley
  Salt, pepper to taste
2 whole white-fleshed fish
  (3 to 4 pounds each),
  cleaned

Sauté onion in oil until soft. Add pine nuts and rice and sauté 3 to 4 minutes, stirring, or until translucent. Add the broth, currants, cinnamon, parsley, salt and pepper. Cook slowly, covered, about 20 minutes, or until the liquid is absorbed and the grains are separate. Wash the fish and wipe dry. Sprinkle inside and out with salt and pepper. Stuff with rice filling and close openings. Place in a greased baking dish and cook in a preheated moderate oven (350° F.), allowing about 10 minutes per pound, until tender. Serve garnished with parsley and lemon wedges, if desired. Serves 4 to 6.

Braised Quail

The Bulgarians are noted for the way they cook quail, served over rice combinations or cooked with other flavorful ingredients.

4 quail, cleaned	1 cup dry red wine
¼ cup butter or margarine	⅛ to ¼ teaspoon cayenne
Salt, pepper to taste	4 rounds buttered white
3 tablespoons tomato paste	bread
1 medium tomato, peeled	
and chopped	

In a large skillet brown quail on all sides in butter. Sprinkle with salt and pepper. Add tomato paste, tomato, wine and cayenne. Mix well; cook slowly, covered, about 30 minutes, or until just tender. Remove to a warm platter. Fry rounds of bread and soak in warm drippings. Serve each quail placed over a round of bread. Spoon remaining sauces into a bowl and serve with quail. Serves 4.

Chicken with Vegetables

A Bulgarian way of cooking chicken or other poultry is by simmering it slowly on top of the stove, which results in a very tender dish. This type of stew is called jachnia.

1 whole broiler-fryer chicken (about 3½ pounds)	4 large onions, peeled and sliced
½ cup oil, butter or shortening	1 garlic clove, crushed
Salt, pepper to taste	2 to 3 teaspoons paprika
4 large tomatoes, peeled and quartered	Dry white wine

Wash chicken and wipe dry. Fry in oil in a heavy casserole or kettle until golden on all sides. Season with salt and pepper. Remove chicken to a plate. Add vegetables, garlic, and paprika; sauté 5 minutes. Return chicken to kettle. Add wine, enough to cover ingredients; bring to a boil. Reduce heat; simmer, covered, about 1 hour, or until tender. Remove chicken to a warm platter and cut into serving pieces. Serve surrounded by cooked vegetables. Serves 4.

Potato Musaka

A dish common to the cuisines of Romania, Bulgaria and Yugoslavia is a baked casserole made with vegetables, meat and seasonings, with a topping of eggs and cream or milk. The dish reflects Greek and Turkish influences. Although the dish is prepared in many ways, the Bulgarians are very fond of this one, since potatoes are a favorite food. The same dish can also be made with eggplant instead of potatoes, if desired.

4 medium potatoes, peeled and sliced	⅛ teaspoon dried thyme or summer savory
¼ cup oil, lard or butter	Salt, pepper to taste
2 medium onions, peeled and chopped	3 tablespoons chopped parsley
2 garlic cloves, crushed	2 eggs, beaten
1 pound ground lean beef	1 cup light cream or milk
1 can (8 ounces) tomato sauce	¼ cup grated Kashkaval, Caciocavallo, or Provolone

Fry potato slices in some of the fat until soft and golden. Drain and set aside. Sauté onions and garlic in remaining oil until tender. Add beef; cook, stirring with a fork, until redness disappears. Add tomato sauce, thyme, salt and pepper; cook 1 or 2 minutes, uncovered, to blend flavors. Stir in parsley.

Arrange half of the potato slices in a greased shallow baking dish. Cover with beef-tomato mixture. Top with remaining potato slices. Combine beaten eggs and milk; pour over ingredients. Sprinkle with cheese. Bake in a preheated moderate oven (350° F.) for 50 minutes, or until the topping is set. To serve, cut into squares. Serves 4.

Note: Eggplants may be substituted for potatoes. Sprinkle eggplant slices with flour and fry in hot olive oil until golden on both sides.

Ghivetch

This meat and vegetable baked dish is common to the cuisines of Bulgaria and Romania, but there are slight differences in the preparation. Bulgarian cooks point out that ghivetch is best when prepared in the summer, with as many as a dozen or more fresh vegetables. Given below is one suggested recipe, but other vegetables may be used as substitutes if desired.

2 pounds boneless lamb shoulder, cut in small cubes, about 1½ inches
Vegetable oil or other fat for frying
2 medium onions, peeled and chopped
1 teaspoon dried hot red peppers, crumbled
Salt, pepper to taste
4 medium potatoes, peeled and cut into 1½-inch cubes

1 medium eggplant, unpeeled and cut into 1½-inch cubes
3 large green or red peppers, cleaned and cut into strips
1½ cups fresh or frozen green beans, cut-up
1 cup okra, cut-up
4 tomatoes, peeled and sliced
3 eggs, beaten
¼ cup chopped fresh parsley

Wipe meat dry and brown on all sides in 3 tablespoons of oil in a large saucepan or kettle. Push meat aside; add onions and more oil, if needed. Sauté onions until tender. Mix in red peppers, salt and pepper. Add water to cover and cook slowly, covered, for 1 hour. While meat is cooking, sauté potatoes, eggplant, peppers, green beans and okra separately in oil. (Or, omit this step and partially cook the vegetables in the stew. The dish will be more flavorful if vegetables are sautéed separately in oil.) Spoon meat and other ingredients in the kettle into a large round casserole; top with sautéed or partially cooked vegetables. Season with salt and pepper; add water to just cover ingredients. Cook in a preheated moderate oven (350° F.) for about 1 hour, or until ingredients are cooked. Put tomato slices over other vegetables 10 minutes before cooking is finished. Combine eggs and parsley and stir with a fork. Spoon over ingredients; leave in oven long enough to set. Cool a little before serving. Serves 6 to 8.

Veal-Vegetable Stew

This is an example of the excellent stews that the Bulgarians make with veal, lamb or pork, well-flavored vegetables and seasonings.

2 pounds boneless veal shoulder, cut into 1½-inch cubes
⅓ cup olive or vegetable oil
Salt, pepper to taste
6 green onions, with tops, cleaned and sliced
2 medium tomatoes, peeled and chopped

1 medium eggplant, cut into 1½-inch cubes
½ teaspoon dried savory
1 tablespoon chopped fresh mint
3 tablespoons chopped fresh parsley

Wipe veal dry and brown in oil in a large kettle. Season with salt and pepper. Push meat aside; add onions. Sauté until tender. Stir in tomatoes and cook 1 minute, until mushy. Barely cover with water; cook slowly, covered, for 1 hour. Add eggplant and savory; continue cooking until tender, 30 minutes or longer. Stir in mint and parsley. Add more water during the cooking, if needed. Serves 6.

Rice with Liver

The Bulgarians cook rice in the Turkish style—sautéed in fat and cooked by itself, or cooked with other foods to make a flavorful pilaf.

1 medium onion, peeled and chopped
5 tablespoons butter or margarine
½ pound calf's liver, chopped

3 cups beef bouillon
1½ cups uncooked rice
Salt, pepper, cayenne to taste
⅓ cup chopped fresh parsley

Sauté onion in 3 tablespoons of butter until tender. Add liver; cook 1 minute. Pour in bouillon; bring to a boil. Stir in rice; season with salt, pepper and cayenne. Mix well. Lower heat and cook slowly, covered, about 25 minutes, or until rice is tender and liquid has been absorbed. Stir in parsley and remaining 2 tablespoons of butter. Correct seasoning, if necessary. Serves 6.

VEGETABLES

Green Beans and Eggs

A favorite Bulgarian dish is made by combining vegetables, eggs and seasonings. It is good luncheon fare.

1 medium onion, peeled and chopped
2 tablespoons oil, butter or other fat
1 tablespoon flour
Salt, pepper, cayenne to taste

1 cup chopped cooked green beans
4 eggs, slightly beaten
½ cup yogurt or sour cream at room temperature
1 tablespoon chopped fresh dill

Sauté onion in oil until tender. Stir in flour, salt, pepper and cayenne. Add green beans and mix well. Stir in eggs; cook, stirring, until almost set. Add yogurt and dill; continue to cook until set. Serves 2.

Potato Casserole

4 medium potatoes, peeled and sliced thinly
Oil for frying
1 large onion, peeled and chopped
1 cup tomato sauce
⅛ teaspoon dried oregano

Salt, pepper to taste
2 tablespoons chopped fresh dill or parsley
2 tablespoons fine dry bread crumbs
⅓ cup grated Kashkeval or Parmesan cheese

Fry potato slices in hot oil in a skillet for 1 minute. Drain on absorbent paper. Sauté onions in oil drippings until tender. Add tomato sauce, oregano, salt, pepper and dill or parsley. Cook, uncovered, 1 minute. Fill a shallow buttered baking dish with layers of potatoes spread with tomato sauce mixture. Sprinkle top with bread crumbs and cheese. Bake in a preheated moderate oven (375° F.) for about 30 minutes, or until potatoes are tender. Serves 4.

Beets with Yogurt

¾ cup plain yogurt
1 tablespoon vinegar
2 tablespoons chopped dill

Salt, pepper, cayenne to taste
2 cans (1 pound each) julienned beets

Combine all ingredients except beets. Blend well and chill. Drain beets and chill. To serve, spoon yogurt mixture over beets. Serves 8.

Mixed Vegetable Salad

This Bulgarian dish is called shopska salata, a name that is derived from the village of Shopka on the outskirts of Sofia.

4 medium green or red peppers, cleaned and sliced
1 medium cucumber, washed and thinly sliced
4 large tomatoes, peeled and thinly sliced
2 medium onions, peeled and thinly sliced

Olive oil
Vinegar
2 tablespoons chopped fresh parsley
1 tablespoon chopped fresh dill
Salt, pepper to taste
½ cup diced white cheese (sirene, feta or farmer's)

On a large plate, arrange vegetables in circles overlapping each other. Sprinkle with oil and vinegar, parsley, dill, salt and pepper. Put cheese over top. Serves 4 to 6.

SAUCES

Black Sea Fish Sauce

1 medium onion, peeled
and minced
3 tablespoons oil, butter
or margarine
2 tablespoons flour
Salt, pepper, cayenne to
taste

3 medium tomatoes, peeled
and chopped
1 cup fish broth
1 cup white wine
½ cup cooked peas
½ cup cooked diced carrots
½ teaspoon crumbled dried
basil

Sauté onion in oil until tender. Stir in flour, salt, pepper and
cayenne; cook 1 minute. Add tomatoes; sauté until mushy. Add
fish broth and wine. Bring to a boil. Reduce heat and cook,
uncovered, for 5 minutes, stirring often. Add peas, carrots and
basil; cook 1 minute. Serve with cooked fish. Makes about 3½
cups.

Yogurt Sauce

2 cups plain yogurt
¼ cup hot meat bouillon
Salt, pepper to taste
2 garlic cloves, crushed
2 tablespoons butter or
margarine

1 teaspoon paprika
2 tablespoons flour
2 tablespoons chopped dill
or parsley

Heat yogurt over a low fire. Add meat bouillon, salt, pepper and
garlic; heat through. Combine butter, paprika, flour and dill;
stir into yogurt. Cook, stirring, about 1 minute. Serve with cooked
vegetables or fish. Makes about 2¼ cups.

DESSERTS

Yogurt Cake

This is an interesting dessert made with yogurt, a staple in Bulgaria.

½ cup butter or margarine	2 cups sifted all-purpose
⅔ cup sugar	flour
2 eggs, beaten	2 teaspoons baking powder
2 teaspoons minced lemon	½ teaspoon baking soda
rind	½ teaspoon salt
1 cup plain yogurt	Confectioners' sugar

Cream butter in a large bowl. Add sugar; beat with a spoon or electric mixer until creamy and light. Add eggs, one at a time, and lemon rind; beat again. Stir in yogurt. Sift flour, baking powder, soda and salt into yogurt mixture; beat until smooth. Pour into a buttered cake pan, 9 inches square; bake in a preheated moderate oven (350° F.) for about 35 minutes, or until cooked. Cool for 5 minutes. Turn out on a rack and sprinkle with confectioners' sugar. Serve while still warm. Serves about 10.

Rice-Milk Pudding

In Bulgaria, as well as other Balkan countries, cold solid milk puddings garnished with finely chopped nuts or ground cinnamon are well-liked desserts and snacks. This is one of the most popular kinds and is called mallebi.

⅓ cup uncooked rice	⅓ cup sugar
1 cup water	1 cinnamon stick
3 tablespoons cornstarch	Finely chopped nuts or
4 cups milk	ground cinnamon

Cook rice in water in a covered saucepan, about 20 minutes, or until liquid is absorbed and grains are tender. Mix cornstarch with

½ cup milk. Combine with remaining milk, cooked rice, sugar and cinnamon stick in a large saucepan; cook over low heat, stirring frequently, until pudding is thickened. Remove and discard cinnamon stick. Spoon into small bowls and chill. Serve garnished with nuts or cinnamon. Serves 4 to 6.

Yugoslavian Cookery

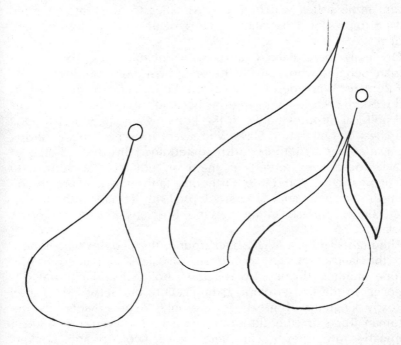

Yugoslavia is a country of contrasts, with great variations in terrain, climate, vegetation and culture. The Yugoslavs still speak three separate languages, have two alphabets, and have three primary religions. It is not surprising, therefore, that the cookery is diverse and exciting.

Largest of the Balkan countries, formed in 1945, the Socialist Federal Republic of Yugoslavia is bordered by Italy, Austria, Hungary, Romania, Bulgaria, Albania and the Adriatic Sea. Because of its east-west crossroads position on historic routes of trade and conquest, the country for a long time had struggles with its neighbors as well as internal conflicts. Thus the cookery reflects external influences as well as inherent regional traditions and differences.

The land of the southern Slavs is a complex of six republics—

Serbia, Croatia, Bosnia-Herzegovina, Slovenia, Macedonia and Montenegro—and two "autonomous regions"—Vojvodina and Kosovo. Each has a different but proud heritage that has been steadfastly preserved over the centuries and that is reflected in innumerable dishes, which, if too diversified to constitute a unified cuisine, represent a national cookery of uncommon interest and appeal.

Originally these Balkan lands were inhabited by Thracian or Illyrian peoples who, shortly before Christ, were subjugated by the Romans. With the division of the Roman Empire into eastern and western sectors, these regions became subject to the religious and political disputes between the Roman Catholic and Orthodox churches. The migrating Slavs who swept into the Balkans during the Dark Ages had their future determined by their choice of locale. Those who settled in the east, notably the Serbs and Macedonians, accepted the Orthodox faith; those living in the west, the Slovenes and Croats, adopted the Roman Catholic rite. Later, under Turkish influence, the Bosnians became converts to Islam.

Although sharing a Slavic background, the peoples who inhabited the lands that now comprise Yugoslavia remained hostile to one another, divided by religious, political and cultural differences. In the first attempt at unification, the Serbs established an early kingdom of great power, only to be crushed by the Ottoman Turks in the fifteenth century. But even the Turkish domination was never complete, since two Adriatic pockets remained under the rule of Venice, and parts of Croatia and Slovenia were attached to Hungary and Austria. Under a succession of foreign overlords, trouble and turmoil became a way of life. The area was a ravaged arena for war, particularly in the conflict between the Hapsburgs and the Ottoman Turks, both of whom left lasting imprints. Finally, however, the country was united in 1918 as the Kingdom of the Serbs, Croats and Slovenes; the name Yugoslavia appeared only in 1929.

In view of this checkered background, it is little wonder that the Yugoslavian bill of fare remains, as in the past, a fascinating melange. Serbians, who enjoy a combination of dishes of Balkan and Hungarian origin, like heavily spiced food and favor pork over lamb. In Bosnia-Herzegovina and Macedonia, Islamic and Turkish or Greek overtones are found. The Slovenes, close to Italy and once part of the Austro-Hungarian Empire, are fond of foods similar to foods of those three countries and are particularly proud of their pastries and cakes. Croatia, of which the lovely Dalmatian coast is a part, has delightful seafood, vegetable and fruit dishes, many resembling those of Central Europe. The cookery of mountainous Montenegro, which in the past was influenced by that of Venice, features interesting seafood soups and grilled specialties, as well as an intriguing number of lamb dishes introduced by the Moslem segment of the population. The strongest imprint on Yugoslavian cookery as a whole was left by the five centuries of Turkish rule. Yugoslavs, for example, still enjoy an array of appetizers called meze, which, as in Turkey, include small pieces of fried liver, white and yellow goat or sheep's milk cheese, nuts, raw and pickled vegetables, spicy preserved meats, and small cheese-filled flaky pastries. With the meze non-Moslems partake of the national drink, slivovitz, a clear plum brandy of considerable potency.

The Yugoslavian menu features such Turkish or Near Eastern creations as musaka—alternating layers of ground meat and eggplant, squash or potatoes with an egg-cream topping—and baked dishes of layered paper-thin pastries with fillings of cheese or meats. Many of the pilaf or rice dishes were adopted, but the Yugoslavs also became, like the Romanians, fond of cornmeal dishes and, like the Italians, devotees of pasta.

Yugoslavia harvests a wide range of vegetables, and high on the list of favorite preparations, other than salads, relishes and pickles, are peppers, tomatoes, squash and eggplants, stuffed with savory rice or meat, inspired by the Near East. Also popular are vine leaves filled with ground lamb and eaten hot, or, as in the Adriatic variation, more akin to Greek cookery, stuffed with rice and eaten cold with a lemon sauce. The Yugoslavian national specialty, however, is sarma, rolled cabbage or sauerkraut leaves stuffed with rice and ground pork, similar to the Bulgarian and Romanian dishes.

A predilection for milk products, particularly those from the east, is evident in the use of yogurt for soups, appetizers, sauces and dressings and in the frequent appearance of sour cream on northern tables. Most widely used is the Serbian kajmak, a thick fresh or fermented cream (sometimes called a cheese), which often appears as a filling for pastries or as a topping or accompaniment for various foods and dishes.

Other reminders of Turkish influence may be found in the

national fondness for small cups of dark, thick coffee, brewed in long-handled pots, and for slatko (heavily sweetened stewed fruit) served with a glass of water as a gesture of hospitality. Yugoslavs are extremely fond of sweet desserts, such as a rich shredded wheat creation called kadaif, the world-famous baklava, cakes drenched with honey or sugar syrups, Turkish delight, and a pudding of sweetened cooked pumpkins, also used as a filling for thin pastry.

Although exceptional fresh fruits and ice creams are well-known desserts, the Yugoslavs also have a rich heritage of baked goods and other mouth-watering delicacies, many of which were derived from other lands. The Slovenes are noted for their sweet noodle creations, fruit-filled dumplings, fried yeast doughs, cakes and cookies. Another delicacy, made in many variations, is potica, a name taken from the Slovenian word *povitica*, meaning "something rolled in." From the Hungarians was acquired a fondness for palacinke, thin pancakes filled with apricot or plum jam or chocolate, and rich tortes. Yugoslav women are famous for pita, a holiday specialty of paper-thin pastry made with various fillings, similar to strudel.

Whether it is a gift from the Near East or a native creation, the art of grilling meats on spits or skewers or over open grates has been mastered by the Yugoslavs. Outdoor cafes and small garden restaurants permeate surrounding areas with the tempting aromas of these specialties sizzling throughout the day and evening. On the bill of fare are usually ražnjići, skewered cubes of pork and veal; sausagelike rolls made with ground pork and beef called ćevapčići; and a flavorful type of hamburger made of a combination of ground meats, named pljeskavica. In Bosnia lamb šiš cévap, similar to shish kebab, is popular. One Yugoslav specialty, a mixed grill meat platter with accompaniments of chopped onions and hot peppers, has also become popular in other lands.

Special mention must be made of the succulent and creative Yugoslav stews and casseroles, marvelous one-dish meals featuring medleys of vegetables, meat, seasonings, and sometimes grains. Two dishes that reflect Near Eastern influence are kapama, lamb cooked with green onions and spinach, and lonac, or pot, a Bosnian specialty made with a deft selection of native ingredients, including a formidable number of whole garlic bulbs. Lonac is baked slowly for many hours to achieve a harmonious blending of flavors.

Djuveč, made with several vegetables, sometimes including rice, and pork, game or fish, is akin to similar dishes of Romania and Bulgaria. A number of goulashes and paprikáshes, well-seasoned meat, poultry or game specialties, have been adapted from Austria and Hungary. A standard everyday Yugoslav dish is pasulj, beans, which also contains pork and hot red peppers. With their Balkan neighbors, Yugoslavs share a penchant for peppers, which are used widely as seasonings, but are also eaten by themselves and included in dishes featuring other foods. Yugoslavian cookery also reflects a distinct fondness for garlic and onions.

Slavic influence is perhaps most notable in the staple soups, using such ingredients as cabbage, sauerkraut, legumes, meatballs and mushrooms. Many of the soups are flavored with sour liquids such as vinegar or fermented fruit juice. Among the Yugoslav soups are also many resembling Near Eastern *čorbas*, such as one made with lamb, rice, onions and yogurt, as well as several soups derived from Central Europe that include noodles and dumplings.

Fish soups are among the best in the Yugoslav repertoire. An excellent example is brodet, which is made with a variety of seafood and includes such seasonings as tomatoes, herbs and wine. One of the most famous specialties is alaska čorba, sometimes compared to bouillabaise, but made with a variety of freshwater fish from the Danube River, such as sterlet, perch and pike, seasoned with herbs and onions.

Inland streams and lakes provide many treasures. One of the best is a salmon trout taken from Lake Ohrid in Macedonia and not found elsewhere in Europe. The Yugoslavs can also draw on the incredible variety of seafood found in the warm waters of the Adriatic—sardines, bonito, tunny, swordfish, squid, anchovies, red mullet, mussels, langouste and scampi. Two favorite ways of preparing fresh fish are to simply grill it over charcoal after brushing with oil and lemon juice and to bake or stew it over a bed of vegetables.

Although Yugoslavian food may differ from region to region, it reflects the general appreciation of good food and enjoyment of the pleasures of the table. Whether native creations or imaginative adaptations, the dishes are only the more interesting for their variety. Some of the best examples are included in this selection of recipes.

MEZE

Serbian Vegetable Appetizer

This flavorful eggplant-pepper combination, called srpski ajvar, is a good relish; or it may be served as a spread for dark bread.

1 medium eggplant, about 1 pound	⅓ cup (approximately) olive or vegetable oil
4 medium green peppers	2 tablespoons vinegar
1 or 2 small garlic cloves, crushed	3 tablespoons chopped fresh parsley
	Salt, pepper to taste

Preheat oven to 475°F. Prick eggplant in several places; put on a cookie sheet with peppers. Bake eggplant about 40 minutes, or until tender, and peppers for about 15 minutes. Remove from stove; cool about 10 minutes. Peel eggplant and chop pulp very finely. Clean peppers, discarding seeds and ribs; chop finely. Mix with remaining ingredients and chill. Serves 4.

Croatian Fried Liver

Cut 1 pound calf or lamb liver into small pieces. Roll in flour previously seasoned with salt, pepper and cayenne. Heat about ⅛ inch oil in a skillet. Fry liver until cooked. Drain on absorbent paper. Serve at once on toothpicks, with sharp mustard or chopped onion. Serves 4.

Slovakian Salami Canapés

1 cup finely chopped salami	3 tablespoons minced dill pickle
6-7 tablespoons butter or margarine	Salt, pepper, cayenne to taste
1 tablespoon minced onion	

Combine ingredients; mix well. Serve on small crusty rolls cut in halves. Makes about 1¾ cups.

Cucumber-Yogurt Appetizer

This refreshing chilled appetizer may be served in cups and eaten as a cold soup or spooned onto a plate and enjoyed with other appetizer foods.

2 medium cucumbers
Salt
1 garlic clove, crushed
2 tablespoons vinegar or fresh lemon juice
2 teaspoons chopped fresh dill

2 cups plain yogurt
Pepper to taste
2 tablespoons olive oil
1 tablespoon chopped fresh mint

Peel cucumbers and quarter lengthwise. Cut into ¼-inch pieces. Sprinkle with salt; let stand 20 minutes. Drain and mix with garlic, vinegar or lemon juice, dill, yogurt and pepper. Sprinkle with oil and mint. Serves 4 to 6.

Montenegrin Bean Appetizer

Dried beans are a staple food in the mountainous regions of Yugoslavia. They are prepared in such interesting ways that each bean dish is like a new culinary creation. This is one example.

2 cups cooked white beans, drained and cooled
Salt, pepper, paprika to taste
1 large red onion, peeled and cut into rings
2 medium tomatoes, peeled and chopped

1 hot green pepper, cleaned and minced
2 tablespoons chopped fresh parsley
Vinegar
Olive or salad oil

Spoon beans onto a large plate. Season with salt, pepper and paprika. Top with onion rings, tomatoes, green pepper and parsley. Sprinkle with vinegar and oil. Chill. Serves 4.

Dalmatian Tuna Fish

Along Yugoslavia's Adriatic coast tunny (tuna) is abundant; it is a favorite appetizer, often enjoyed only with olive oil. It may also, however, be served in this manner.

Drain 1 can (7 ounces) tuna fish chunks and arrange on a plate. Sprinkle with minced green onions and fresh parsley, lemon juice, pepper and cayenne. Garnish with black or green olives. Serves 4.

Macedonian Fried Eggplant

Wash 2 medium eggplants and remove stems. Cut crosswise into ¼-inch slices. Season with salt and pepper. Coat with fine dry bread crumbs; dip in beaten egg; coat again with bread crumbs. Pour about ⅛ inch of olive oil in a skillet; heat. Fry slices on both sides until golden and crisp. Drain on absorbent paper and serve at once. Serves 6 to 8.

SOUPS

Lamb-Spinach Čorba with Rice

The Yugoslavs are fond of nourishing thick soups that can be entire meals in themselves. This interesting soup is made with frozen instead of fresh spinach.

2 pounds breast of lamb, cut into large pieces

3 tablespoons butter or margarine

1 large onion, peeled and
chopped
1 tablespoon paprika
Salt, pepper to taste
½ cup uncooked rice
2 packages (10 ounces each)
frozen spinach

2 tablespoons chopped fresh
parsley
1 cup plain yogurt at
room temperature
2 tablespoons chopped fresh
dill

Wipe lamb pieces dry and brown in butter in a large kettle. Push meat aside; add onion. Sauté until tender. Stir in paprika, salt and pepper. Add 2½ quarts water; bring to a boil. Skim. Lower heat and cook slowly, covered, for 2 hours. Add rice, spinach and parsley; cook another 30 minutes, or until rice and vegetables are tender. Take out lamb; cut off lean pieces. Discard fat and bones. Return small pieces of lamb to soup. Combine yogurt and dill; stir into soup just before serving. Serves 8 to 10.

Macedonian White Bean Soup

This is one of the best of the flavorful Yugoslav bean soups. The vegetables and seasonings give zest to the bland beans.

1½ cups dried white beans
½ cup olive or vegetable oil
2 medium onions, peeled
and chopped
2 garlic cloves, crushed
1 large carrot, scraped and
minced

2 tomatoes, peeled and
chopped
½ teaspoon crumbled dried
thyme
Salt, pepper to taste

Soak beans overnight or for several hours in 8 cups water. Put on stove in the same water; bring to a boil. Lower heat; cook slowly, covered. Meanwhile, heat oil in a skillet. Add onions; sauté until limp. Stir in garlic, carrot and tomatoes. Sauté 5 minutes; stir into beans. Add thyme and season with salt and pepper. Continue to cook until beans and carrot are tender, about 1½ hours. Serves 6 to 8.

Croatian Onion-Tomato Soup

A basic but flavorful soup.

5 cups sliced onions	2 tablespoons chopped fresh
2 garlic cloves, crushed	dill
¼ cup butter or margarine	Salt, pepper, cayenne to
6 cups tomato juice	taste
½ teaspoon celery seed	Sour cream or plain yogurt
(optional)	

In a large saucepan, sauté onions and garlic in butter until onions are limp. Add tomato juice and celery seed; simmer 30 minutes. Stir in dill; season with salt, pepper and cayenne. Top each serving with a spoonful of sour cream or yogurt. Serves 6 to 8.

Slovenian Chicken Noodle Soup

In Slovenia there are many Austrian-inspired dishes, such as this soup, which can be served with crusty bread for a one-dish luncheon or supper.

1 stewing chicken, about 4 pounds, washed and cut up	1 cup chopped mushrooms
1 bouquet garni (parsley sprigs, thyme, bay leaf)	1 package (½ pound) fine egg noodles
Salt, pepper to taste	2 tablespoons butter or margarine
1 cup uncooked green peas	2 tablespoons chopped fresh
1 green pepper, cleaned and chopped	chives

Put cut-up chicken in a large kettle with bouquet garni, salt, pepper and 4 quarts water. Bring to a boil; skim. Reduce heat; cook slowly, covered, for 1 hour or until tender. Take chicken pieces from broth; cut off meat, discarding skin and bones. Return chicken to broth. Add peas, green pepper and mushrooms; cook slowly, covered, for 20 minutes, or until vegetables are tender. Add noodles during last 10 minutes of cooking. Stir in butter and chives just before removing from heat. Serves 8 to 10.

ENTRÉES

Serbian Gardeners' Omelet

This is a good luncheon or supper dish.

2 medium onions, peeled and chopped	1½ cups diced cooked potatoes
2 garlic cloves, crushed	8 eggs
4 slices bacon, diced	Salt, pepper, cayenne to
1 cup diced cooked carrots	taste
1 cup cooked peas	2 tablespoons chopped fresh parsley

In a skillet, sauté onions and garlic with bacon until onions are soft. Pour off all except 3 tablespoons fat. Add carrots, peas and potatoes; sauté 1 or 2 minutes. Beat eggs slightly; season with salt, pepper and cayenne. Stir in parsley; add mixture to vegetables. Cook over low heat until set and the surface is dry. Cut into wedges to serve. Serves 4 to 6.

Macedonian Poached Eggs in Spinach with Yogurt

This is a well-known luncheon dish in Macedonia.

2 packages (10 ounces each) frozen chopped spinach, cooked and drained	1½ cups yogurt
	½ cup grated yellow cheese
	3 tablespoons chopped fresh parsley
8 eggs	
2 garlic cloves, crushed	

Arrange spinach in a buttered shallow baking dish; make 8 depressions in spinach with back of a spoon. Break 1 egg into each depression. Combine garlic, yogurt and grated cheese; spoon over eggs. Sprinkle with chopped parsley. Put under a preheated broiler long enough to become hot and bubbly. Serves 4.

Bosnian Eggs with Tomatoes

3 tablespoons olive or salad oil
1 large onion, peeled and chopped
2 garlic cloves, crushed
4 medium tomatoes, peeled and chopped

¼ teaspoon dried oregano
Salt, pepper to taste
4 eggs, slightly beaten
⅓ cup grated Parmesan cheese

Heat oil in a skillet; sauté onion and garlic in oil until soft. Mix in tomatoes and oregano. Season with salt and pepper. Cook over low heat, uncovered, for 10 minutes. Combine eggs and cheese; pour over tomato mixture. Cook, stirring, until eggs are set. Serves 2.

Omelet, Dubrovnik Style

Wives of the coastal fishermen have devised numerous, delectable dishes using leftover cooked fish. This one is sometimes served as a second breakfast in mid-morning to early rising seafarers who have been fishing in the Adriatic. The seasoning depends on what fresh or dried herbs are available.

3 tablespoons vegetable oil
6 green onions, with tops, minced
2 tablespoons tomato paste
1 tablespoon lemon juice
Salt, pepper, cayenne to taste

2 cups diced cooked white fish
3 tablespoons chopped dill or parsley
6 eggs, beaten

Heat oil in a small saucepan; sauté onions in oil. Add tomato paste and lemon juice; cook, stirring, 1 minute. Season with salt, pepper and cayenne. Add with fish and dill to eggs. Mix well. Pour into a well-greased skillet; cook over low heat until mixture is set and top is dry. Fold in half and serve at once. Serves 4.

Baked Mackerel with Yogurt Sauce

This is an interesting preparation for mackerel, skuše, of which the Yugoslavs are fond. Any other white-fleshed fish could be used.

1 whole mackerel, about
4 pounds, cleaned
3 large onions, peeled and
sliced
2-3 garlic cloves, crushed
⅓ cup.olive or salad oil
1 tablespoon paprika
3 tablespoons tomato paste

3 tablespoons chopped
fresh parsley
Salt, pepper to taste
1 cup dry white wine or
water
2 tablespoons flour
1 cup yogurt

Arrange fish in a greased baking dish. Sauté onions and garlic in hot oil until tender. Add paprika; cook 1 minute. Stir in tomato paste, parsley, salt, pepper and wine. Pour over fish; bake in a preheated moderate oven (350°F.), allowing about 10 minutes per pound, until tender, basting occasionally with pan juices. Remove fish to a hot platter. Stir flour into pan juices. Add yogurt; mix well. Cook over low heat, stirring, for 5 minutes. Serve with fish. Serves 4.

Adriatic Tuna with Tomato Sauce

1 medium onion, peeled
and chopped
1 garlic clove, crushed
2 tablespoons olive or
vegetable oil
3 tablespoons tomato paste
1½ cups dry white wine
1 bay leaf

½ teaspoon dried thyme
Salt, pepper to taste
2 tablespoons chopped fresh
parsley
4 fresh tuna steaks or 2 cans
(7 ounces each) tuna,
drained and flaked

Sauté onion and garlic in oil until tender. Add tomato paste, white wine, bay leaf, thyme, salt and pepper; mix well. Bring to a boil. Lower heat; simmer, uncovered, 10 minutes. Add parsley. Fry tuna steaks or heat flaked tuna. Serve warm, covered with sauce. Serves 4.

Spicy Fish, Slovenian Style

1 large onion, peeled and
chopped
¼ cup olive or salad oil
1-2 tablespoons paprika
8 slices or pieces white-
fleshed fish

3 tablespoons tomato paste
1 tablespoon vinegar or
lemon juice
2 garlic cloves, crushed
1 bay leaf
Salt, pepper to taste

In a frying pan, sauté onion in oil until tender. Add paprika;
cook 1 minute. Add fish and brown in drippings, adding more
oil if necessary. Stir in tomato paste, vinegar and ¼ cup water.
Add garlic, bay leaf, salt and pepper. Cook slowly, covered,
about 10 minutes, or until fish is cooked. Time will depend on
thickness of fish. Serves 4.

Bosnian Chicken with Okra

Favorite dishes in Bosnia are well-seasoned stews that are cooked
slowly to blend the flavors. This is one of the best kinds.

2 frying chickens, about 2½
pounds each, cut up
3 tablespoons butter or
margarine
Salt, pepper-to taste
2 large onions, peeled and
sliced
⅛ teaspoon cayenne

2 cups sliced uncooked okra
1 cup chopped green
peppers
1 cup (approximately) hot
chicken broth
3 tablespoons tomato paste
3 tablespoons chopped fresh
parsley

Wipe chicken pieces dry and fry on both sides in butter in a
skillet. Remove to a heavy casserole. Season with salt and pepper.
Sauté onions in drippings. Mix in cayenne; spoon over chicken.
Top with okra and green peppers. In another pan, combine
1 cup of hot chicken broth and tomato paste. Bring to a boil;
pour over chicken and vegetables. Cook very slowly, covered,
about 35 minutes, or until chicken is tender. Add a little more
broth during cooking, if necessary. Stir in parsley. Serves 4 to 6.

Roast Goose with Sour Cream Sauce

The goose has an honored place on Yugoslav tables and is cooked in interesting dishes such as this one.

2 medium onions, peeled and sliced	Salt
3 tablespoons lard or other fat	10 peppercorns
1 bay leaf	1 small young goose (about 5 pounds), cut up
1 lemon, sliced	1 cup sour cream at room temperature

In a saucepan, sauté onions in lard until tender. Add bay leaf, lemon slices, salt, peppercorns and 1 cup water. Bring just to a boil. Pour into a roasting pan. Rub pieces of goose with salt; prick skin in several places. Arrange over onion mixture. Roast in a preheated slow oven (325°F.) about 3 hours, or until tender. Spoon off any accumulated fat. While cooking, turn over pieces a few times. When cooked, remove goose to a platter. Remove and discard bay leaf and peppercorns. Add sour cream to pan drippings. Mix well and heat through. Strain and pour over goose. Serves 6.

Serbian Duckling with Sauerkraut

1 duckling, 4 to 5 pounds	2-3 tablespoons paprika
Salt, pepper to taste	2 pounds sauerkraut, drained
2 large onions, peeled and chopped	2 tablespoons chopped fresh dill
2 tablespoons lard or vegetable oil	

Wash duckling and wipe dry. Sprinkle with salt and pepper. Prick skin in several places. Place in a roasting pan; cook in a preheated slow oven (325°F.) for 1½ hours. Meanwhile, sauté onions in lard in a saucepan. Add paprika; cook 1 minute. Stir in sauerkraut; add 2 cups water. Cook slowly, covered, for 30 minutes. When duckling has cooked for 1½ hours, take from oven. Remove to a platter. Spoon off all except 2 tablespoons fat. Add sauerkraut mixture to pan; mix with drippings. Place duckling over sauerkraut. Return to oven and cook another 30 to 45 minutes, or until duckling is tender. Serve sprinkled with chopped dill and surrounded with sauerkraut. Serves 4 to 6.

Macedonian Rice-Lamb Musaka

This Turkish-inspired casserole is another variation of musaka, which is eaten in all the Balkan countries.

1 large onion, peeled and minced	2 large tomatoes, peeled and chopped
2 garlic cloves, crushed	1 teaspoon paprika
2 tablespoons butter or margarine	Salt, pepper to taste
	½ cup uncooked rice
1 pound ground lean lamb	1½ cups tomato juice
½ cup minced green pepper	2 eggs, beaten
	1 cup milk

Sauté onion and garlic in butter until tender. Add lamb; cook, mixing with a fork, until redness disappears. Stir in green pepper, tomatoes, paprika, salt and pepper; cook 1 minute. Add rice and tomato juice; mix well. Spoon into a greased shallow baking dish. Combine eggs and milk; pour over mixture. Bake in a preheated moderate oven (350°F.) 50 to 60 minutes, or until topping is set. Serves 4.

Serbian Pork and Beans

This characteristic country dish, pasulj, can be flavored with varying amounts of peppers or paprika according to the desired strength. The ingredients are cooked slowly for a long time to blend the flavors.

1 pound dried white beans, washed	2-3 garlic cloves, crushed
	Salt, pepper to taste
1½ pounds boneless smoked pork	2 medium onions, peeled and chopped

3 tablespoons lard or other fat 1-2 tablespoons paprika	1 teaspoon crumbled hot red peppers (optional)

Put beans in a heavy casserole or kettle and cover with water. Bring to a boil; boil 2 minutes. Take from heat; leave, covered, 1 hour. Add smoked pork, salt and pepper; cook slowly, covered, 1 hour. Meanwhile, sauté onions and garlic in hot lard until tender. Stir in paprika; cook 1 minute. Add to beans and pork; continue to cook until beans are tender, about 40 minutes. If desired, sprinkle top with hot peppers. The final dish should have a very thick sauce. Slice pork before serving. Serves 4 to 6.

Djuveč

This Yugoslavian national dish, made with baked meat and vegetables, is similar to one prepared in Bulgaria and Romania. The ingredients vary somewhat from one region to another. Potatoes, for example, could replace rice in this dish.

4 medium onions, peeled and sliced ½ cup olive oil 2 pounds lean boneless pork, cut into 1½-inch cubes 1 pound boneless lamb, cut into 1½-inch cubes Salt, pepper to taste	6 medium tomatoes, peeled and sliced 1 medium eggplant, cubed 2 zucchini, sliced 4 green peppers, cleaned and sliced 1 cup cut-up green beans 1 cup uncooked rice

In a casserole or skillet, sauté onions in oil until tender. Add pork and lamb cubes; brown. Season with salt and pepper. Arrange onions, meat, vegetables and rice in layers in a large shallow baking dish, topping with a layer of tomato slices. Add enough water to cover ingredients. Bake, covered, in a preheated medium oven (350°F.) about 1½ hours, or until ingredients are cooked. Uncover during last 30 minutes of cooking. Serves 8 to 10.

Ćevapčići

These favorite Serbian skewered meatballs are commonly sold throughout Yugoslavia from sidewalk stalls or small open-air restaurants. Their captivating aroma permeates the city and village streets. Ćevapčići are eaten as snacks, appetizers or entrées.

1½ pounds ground lean pork	Salt, freshly ground pepper
1½ pounds ground lean veal	to taste
or beef	Finely chopped onions

Put meat through a meat grinder 2 to 3 times. Season with salt and pepper. Shape into small sausage forms; thread on a skewer. Cook over charcoal or under a broiler, turning once, until done. Serve with grated onions. Serves 6 as an entrée.

Lamb Pilaf with Yogurt Sauce

From the Turks, the Yugoslavs acquired a fondness for rich rice dishes, made with or without meat, called pilafs. They are well-seasoned and flavorful creations.

1 pound lean boneless lamb shoulder, cut into 1-inch cubes	2 medium tomatoes, peeled and chopped
½ cup olive or salad oil	½ teaspoon crumbled dried thyme
2 medium onions, peeled and chopped	Salt, pepper to taste
2 garlic cloves, crushed	¾ cup uncooked rice
1 can (6 ounces) tomato paste	1 cup yogurt
	2 tablespoons butter or margarine
	1 teaspoon cayenne pepper

Wipe lamb dry and brown in oil in a large kettle or casserole. Add onions and garlic; sauté until onions are tender. Stir in tomato paste, tomatoes and 3½ cups hot water. Season with thyme, salt and pepper. Bring to a boil; stir in rice. Cook over very low fire, tightly covered, about 30 minutes, or until rice and meat are tender and liquid is absorbed. Gently heat yogurt. Stir in butter and cayenne. To serve, pour yogurt mixture over cooked rice and lamb. Serves 6 to 8.

GRAINS

Croatian Rice-Vegetable Medley

This dish is occasionally served with spicy sausages and grilled well-seasoned lamb chops.

1 large onion, peeled and chopped	1 cup uncooked diced squash
2 garlic cloves, crushed	Salt, pepper, paprika to taste
½ cup lard or other fat	
1½ cups uncooked rice	2 tablespoons chopped fresh parsley
3 cups beef bouillon	
1 cup uncooked green peas	3 tablespoons chopped fresh dill

Sauté onion and garlic in lard in a skillet until onion is tender. Add rice; sauté until well coated with shortening. Add beef bouillon, peas and squash. Season with salt, pepper and paprika. Stir well. Cook over a low fire, covered, about 30 minutes, or until rice is tender, liquid is absorbed and vegetables are cooked. Stir in parsley and dill. Serves 6 to 8.

Savory Rice Stuffing

This pilaf, of Turkish origin, is often served as an accompaniment to meat or poultry, but it is also a popular stuffing for vegetables, meats, poultry and game. In the spring it is particularly delectable as a filling for baby lamb. If it is to be served as an entrée, cubes of liver may be also included in the pilaf. Makes about 4 cups, enough to fill a 6 to 8 pound turkey.

1 medium onion, peeled
  and finely chopped
6 green onions, with tops,
  minced
3 tablespoons butter or
  margarine
⅓ cup pine nuts
1 cup uncooked rice
⅓ cup chopped currants or
  raisins

Salt, pepper to taste
2 cups hot chicken bouillon
1 tablespoon sugar
2 teaspoons cinnamon
⅓ cup chopped fresh dill or
  parsley
1 chicken liver, chopped
  (optional)

In a large skillet, sauté onion and green onions in butter until just tender. Do not brown. Add pine nuts; sauté 2 minutes. Stir in rice; sauté, stirring constantly, 5 minutes, or until rice is transparent and nuts are golden. Add currants, salt, pepper and hot bouillon; mix well. Cook over low fire, tightly covered, about 30 minutes, or until rice is tender and all liquid has been absorbed. Add sugar, cinnamon and dill or parsley; cook another 1 or 2 minutes.

Note: If chicken liver is to be added, sauté in butter for 5 minutes and mix into rice with sugar, cinnamon and dill.

VEGETABLES

Eggplant-Vegetable Stew, Bosnian Style

In the Balkans, a favorite way of preparing vegetables is to cook one or more of them with seasonings to make a vegetable stew. The dish, cooked very slowly, has a rich thick sauce. This recipe can also be prepared with green beans, okra, squash or cauliflower and can be served hot or cold.

2 medium eggplants, washed
1 cup olive oil
2 medium onions, peeled
  and chopped
3 medium tomatoes, peeled
  and chopped

2 garlic cloves, crushed
¼ cup chopped fresh parsley
½ teaspoon dried marjoram
  Salt, pepper to taste

Remove stems from eggplants and cut into cubes. Heat oil in a saucepan; sauté onions in oil until tender. Add eggplant cubes; sauté 1 or 2 minutes. Stir in other ingredients; cook slowly, covered, about 25 minutes, or until eggplant is cooked. Stir occasionally while cooking. Serves 8.

Serbian Braised Carrots with Yogurt

8 medium carrots, scraped and cut into ¼-inch slices
½ cup sliced green onions, with tops
¼ cup butter or margarine
1 teaspoon sugar

¼ teaspoon cayenne
Salt, pepper to taste
1 cup plain yogurt at room temperature
2 tablespoons chopped fresh dill

In a tightly covered saucepan, braise carrot slices and green onions in butter and sugar until tender. Season with cayenne, salt and pepper. Combine yogurt and dill; stir into carrot mixture. Serves 4 to 6.

Serbian Spinach with Rice

1 medium onion, peeled and chopped
¼ cup olive or salad oil
1 cup uncooked rice
1 pound spinach, washed

2 tablespoons chopped dill or parsley
Salt, pepper to taste
1 cup sour cream

Sauté onion in oil in a saucepan until tender. Add rice; sauté, stirring occasionally, for 15 minutes. Pour in 2 cups hot water; add spinach and dill or parsley. Season with salt and pepper; mix well. Cook slowly, covered, about 20 minutes, or until rice and spinach are tender. Serve with sour cream. Serves 4.

Serbian Potato-Egg Pancakes

This is a delectable breakfast dish or a good accompaniment for roast meat, particularly pork.

4 large sized potatoes, peeled	4 tablespoons sour cream
Salt, pepper, paprika to taste	1 egg, beaten
3 tablespoons minced green onions, with tops	3 tablespoons grated Parmesan cheese
	Fat for frying

Cook potatoes and, while still warm, mash until smooth. Beat with other ingredients except fat. Chill in refrigerator 15 minutes. Melt enough fat in a skillet to cover surface. Drop in 2 heaping tablespoons of the potato-egg mixture; shape with a spoon to form a pancake. Repeat until all mixture is used. Fry until golden and crisp on both sides. Serves 4.

SALADS

Pepper-Cucumber Salad

This Yugoslav salad is called srpska salata and contains the well-liked red and green peppers.

2 medium green peppers	Olive or vegetable oil
2 medium sweet red peppers	Vinegar or fresh lemon juice
1 medium cucumber, peeled and sliced thinly	Salt, pepper to taste
Lettuce leaves	

Clean peppers. Remove and discard seeds and ribs. Cut into strips. Arrange with cucumber slices over lettuce leaves. Sprinkle with oil, vinegar, salt and pepper. Serves 4.

Macedonian Bean Salad

3 cups cooked white beans	1 garlic clove, crushed
1 large red onion, peeled and sliced thinly	6 green onions, with tops, minced

⅓ cup olive or salad oil   Pinch oregano
    Juice of 1 lemon   Salt, pepper to taste

Combine all ingredients and chill. Serves 4 to 6.

DESSERTS

Palacinke

The Yugoslavs are very fond of thin pancakes called palacinke, which
they prepare with interesting fillings.

2 eggs, separated	2 tablespoons brandy or rum
½ cup milk	1 cup all-purpose flour
½ cup water	Butter for frying
1 tablespoon sugar	Fruit jelly
¼ teaspoon salt	Confectioners' sugar

Mix egg yolks with milk, water, sugar, salt and brandy or rum.
Stir in flour; mix well. Beat egg whites until stiff; fold into
mixture. Heat a lightly greased 7- or 8-inch skillet; add 3 tablespoons batter all at once. Tilt pan to spread evenly. Cook over
medium heat until underside is golden. Turn over with a spatula
and cook on the other side. Slip onto a warm plate and keep
warm in a preheated 250°F. oven. Continue to cook other pancakes. Spread each with a thin layer of jelly; fold into quarters.
Serve at once sprinkled with confectioners' sugar. Serves about 6.

Baklava

This internationally known dessert is well-liked in Yugoslavia,
where the recipes vary from one household to another. Although
the paperthin pastry can be made at home, the process is very
difficult; usually, the pastry is purchased. In America it can
be bought at specialty food stores or Greek and Middle Eastern
groceries.

1 pound *fillo* or *phyllo*
pastry sheets
½ pound (approximately)
butter, melted
1 pound walnuts, chopped
½ cup chopped blanched
almonds

2 cups sugar
2 teaspoons cinnamon
(optional)
1½ cups water
3 tablespoons lemon juice

Arrange ⅓ of the pastry sheets, each sheet brushed with melted butter, in a baking dish that is a suitable size for pastry sheets. Combine nuts, ½ cup sugar and cinnamon. Sprinkle ½ of mixture over fillo sheets. Place another third of the pastry sheets, each sheet brushed with melted butter, over nut mixture. Repeat with another layer of nut mixture and remaining ⅓ of the pastry sheets. With a sharp knife, cut into diamond-shaped pieces. Bake in a preheated moderate oven (350°F.) for 1 hour, or until cooked. Remove from oven and cool a little. Meanwhile, combine remaining 1½ cups of sugar, water and lemon juice in a saucepan; bring to a boil. Lower heat; simmer until mixture thickens. Pour, while still warm, over the baklava; leave at room temperature until ready to serve. Makes about 20 pieces.

Serbian Cinnamon Cookies

2 eggs, beaten
1 cup sugar
1⅔ cups sifted all-purpose
flour
1 teaspoon ground
cinnamon

⅓ cup blanched
almond slivers
1 tablespoon fresh lemon
juice
2 teaspoons grated lemon
peel

Combine eggs and sugar in a bowl; mix well. Add flour and cinnamon; mix again. Stir in almonds, lemon juice and lemon peel. Mix until ingredients are thoroughly combined. Chill in refrigerator for 1 hour. Roll out on a floured board to a thickness of ¼ inch. Cut into 3 x ½-inch strips. Arrange on a greased and floured baking sheet. Bake in a preheated moderate (350°F.) oven about 15 minutes, or until cooked. Makes about 6 dozen.

Serbian Baked Pancakes

2 eggs, beaten	1½ cups all-purpose flour
1½ cups milk	Butter for frying
¼ teaspoon salt	Jam or jelly
1 tablespoon sugar	Slivered almonds
2 teaspoons grated lemon rind	1 cup light cream
	Confectioners' sugar

Combine eggs, milk, salt, sugar and lemon rind in a bowl. Stir in flour and mix well. Heat a 7- or 8-inch skillet; grease lightly. Add 3 tablespoons batter; quickly tilt pan to spread evenly. Cook over medium heat until underside is golden. Turn over and cook on other side. Keep warm in a preheated 250°F. oven. Continue to cook other pancakes. Spread each with jam or jelly; sprinkle with slivered almonds and confectioners' sugar. Roll up and arrange, folded sides underneath, side by side, in a buttered shallow baking dish. Cover with cream. Bake, covered with foil, in a preheated moderate oven (350°F.) 20 minutes. Makes about 14.

Albanian Cookery

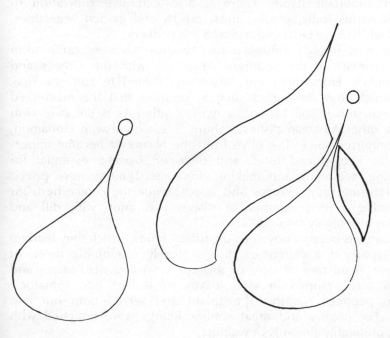

Albania, the smallest and least known of the Eastern European countries, is called by its inhabitants Shqiperi—"land of eagles." The name is quite appropriate to this rugged land of harsh mountains, beautiful seascapes and fierce individualists. Its cookery, like its history, reflects the effects of centuries of warfare with invading Goths, Serbs, Venetians, Turks and Italians. Nevertheless, the traditional spirit of isolation and independence has always survived, and Albanian dishes have just enough differences to distinguish them from those of their neighbors and former foes.

Situated between Yugoslavia and Greece on the coast of the Adriatic Sea facing Italy, Albania has long been coveted for its strategic position. Its first settlers, the ancient Illyrians, a non-Slavic Indo-European people, were among the earliest in Europe.

The Peoples Republic of Albania, formed in 1945, is primarily a primitive agricultural and pastoral country, largely devoted to grazing animals, particularly sheep and goats, and to growing such cereal crops as wheat, barley, oats, rye and corn, which is an important staple. There is also extensive cultivation of olives, citrus fruits, grapes, nuts, raisins and garden vegetables, all of which have been important to the cookery.

The first foreign influence on Albanian cookery came from early contact of the southern Albanians with the Greeks and Byzantines. From them the Albanians learned to cultivate rice, for which they developed such a fondness that the most-liked national dish is still kabuni, a type of pilaf. As is the case with many other Albanian dishes, kabuni is seasoned with cinnamon, the preferred spice. The olive from the Near East became important as a crop and food, and olive oil became essential for cooking, seasoning and making dressings. Lemons were prized for flavoring soups, sauces and salads, while the choice herb for seasoning a wide number of dishes was mint, with dill and parsley also highly favored.

Albanians became devotees of stuffed foods, which they learned to prepare in a variety of dishes closely resembling those of Greece. A mixture of rice, or ground meat and rice, spices and herbs was wrapped in vine leaves or stuffed into tomatoc green peppers, squash or eggplant and served both hot and cold. For poultry and meat similar fillings were enriched with nuts, preferably almonds or walnuts.

The Turkish rule of Albania, which lasted some 350 years, had a most pronounced effect on the eating customs and cookery. Notably Albania became a predominantly Moslem country, with a great percentage of the population adhering to the religious taboos against alcohol and pork. Thus lamb and mutton, especially when skewered or grilled over outdoor charcoal or wood fires, became the preferred meats. The two significant minorities, the Roman Catholics and Orthodox Christians, drank the anise-flavored rakı of Turkey and native wines, and favored highly seasoned pork dishes, made very hot with peppers.

From the Turks the Albanians also acquired a fondness for meat-filled thin pastries prepared in various forms, as well as for rich sweets, flavored primarily with honey and oozing with syrups and nuts. Yogurt became the preferred form of milk, and was widely used to make vegetable and herb-flavored appetizers and soups, as well as main dishes and sauces. The Albanians also adopted small cups of thick dark Turkish coffee, and white and yellow cheeses made from sheep's and goat's milk.

It was probably from the Italians, with whom they had early encounters across the Adriatic, that the Albanians acquired New World foods—the tomato, corn and later the potato, all of which became staples. The Albanians also share with the Italians a fondness for pasta and the age-old tradition of preparing hearty seafood soups and stews with a medley of the day's catch.

This collection of recipes is typical of the food that is still being prepared and enjoyed as it has been for centuries, for the cookery of Albania has changed but little over the years.

APPETIZERS

Stuffed Green Peppers

Favorite appetizers in Albania are flavorful rice-stuffed green peppers called dolma me vaj. The exact amount of stuffing required will vary according to the size of the peppers.

6 medium green peppers	2 large tomatoes, peeled and
1 large onion, peeled and	chopped
chopped	2 tablespoons lemon juice
2 garlic cloves, crushed	Salt, pepper to taste
1 cup olive or salad oil	⅓ cup chopped fresh parsley
1 cup uncooked rice	
¼ cup chopped pine nuts	
(optional)	

Cut tops from peppers; scoop out seeds and membranes. Wash and invert to drain. Sauté onion and garlic in oil until tender. Add rice and pine nuts; sauté several minutes, until rice becomes translucent. Mix in tomatoes, lemon juice, salt and pepper. Cook slowly, stirring frequently, for 10 minutes. Add parsley; mix well. Spoon into drained peppers, filling loosely. Arrange in a kettle; add boiling water to half cover vegetables. Cook slowly, tightly covered, about 45 minutes, or until rice filling is cooked. Serve hot or cold. Serves 6.

Cucumber-Walnut Appetizer

The combination of walnuts and cucumbers, found in the cuisines of both Albania and Bulgaria, is a pleasing culinary marriage. This dish makes an excellent spread for thick dark bread.

½ cup finely chopped walnuts
2 garlic cloves, crushed
2 cups peeled and diced cucumbers

1 tablespoon wine vinegar
¼ cup olive or vegetable oil
Salt, pepper to taste

Combine all ingredients; mix well. Chill. Serve garnished with chopped fresh mint, if desired. Serves 6.

Cheese-filled Pastry

The Albanians are fond of the very thin pastry that is called fillo in Greece and Turkey and is filled with cheese. The pastry is served as an appetizer, first course or entrée.

½ pound (about 2 cups) white or feta cheese, crumbled
4 cups small-curd cottage cheese
4 eggs, beaten

2 tablespoons light cream or milk
½ cup chopped fresh parsley
½ pound prepared fillo dough
½ pound butter, melted

Combine cheeses, eggs, cream and parsley; beat well. Line a buttered baking dish, 8 inches square, with ½ of the fillo sheets, brushing each sheet with melted butter before putting in dish. Spread cheese mixture over the sheets of fillo. Top with remaining sheets after brushing each with melted butter. Butter top generously. Trim off any overhanging pastry. Mark off filo dough into squares or diamonds. Bake in preheated moderate oven (350°F.) about 1¼ hours, or until filling is set and top is golden. Serve warm. Makes 12 pieces.

Tirana's Romaine Salad

Albania's capital enjoys a warm climate in which garden crops flourish. This is a salad served in local restaurants as an appetizer, but it can be served as an accompaniment to meats as well. Wash 1 head romaine; separate leaves. Break into bite-sized pieces. Garnish with chopped green onions and sliced hard-cooked eggs. Season with salt and pepper. Just before serving, sprinkle with olive oil and lemon juice. Serves 4.

Stuffed Grape Leaves

In Albania these appetizers are made with leaves from the vineyards. In Ámerica the vine leaves can be purchased in specialty food stores or Near Eastern or Greek groceries.

1 pound or 1 jar (12 ounces) grape leaves
½ cup olive or salad oil
1 cup finely chopped onions
2 tablespoons chopped pine nuts
1 cup uncooked rice
1 large tomato, peeled and chopped

2 cups chicken broth
2 tablespoons currants
1 teaspoon ground cinnamon
⅛ teaspoon ground cloves
Salt, pepper to taste
3 tablespoons chopped fresh parsley

Drain grape leaves. Separate and rinse in cold water. Set aside. Heat oil in a large frying pan; sauté onions until tender, being careful not to brown. Add pine nuts and rice; continue to sauté, stirring continuously, until rice is transparent and well coated with oil. Add tomato, broth, currants, cinnamon, cloves, salt and pepper. Mix well. Cook over a low fire, uncovered, about 10 minutes, long enough for most of liquid to evaporate. Stir in parsley; remove from heat. Cool.

Arrange each leaf, glossy side down, on a flat surface. Cut off any stem from each leaf. Mix stuffing well; place a spoonful of stuffing in center of each grape leaf. The exact amount will differ according to the size of the leaf. Roll up, beginning at bottom, and fold in sides. Be sure that stuffing is well enclosed. Place, one on top of the other, in a large saucepan. Heat 2 cups water in the frying pan in which stuffing was cooked; slowly pour over the grape leaf packets. Cook slowly, covered, for 40 minutes. Take from dish and cool. Serve cold with yogurt or lemon wedges. Makes about 55.

Egg and Lemon Soup

The Albanians, like the Greeks, are devotees of a flavorful rich light soup that is an excellent first course. The soup may be partially prepared beforehand, but the egg yolks and lemon juice have to be added just before the soup is served. It is called supe ves limua.

2 quarts chicken broth	2 egg yolks, beaten
½ cup uncooked rice	Juice of 2 lemons
Salt, pepper to taste	2 teaspoons chopped fresh
1 tablespoon butter or	mint
margarine	

Bring broth to a boil in a large saucepan. Add rice; lower heat. Cook slowly, covered, until rice is tender, about 20 minutes. Season with salt and pepper. Stir in butter. Combine egg yolks and lemon juice. Add a little hot soup to them, stirring constantly. Mix into remaining soup; leave over low heat, stirring constantly, 2 to 3 minutes. Serve at once. Do not reheat. Serve garnished with mint. Serves 6 to 8.

ENTRÉES

Scrambled Eggs with White Cheese

½ cup crumbled white cheese	⅓ cup milk
(feta or farmer's)	8 eggs, beaten
⅓ cup golden raisins	Oil for frying

Combine all ingredients except oil; mix well. Heat oil in a skillet; pour in the egg mixture. Cook, stirring, until eggs are set. Serves 4.

Skewered Fish

The Albanians are fond of cooking their Adriatic Sea fish on skewers over outdoor open fires. This dish, however, can be broiled indoors as well.

2 pounds swordfish (or other firm-fleshed fish), cut into 1½-inch cubes	¾ cup olive or vegetable oil
1 medium onion, finely chopped	¾ teaspoon crumbled dried oregano
¼ cup fresh lemon juice	Salt, pepper to taste
	Onion slices
	Bay leaves

Remove any skin from fish; put fish in a large bowl. Cover with onion, lemon juice, oil, oregano, salt and pepper. Leave to marinate, mixing about occasionally, for 1 hour. Thread fish cubes on skewers alternately with onion slices and bay leaf pieces. Arrange on a piece of foil. Cover with remaining marinade. Broil about 15 minutes, turning once or twice, or until fish is tender. Serve on skewers. Serves 6.

Mixed Fish Stew with Potatoes

This thick soup or stew is made with a medley of fish, whatever is in the daily catch, by the coastal fishermen. It can be seasoned in many ways.

2 large onions, peeled and sliced	¼ teaspoon crumbled dried basil
2 garlic cloves, crushed	1 bay leaf
3 tablespoons olive or vegetable oil	Salt, pepper, cayenne to taste
¼ cup tomato paste	2 pounds mixed white-fleshed fish, cut up
2 cups fish broth or water	3 tablespoons chopped fresh parsley
1 cup dry white wine	
6 potatoes, peeled and sliced thinly	

In a large saucepan, sauté onions and garlic in oil until tender. Stir in tomato paste; mix well. Add fish broth, wine, potatoes, basil, bay leaf, salt, pepper and cayenne. Cook, covered, 15 minutes. Add fish; cook slowly another 12 minutes, or until potatoes and fish are tender. Serve sprinkled with parsley. Serves 4 to 6.

Rice-Nut Stuffed Chicken

Pule medrop is chicken stuffed with a flavorful nut-rice mixture that is generally sweetened with a little sugar.

1 roasting chicken (about 4 pounds)	⅓ cup chopped shelled walnuts
Salt, pepper to taste	1 tablespoon sugar
½ cup raw rice	1 teaspoon ground cinnamon
1 cup chicken broth	(optional)
¼ cup currants or seedless raisins	

Wash chicken and wipe dry. Season with salt and pepper. Cook rice in chicken broth about 15 minutes, or until liquid has been absorbed and rice is tender. Mix with currants, nuts, sugar and cinnamon. Season with salt and pepper. Stuff chicken with rice mixture. Arrange in a roasting pan; cook, uncovered, in a preheated slow oven (325°F.) for 2½ to 3 hours, or until tender. Serves 6.

Chicken and Rice Casserole

This Turkish-inspired dish can be made with game as well as with chicken.

4 large chicken breasts	½ teaspoon crumbled dried oregano
1 large onion, peeled and chopped	2½ cups chicken broth
¼ cup butter or margarine	1 cup uncooked rice
Salt, pepper to taste	½ cup chopped, blanched walnuts or almonds
3 medium tomatoes, peeled and chopped	¼ cup chopped fresh parsley

With tip of a sharp knife, carefully remove meat from chicken breasts. Cut into thin pieces 2-3 inches long. In a saucepan, sauté chicken and onion in butter until onion is tender. Season with salt and pepper. Add tomatoes and oregano; cook, stirring, 1 minute. Pour in broth and bring to a boil. Stir in rice and walnuts. Lower heat; cook slowly, covered, about 25 minutes, or until rice and chicken are tender. Mix in parsley just before serving. Serves 6.

Mint-Flavored Meatballs

Quofte me mente are typical of the Albanian mint- and cinnamon-flavored meat dishes.

1 pound ground lamb	½ teaspoon cinnamon
3 eggs, beaten	2 teaspoons flour
1 garlic clove, crushed	Salt, to taste
3 cups fine dry bread crumbs	Oil for frying
¼ cup chopped fresh mint	

Combine all ingredients except oil. Leave, covered, for 1 hour to blend flavors. Shape into small balls, about 1 inch in diameter. Fry in hot oil in a skillet until brown on all sides. Drain. Serve with rice or pilaf. Serves 4.

Lamb Stew with Okra

This piquantly flavored lamb stew called mish me bamje is a favorite spring or early summer dish. It can be prepared with greens or small artichokes as well as with okra.

2 pounds lean lamb shoulder, cut in 1½-inch cubes	2 medium onions, peeled and chopped
3 tablespoons olive or vegetable oil	3 tablespoons chopped fresh dill or parsley
4 green onions, cleaned and chopped	Salt, pepper to taste
	1 pound fresh okra, cleaned

3 egg yolks   Juice of 1 lemon
1 tablespoon water

Brown lamb cubes in oil in a saucepan. Add onions; sauté until
tender. Add dill, salt, pepper and water to cover. Cook slowly,
tightly covered, about 1 hour or until meat is tender. Add more
water while cooking, if needed. Add okra; continue to cook
another 30 minutes, or until meat and okra are tender. Combine
egg yolks, water and lemon juice. Add some hot broth to mixture;
stir into stew, mixing constantly. Leave over heat just long enough
to thicken. Serves 4 to 6.
Note: Use frozen or canned okra, if desired.

Lamb-Stuffed Vegetables

Favorite main dishes in Albania and other Balkan countries are
vegetables stuffed with rice and meat (generally lamb but sometimes beef or pork). These are flavored according to regional
tastes and may be eaten warm or cold, with or without a sauce.
This is a general recipe that may be used for stuffing green
peppers, tomatoes, eggplants or zucchini. The necessary amount
of stuffing will vary according to the size of the vegetables.
Any leftover stuffing can be shaped into small meatballs and
cooked with the vegetables. To prepare vegetables, scoop out
the centers, rinse and drain. The cooking liquid may be a rich
meat stock, a vegetable bouillon or water.

1 medium onion, peeled   Salt, pepper to taste
   and minced   8 (approximately) prepared
1 pound ground lamb   green peppers, tomatoes,
½ cup uncooked rice   eggplants or zucchini
2 tablespoons chopped fresh   1 cup meat or vegetable
   dill, mint or parsley   bouillon
1 egg   ¼ cup olive or salad oil
3 tablespoons tomato paste

Combine minced onion, ground meat, rice, dill, egg, tomato
paste, salt and pepper. Mix well to thoroughly combine ingredients.
Spoon into prepared vegetables, stuffing lightly. Place in a

kettle. Add bouillon, oil and enough hot water to half cover vegetables. Cook, tightly covered, over low heat about 40 minutes, or until rice is thoroughly cooked. Serve hot or cold.

Rice with Raisins

This simple and delectable national dish called Kabuni is made preferably with sweet, golden raisins. It is an excellent accompaniment to chicken.

¼ cup butter or margarine	1 cup golden raisins
1 cup uncooked rice	2 tablespoons (about) sugar
2½ cups chicken broth	1 teaspoon ground cinnamon

Melt the butter in a saucepan. Add the rice and sauté 1 or 2 minutes, stirring, until the grains are well coated with butter. Add the broth and bring to a boil. Mix in the raisins and lower the heat. Cook slowly, covered, about 25 minutes or until the rice is tender and all the liquid is absorbed. Add sugar according to taste, add cinnamon and mix into the rice just before serving. Serves 4.

VEGETABLES

Baked Mixed Vegetables

Characteristic Albanian dishes are those that contain one or more vegetables with seasonings, baked or stewed. The dishes are good accompaniments for grilled or roasted meats, game or poultry. If desired, other vegetables may be used as substitutes for those listed below.

3 medium potatoes, peeled and thinly sliced	3 medium tomatoes, peeled and sliced
Fat for frying	2 medium zucchini, thinly sliced
Butter	

½ cup uncooked green peas   2 tablespoons chopped fresh
½ cup tomato paste   mint
½ cup olive or salad oil   ½ cup chopped fresh parsley
    Salt, pepper to taste

Fry potatoes in hot fat until soft. Drain. In a buttered casserole, arrange with tomatoes, zucchini and green peas in layers. Combine tomato paste with 1 cup water; bring to a boil. Stir in oil, salt and pepper. Add mint and parsley; pour over vegetables. Bake in a preheated moderate oven (350°F.) about 35 minutes, or until vegetables are cooked. Serves 6 to 8.

Fried Squash with Sour Cream Sauce

Kungull me kos is an interesting Albanian vegetable dish.

1 cup sour cream or plain   1 cup flour
    yogurt   Salt, to taste
1 garlic clove, crushed   1 egg, slightly beaten
2 pounds (approximately)   ½ cup (approximately) water
    zucchini, yellow or summer   Oil or fat for deep frying
    squash

Combine sour cream and garlic; set aside. Wash squash and remove stems. Cut unpeeled squash crosswise into thin slices. Mix flour, salt, egg and water to make a batter. Dip squash in it; then fry in hot oil or fat until golden on both sides. Serve with the prepared sour cream and garlic sauce. Serves 4 to 6.

SAUCES

Basic Tomato Sauce

1 large onion, peeled and   2 tablespoons olive or salad
    chopped   oil
2 garlic cloves, crushed   1 can (6 ounces) tomato paste

1 cup (approximately) water
2 teaspoons crumbled dried
  herbs (basil, thyme,
marjoram and oregano)
1 bay leaf
Salt, pepper to taste

In a skillet, sauté chopped onion and garlic in oil until tender. Add tomato paste; mix well. Add remaining ingredients; cook slowly, uncovered, 30 minutes. Thin with more water while cooking, if desired. Remove and discard bay leaf. Serve with cooked fish, noodles, cornmeal dishes, or stuffed vegetables. Makes about 2 cups.

Egg and Lemon Sauce

3 egg yolks
Juice of 2 lemons
1 cup hot chicken bouillon
Salt, pepper to taste

Beat the egg yolks until light. Add the lemon juice, drop by drop, stirring constantly. Gradually add the hot bouillon, stirring constantly. Season with salt and pepper. Be careful not to boil the sauce while adding the bouillon. Makes about 1½ cups. Serve with cooked vegetables or fish.

Mint Sauce

1 cup chopped fresh mint
  leaves
1 tablespoon sugar
2 tablespoons lemon juice
1 cup hot chicken bouillon
Salt to taste

Combine all the ingredients and mix well. Cool. Serve with cold cooked meats. Makes about 1½ cups.

DESSERTS

Almond Cake

This cake is called ematur, which means "the counted" or "exactly done thing."

1 cup water   1 cup sugar
1 cup butter   2 cups sifted flour
                                     Blanched almonds

Bring water to a boil. Add butter and sugar; boil 2-3 minutes. Slowly add flour, stirring as adding. Spread in a greased 8-inch square pan. Cut into diamond-shaped sections. Put an almond in center of each. Bake in a preheated hot oven (450°F.) for 15 minutes. Lower heat and continue to bake until done.

Albanian Walnut Cake

Albanians are very fond of either a plain or nut-flavored cake, which is covered with a thick syrup. This is one variety.

½ cup butter or margarine   1 teaspoon baking soda
2½ cups sugar   ½ teaspoon ground cinnamon
2 eggs, beaten slightly   ⅔ cup sour milk
2 cups sifted all-purpose   1 cup chopped walnuts
   flour   Grated rind of 1 lemon
1 teaspoon baking powder   1 cup water

Cream butter in a large bowl. Mix in 1 cup sugar and eggs to blend well. Sift the dry ingredients and add alternately with the sour milk. Stir in the nuts and lemon rind and mix until well combined. Pour into a greased baking dish, 13 x 9 x 2", and bake in a preheated moderate oven (350°F.) for about 45 minutes.

Meanwhile, make a thick syrup by boiling together the remaining 1½ cups sugar and the water for 15 minutes. Pour over the cake while it is still warm and put back into oven just after it has been turned off. Leave 5 minutes and then cut into diamond shapes. Serves warm or cooled. Makes about 16 pieces.

Index

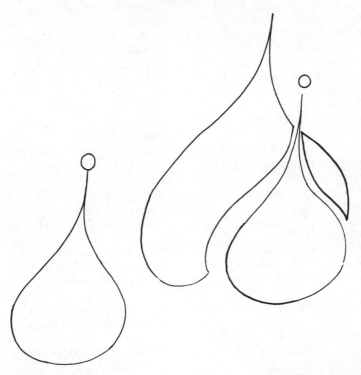

A CATALOGUE OF SELECTED DOVER BOOKS
IN ALL FIELDS OF INTEREST

A CATALOGUE OF SELECTED DOVER
BOOKS IN ALL FIELDS OF INTEREST

RACKHAM'S COLOR ILLUSTRATIONS FOR WAGNER'S RING. Rackham's finest mature work—all 64 full-color watercolors in a faithful and lush interpretation of the *Ring*. Full-sized plates on coated stock of the paintings used by opera companies for authentic staging of Wagner. Captions aid in following complete Ring cycle. Introduction. 64 illustrations plus vignettes. 72pp. 8⅝ x 11¼.   23779-6 Pa. $6.00

CONTEMPORARY POLISH POSTERS IN FULL COLOR, edited by Joseph Czestochowski. 46 full-color examples of brilliant school of Polish graphic design, selected from world's first museum (near Warsaw) dedicated to poster art. Posters on circuses, films, plays, concerts all show cosmopolitan influences, free imagination. Introduction. 48pp. 9⅜ x 12¼.
23780-X Pa. $6.00

GRAPHIC WORKS OF EDVARD MUNCH, Edvard Munch. 90 haunting, evocative prints by first major Expressionist artist and one of the greatest graphic artists of his time: *The Scream, Anxiety, Death Chamber, The Kiss, Madonna,* etc. Introduction by Alfred Werner. 90pp. 9 x 12.
23765-6 Pa. $5.00

THE GOLDEN AGE OF THE POSTER, Hayward and Blanche Cirker. 70 extraordinary posters in full colors, from Maitres de l'Affiche, Mucha, Lautrec, Bradley, Cheret, Beardsley, many others. Total of 78pp. 9⅜ x 12¼.   22753-7 Pa. $5.95

THE NOTEBOOKS OF LEONARDO DA VINCI, edited by J. P. Richter. Extracts from manuscripts reveal great genius; on painting, sculpture, anatomy, sciences, geography, etc. Both Italian and English. 186 ms. pages reproduced, plus 500 additional drawings, including studies for *Last Supper,* Sforza monument, etc. 860pp. 7⅞ x 10¾. (Available in U.S. only)
22572-0, 22573-9 Pa., Two-vol. set $15.90

THE CODEX NUTTALL, as first edited by Zelia Nuttall. Only inexpensive edition, in full color, of a pre-Columbian Mexican (Mixtec) book. 88 color plates show kings, gods, heroes, temples, sacrifices. New explanatory, historical introduction by Arthur G. Miller. 96pp. 11⅜ x 8½. (Available in U.S. only)   23168-2 Pa. $7.95

UNE SEMAINE DE BONTÉ, A SURREALISTIC NOVEL IN COLLAGE, Max Ernst. Masterpiece created out of 19th-century periodical illustrations, explores worlds of terror and surprise. Some consider this Ernst's greatest work. 208pp. 8⅛ x 11.   23252-2 Pa. $5.00

CATALOGUE OF DOVER BOOKS

AN AUTOBIOGRAPHY, Margaret Sanger. Exciting personal account of hard-fought battle for woman's right to birth control, against prejudice, church, law. Foremost feminist document. 504pp. 5⅜ x 8½.
20470-7 Pa. $5.50

MY BONDAGE AND MY FREEDOM, Frederick Douglass. Born as a slave, Douglass became outspoken force in antislavery movement. The best of Douglass's autobiographies. Graphic description of slave life. Introduction by P. Foner. 464pp. 5⅜ x 8½. 22457-0 Pa. $5.50

LIVING MY LIFE, Emma Goldman. Candid, no holds barred account by foremost American anarchist: her own life, anarchist movement, famous contemporaries, ideas and their impact. Struggles and confrontations in America, plus deportation to U.S.S.R. Shocking inside account of persecution of anarchists under Lenin. 13 plates. Total of 944pp. 5⅜ x 8½.
22543-7, 22544-5 Pa., Two-vol. set $11.00

LETTERS AND NOTES ON THE MANNERS, CUSTOMS AND CONDITIONS OF THE NORTH AMERICAN INDIANS, George Catlin. Classic account of life among Plains Indians: ceremonies, hunt, warfare, etc. Dover edition reproduces for first time all original paintings. 312 plates. 572pp. of text. 6⅛ x 9¼. 22118-0, 22119-9 Pa.. Two-vol. set $11.50

THE MAYA AND THEIR NEIGHBORS, edited by Clarence L. Hay, others. Synoptic view of Maya civilization in broadest sense, together with Northern, Southern neighbors. Integrates much background, valuable detail not elsewhere. Prepared by greatest scholars: Kroeber, Morley, Thompson, Spinden, Vaillant, many others. Sometimes called Tozzer Memorial Volume. 60 illustrations, linguistic map. 634pp. 5⅜ x 8½.
23510-6 Pa. $7.50

HANDBOOK OF THE INDIANS OF CALIFORNIA, A. L. Kroeber. Foremost American anthropologist offers complete ethnographic study of each group. Monumental classic. 459 illustrations, maps. 995pp. 5⅜ x 8½.
23368-5 Pa. $10.00

SHAKTI AND SHAKTA, Arthur Avalon. First book to give clear, cohesive analysis of Shakta doctrine, Shakta ritual and Kundalini Shakti (yoga). Important work by one of world's foremost students of Shaktic and Tantric thought. 732pp. 5⅜ x 8½. (Available in U.S. only)
23645-5 Pa. $7.95

AN INTRODUCTION TO THE STUDY OF THE MAYA HIEROGLYPHS, Syvanus Griswold Morley. Classic study by one of the truly great figures in hieroglyph research. Still the best introduction for the student for reading Maya hieroglyphs. New introduction by J. Eric S. Thompson. 117 illustrations. 284pp. 5⅜ x 8½. 23108-9 Pa. $4.00

A STUDY OF MAYA ART, Herbert J. Spinden. Landmark classic interprets Maya symbolism, estimates styles, covers ceramics, architecture, murals, stone carvings as artforms. Still a basic book in area. New introduction by J. Eric Thompson. Over 750 illustrations. 341pp. 8⅜ x 11¼.
21235-1 Pa. $6.95

HOLLYWOOD GLAMOUR PORTRAITS, edited by John Kobal. 145 photos capture the stars from 1926-49, the high point in portrait photography. Gable, Harlow, Bogart, Bacall, Hedy Lamarr, Marlene Dietrich, Robert Montgomery, Marlon Brando, Veronica Lake; 94 stars in all. Full background on photographers, technical aspects, much more. Total of 160pp. 8⅜ x 11¼.   23352-9 Pa. $6.00

THE NEW YORK STAGE: FAMOUS PRODUCTIONS IN PHOTO-GRAPHS, edited by Stanley Appelbaum. 148 photographs from Museum of City of New York show 142 plays, 1883-1939. *Peter Pan, The Front Page, Dead End, Our Town,* O'Neill, hundreds of actors and actresses, etc. Full indexes. 154pp. 9½ x 10.   23241-7 Pa. $6.00

MASTERS OF THE DRAMA, John Gassner. Most comprehensive history of the drama, every tradition from Greeks to modern Europe and America, including Orient. Covers 800 dramatists, 2000 plays; biography, plot summaries, criticism, theatre history, etc. 77 illustrations. 890pp. 5⅜ x 8½.
                                                              20100-7 Clothbd. $10.00

THE GREAT OPERA STARS IN HISTORIC PHOTOGRAPHS, edited by James Camner. 343 portraits from the 1850s to the 1940s: Tamburini, Mario, Caliapin, Jeritza, Melchior, Melba, Patti, Pinza, Schipa, Caruso, Farrar, Steber, Gobbi, and many more—270 performers in all. Index. 199pp. 8⅜ x 11¼.   23575-0 Pa. $6.50

J. S. BACH, Albert Schweitzer. Great full-length study of Bach, life, background to music, music, by foremost modern scholar. Ernest Newman translation. 650 musical examples. Total of 928pp. 5⅜ x 8½. (Available in U.S. only)   21631-4, 21632-2 Pa., Two-vol. set $10.00

COMPLETE PIANO SONATAS, Ludwig van Beethoven. All sonatas in the fine Schenker edition, with fingering, analytical material. One of best modern editions. Total of 615pp. 9 x 12. (Available in U.S. only)
                                            23134-8, 23135-6 Pa., Two-vol. set $15.00

KEYBOARD MUSIC, J. S. Bach. Bach-Gesellschaft edition. For harpsichord, piano, other keyboard instruments. English Suites, French Suites, Six Partitas, Goldberg Variations, Two-Part Inventions, Three-Part Sinfonias. 312pp. 8⅛ x 11. (Available in U.S. only)   22360-4 Pa. $6.95

FOUR SYMPHONIES IN FULL SCORE, Franz Schubert. Schubert's four most popular symphonies: No. 4 in C Minor ("Tragic"); No. 5 in B-flat Major; No. 8 in B Minor ("Unfinished"); No. 9 in C Major ("Great"). Breitkopf & Hartel edition. Study score. 261pp. 9⅜ x 12¼.
                                                                  23681-1 Pa. $6.50

THE AUTHENTIC GILBERT & SULLIVAN SONGBOOK, W. S. Gilbert, A. S. Sullivan. Largest selection available; 92 songs, uncut, original keys, in piano rendering approved by Sullivan. Favorites and lesser-known fine numbers. Edited with plot synopses by James Spero. 3 illustrations. 399pp. 9 x 12.   23482-7 Pa. $7.95

HOUSEHOLD STORIES BY THE BROTHERS GRIMM. All the great Grimm stories: "Rumpelstiltskin," "Snow White," "Hansel and Gretel," etc., with 114 illustrations by Walter Crane. 269pp. 5⅜ x 8½.
21080-4 Pa. $3.00

SLEEPING BEAUTY, illustrated by Arthur Rackham. Perhaps the fullest, most delightful version ever, told by C. S. Evans. Rackham's best work. 49 illustrations. 110pp. 7⅞ x 10¾. 22756-1 Pa. $2.50

AMERICAN FAIRY TALES, L. Frank Baum. Young cowboy lassoes Father Time; dummy in Mr. Floman's department store window comes to life; and 10 other fairy tales. 41 illustrations by N. P. Hall, Harry Kennedy, Ike Morgan, and Ralph Gardner. 209pp. 5⅜ x 8½. 23643-9 Pa. $3.00

THE WONDERFUL WIZARD OF OZ, L. Frank Baum. Facsimile in full color of America's finest children's classic. Introduction by Martin Gardner. 143 illustrations by W. W. Denslow. 267pp. 5⅜ x 8½.
20691-2 Pa. $3.50

THE TALE OF PETER RABBIT, Beatrix Potter. The inimitable Peter's terrifying adventure in Mr. McGregor's garden, with all 27 wonderful, full-color Potter illustrations. 55pp. 4¼ x 5½. (Available in U.S. only)
22827-4 Pa. $1.25

THE STORY OF KING ARTHUR AND HIS KNIGHTS, Howard Pyle. Finest children's version of life of King Arthur. 48 illustrations by Pyle. 131pp. 6⅛ x 9¼. 21445-1 Pa. $4.95

CARUSO'S CARICATURES, Enrico Caruso. Great tenor's remarkable caricatures of self, fellow musicians, composers, others. Toscanini, Puccini, Farrar, etc. Impish, cutting, insightful. 473 illustrations. Preface by M. Sisca. 217pp. 8⅜ x 11¼. 23528-9 Pa. $6.95

PERSONAL NARRATIVE OF A PILGRIMAGE TO ALMADINAH AND MECCAH, Richard Burton. Great travel classic by remarkably colorful personality. Burton, disguised as a Moroccan, visited sacred shrines of Islam, narrowly escaping death. Wonderful observations of Islamic life, customs, personalities. 47 illustrations. Total of 959pp. 5⅜ x 8½.
21217-3, 21218-1 Pa., Two-vol. set $12.00

INCIDENTS OF TRAVEL IN YUCATAN, John L. Stephens. Classic (1843) exploration of jungles of Yucatan, looking for evidences of Maya civilization. Travel adventures, Mexican and Indian culture, etc. Total of 669pp. 5⅜ x 8½. 20926-1, 20927-X Pa., Two-vol. set $7.90

AMERICAN LITERARY AUTOGRAPHS FROM WASHINGTON IRVING TO HENRY JAMES, Herbert Cahoon, et al. Letters, poems, manuscripts of Hawthorne, Thoreau, Twain, Alcott, Whitman, 67 other prominent American authors. Reproductions, full transcripts and commentary. Plus checklist of all American Literary Autographs in The Pierpont Morgan Library. Printed on exceptionally high-quality paper. 136 illustrations. 212pp. 9⅛ x 12¼. 23548-3 Pa. $7.95

AMERICAN BIRD ENGRAVINGS, Alexander Wilson et al. All 76 plates. from Wilson's *American Ornithology* (1808-14), most important ornithological work before Audubon, plus 27 plates from the supplement (1825-33) by Charles Bonaparte. Over 250 birds portrayed. 8 plates also reproduced in full color. 111pp. 9⅜ x 12½.   23195-X Pa. $6.00

CRUICKSHANK'S PHOTOGRAPHS OF BIRDS OF AMERICA, Allan D. Cruickshank. Great ornithologist, photographer presents 177 closeups, groupings, panoramas, flightings, etc., of about 150 different birds. Expanded *Wings in the Wilderness*. Introduction by Helen G. Cruickshank. 191pp. 8¼ x 11.   23497-5 Pa. $6.00

AMERICAN WILDLIFE AND PLANTS, A. C. Martin, et al. Describes food habits of more than 1000 species of mammals, birds, fish. Special treatment of important food plants. Over 300 illustrations. 500pp. 5⅜ x 8½.
20793-5 Pa. $4.95

THE PEOPLE CALLED SHAKERS, Edward D. Andrews. Lifetime of research, definitive study of Shakers: origins, beliefs, practices, dances, social organization, furniture and crafts, impact on 19th-century USA, present heritage. Indispensable to student of American history, collector. 33 illustrations. 351pp. 5⅜ x 8½.   21081-2 Pa. $4.00

OLD NEW YORK IN EARLY PHOTOGRAPHS, Mary Black. New York City as it was in 1853-1901, through 196 wonderful photographs from N.-Y. Historical Society. Great Blizzard, Lincoln's funeral procession, great buildings. 228pp. 9 x 12.   22907-6 Pa. $7.95

MR. LINCOLN'S CAMERA MAN: MATHEW BRADY, Roy Meredith. Over 300 Brady photos reproduced directly from original negatives, photos. Jackson, Webster, Grant, Lee, Carnegie, Barnum; Lincoln; Battle Smoke, Death of Rebel Sniper, Atlanta Just After Capture. Lively commentary. 368pp. 8⅜ x 11¼.   23021-X Pa. $8.95

TRAVELS OF WILLIAM BARTRAM, William Bartram. From 1773-8, Bartram explored Northern Florida, Georgia, Carolinas, and reported on wild life, plants, Indians, early settlers. Basic account for period, entertaining reading. Edited by Mark Van Doren. 13 illustrations. 141pp. 5⅜ x 8½.   20013-2 Pa. $4.50

THE GENTLEMAN AND CABINET MAKER'S DIRECTOR, Thomas Chippendale. Full reprint, 1762 style book, most influential of all time; chairs, tables, sofas, mirrors, cabinets, etc. 200 plates, plus 24 photographs of surviving pieces. 249pp. 9⅞ x 12¾.   21601-2 Pa. $6.50

AMERICAN CARRIAGES, SLEIGHS, SULKIES AND CARTS, edited by Don H. Berkebile. 168 Victorian illustrations from catalogues, trade journals, fully captioned. Useful for artists. Author is Assoc. Curator, Div. of Transportation of Smithsonian Institution. 168pp. 8½ x 9½.
23328-6 Pa. $5.00

CATALOGUE OF DOVER BOOKS

"OSCAR" OF THE WALDORF'S COOKBOOK, Oscar Tschirky. Famous American chef reveals 3455 recipes that made Waldorf great; cream of French, German, American cooking, in all categories. Full instructions, easy home use. 1896 edition. 907pp. 6⅝ x 9⅜.   20790-0 Clothbd. $15.00

COOKING WITH BEER, Carole Fahy. Beer has as superb an effect on food as wine, and at fraction of cost. Over 250 recipes for appetizers, soups, main dishes, desserts, breads, etc. Index. 144pp. 5⅜ x 8½. (Available in U.S. only)   23661-7 Pa. $2.50

STEWS AND RAGOUTS, Kay Shaw Nelson. This international cookbook offers wide range of 108 recipes perfect for everyday, special occasions, meals-in-themselves, main dishes. Economical, nutritious, easy-to-prepare: goulash, Irish stew, boeuf bourguignon, etc. Index. 134pp. 5⅜ x 8½.
23662-5 Pa. $2.50

DELICIOUS MAIN COURSE DISHES, Marian Tracy. Main courses are the most important part of any meal. These 200 nutritious, economical recipes from around the world make every meal a delight. "I . . . have found it so useful in my own household,"—N.Y. Times. Index. 219pp. 5⅜ x 8½.   23664-1 Pa. $3.00

FIVE ACRES AND INDEPENDENCE, Maurice G. Kains. Great back-to-the-land classic explains basics of self-sufficient farming: economics, plants, crops, animals, orchards, soils, land selection, host of other necessary things. Do not confuse with skimpy faddist literature; Kains was one of America's greatest agriculturalists. 95 illustrations. 397pp. 5⅜ x 8½.
20974-1 Pa. $3.95

A PRACTICAL GUIDE FOR THE BEGINNING FARMER, Herbert Jacobs. Basic, extremely useful first book for anyone thinking about moving to the country and starting a farm. Simpler than Kains, with greater emphasis on country living in general. 246pp. 5⅜ x 8½.
23675-7 Pa. $3.50

A GARDEN OF PLEASANT FLOWERS (PARADISI IN SOLE: PARADISUS TERRESTRIS), John Parkinson. Complete, unabridged reprint of first (1629) edition of earliest great English book on gardens and gardening. More than 1000 plants & flowers of Elizabethan, Jacobean garden fully described, most with woodcut illustrations. Botanically very reliable, a "speaking garden" of exceeding charm. 812 illustrations. 628pp. 8½ x 12¼.   23392-8 Clothbd. $25.00

ACKERMANN'S COSTUME PLATES, Rudolph Ackermann. Selection of 96 plates from the *Repository of Arts,* best published source of costume for English fashion during the early 19th century. 12 plates also in color. Captions, glossary and introduction by editor Stella Blum. Total of 120pp. 8⅜ x 11¼.   23690-0 Pa. $4.50

TONE POEMS, SERIES II: TILL EULENSPIEGELS LUSTIGE STREICHE, ALSO SPRACH ZARATHUSTRA, AND EIN HELDEN-LEBEN, Richard Strauss. Three important orchestral works, including very popular *Till Eulenspiegel's Marry Pranks,* reproduced in full score from original editions. Study score. 315pp. 9⅜ x 12¼. (Available in U.S. only)
23755-9 Pa. $7.50

TONE POEMS, SERIES I: DON JUAN, TOD UND VERKLARUNG AND DON QUIXOTE, Richard Strauss. Three of the most often performed and recorded works in entire orchestral repertoire, reproduced in full score from original editions. Study score. 286pp. 9⅜ x 12¼. (Available in U.S. only)
23754-0 Pa. $7.50

11 LATE STRING QUARTETS, Franz Joseph Haydn. The form which Haydn defined and "brought to perfection." *(Grove's).* 11 string quartets in complete score, his last and his best. The first in a projected series of the complete Haydn string quartets. Reliable modern Eulenberg edition, otherwise difficult to obtain. 320pp. 8⅜ x 11¼. (Available in U.S. only)
23753-2 Pa. $6.95

FOURTH, FIFTH AND SIXTH SYMPHONIES IN FULL SCORE, Peter Ilyitch Tchaikovsky. Complete orchestral scores of Symphony No. 4 in F Minor, Op. 36; Symphony No. 5 in E Minor, Op. 64; Symphony No. 6 in B Minor, "Pathetique," Op. 74. Bretikopf & Hartel eds. Study score. 480pp. 9⅜ x 12¼.
23861-X Pa. $10.95

THE MARRIAGE OF FIGARO: COMPLETE SCORE, Wolfgang A. Mozart. Finest comic opera ever written. Full score, not to be confused with piano renderings. Peters edition. Study score. 448pp. 9⅜ x 12¼. (Available in U.S. only)
23751-6 Pa. $11.95

"IMAGE" ON THE ART AND EVOLUTION OF THE FILM, edited by Marshall Deutelbaum. Pioneering book brings together for first time 38 groundbreaking articles on early silent films from *Image* and 263 illustrations newly shot from rare prints in the collection of the International Museum of Photography. A landmark work. Index. 256pp. 8¼ x 11.
23777-X Pa. $8.95

AROUND-THE-WORLD COOKY BOOK, Lois Lintner Sumption and Marguerite Lintner Ashbrook. 373 cooky and frosting recipes from 28 countries (America, Austria, China, Russia, Italy, etc.) include Viennese kisses, rice wafers, London strips, lady fingers, hony, sugar spice, maple cookies, etc. Clear instructions. All tested. 38 drawings. 182pp. 5⅜ x 8.
23802-4 Pa. $2.50

THE ART NOUVEAU STYLE, edited by Roberta Waddell. 579 rare photographs, not available elsew'ere, of works in jewelry, metalwork, glass, ceramics, textiles, architecture and furniture by 175 artists—Mucha, Seguy, Lalique, Tiffany, Gaudin, Hohlwein, Saarinen, and many others. 288pp. 8⅜ x 11¼.
23515-7 Pa. $6.95

THE COMPLETE BOOK OF DOLL MAKING AND COLLECTING, Catherine Christopher. Instructions, patterns for dozens of dolls, from rag doll on up to elaborate, historically accurate figures. Mould faces, sew clothing, make doll houses, etc. Also collecting information. Many illustrations. 288pp. 6 x 9. 22066-4 Pa. $4.50

THE DAGUERREOTYPE IN AMERICA, Beaumont Newhall. Wonderful portraits, 1850's townscapes, landscapes; full text plus 104 photographs. The basic book. Enlarged 1976 edition. 272pp. 8¼ x 11¼.
23322-7 Pa. $7.95

CRAFTSMAN HOMES, Gustav Stickley. 296 architectural drawings, floor plans, and photographs illustrate 40 different kinds of "Mission-style" homes from *The Craftsman* (1901-16), voice of American style of simplicity and organic harmony. Thorough coverage of Craftsman idea in text and picture, now collector's item. 224pp. 8⅛ x 11. 23791-5 Pa. $6.00

PEWTER-WORKING: INSTRUCTIONS AND PROJECTS, Burl N. Osborn. & Gordon O. Wilber. Introduction to pewter-working for amateur craftsman. History and characteristics of pewter; tools, materials, step-by-step instructions. Photos, line drawings, diagrams. Total of 160pp. 7⅞ x 10¾. 23786-9 Pa. $3.50

THE GREAT CHICAGO FIRE, edited by David Lowe. 10 dramatic, eyewitness accounts of the 1871 disaster, including one of the aftermath and rebuilding, plus 70 contemporary photographs and illustrations of the ruins—courthouse, Palmer House, Great Central Depot, etc. Introduction by David Lowe. 87pp. 8¼ x 11. 23771-0 Pa. $4.00

SILHOUETTES: A PICTORIAL ARCHIVE OF VARIED ILLUSTRATIONS, edited by Carol Belanger Grafton. Over 600 silhouettes from the 18th to 20th centuries include profiles and full figures of men and women, children, birds and animals, groups and scenes, nature, ships, an alphabet. Dozens of uses for commercial artists and craftspeople. 144pp. 8⅜ x 11¼.
23781-8 Pa. $4.00

ANIMALS: 1,419 COPYRIGHT-FREE ILLUSTRATIONS OF MAMMALS, BIRDS, FISH, INSECTS, ETC., edited by Jim Harter. Clear wood engravings present, in extremely lifelike poses, over 1,000 species of animals. One of the most extensive copyright-free pictorial sourcebooks of its kind. Captions. Index. 284pp. 9 x 12. 23766-4 Pa. $7.95

INDIAN DESIGNS FROM ANCIENT ECUADOR, Frederick W. Shaffer. 282 original designs by pre-Columbian Indians of Ecuador (500-1500 A.D.). Designs include people, mammals, birds, reptiles, fish, plants, heads, geometric designs. Use as is or alter for advertising, textiles, leathercraft, etc. Introduction. 95pp. 8¾ x 11¼. 23764-8 Pa. $3.50

SZIGETI ON THE VIOLIN, Joseph Szigeti. Genial, loosely structured tour by premier violinist, featuring a pleasant mixture of reminiscenes, insights into great music and musicians, innumerable tips for practicing violinists. 385 musical passages. 256pp. 5⅝ x 8¼. 23763-X Pa. $3.50

THE SENSE OF BEAUTY, George Santayana. Masterfully written discussion of nature of beauty, materials of beauty, form, expression; art, literature, social sciences all involved. 168pp. 5⅜ x 8½.   20238-0 Pa. $2.50

ON THE IMPROVEMENT OF THE UNDERSTANDING, Benedict Spinoza. Also contains *Ethics, Correspondence,* all in excellent R. Elwes translation. Basic works on entry to philosophy, pantheism, exchange of ideas with great contemporaries. 402pp. 5⅜ x 8½.   20250-X Pa. $4.50

THE TRAGIC SENSE OF LIFE, Miguel de Unamuno. Acknowledged masterpiece of existential literature, one of most important books of 20th century. Introduction by Madariaga. 367pp. 5⅜ x 8½.
20257-7 Pa. $4.50

THE GUIDE FOR THE PERPLEXED, Moses Maimonides. Great classic of medieval Judaism attempts to reconcile revealed religion (Pentateuch, commentaries) with Aristotelian philosophy. Important historically, still relevant in problems. Unabridged Friedlander translation. Total of 473pp. 5⅜ x 8½.   20351-4 Pa. $6.00

THE I CHING (THE BOOK OF CHANGES), translated by James Legge. Complete translation of basic text plus appendices by Confucius, and Chinese commentary of most penetrating divination manual ever prepared. Indispensable to study of early Oriental civilizations, to modern inquiring reader. 448pp. 5⅜ x 8½.   21062-6 Pa. $4.00

THE EGYPTIAN BOOK OF THE DEAD, E. A. Wallis Budge. Complete reproduction of Ani's papyrus, finest ever found. Full hieroglyphic text, interlinear transliteration, word for word translation, smooth translation. Basic work, for Egyptology, for modern study of psychic matters. Total of 533pp. 6½ x 9¼. (Available in U.S. only)   21866-X Pa. $5.95

THE GODS OF THE EGYPTIANS, E. A. Wallis Budge. Never excelled for richness, fullness: all gods, goddesses, demons, mythical figures of Ancient Egypt; their legends, rites, incarnations, variations, powers, etc. Many hieroglyphic texts cited. Over 225 illustrations, plus 6 color plates. Total of 988pp. 6⅛ x 9¼. (Available in U.S. only)
22055-9, 22056-7 Pa., Two-vol. set $12.00

THE ENGLISH AND SCOTTISH POPULAR BALLADS, Francis J. Child. Monumental, still unsuperseded; all known variants of Child ballads, commentary on origins, literary references, Continental parallels, other features. Added: papers by G. L. Kittredge, W. M. Hart. Total of 2761pp. 6½ x 9¼.
21409-5, 21410-9, 21411-7, 21412-5, 21413-3 Pa., Five-vol. set $37.50

CORAL GARDENS AND THEIR MAGIC, Bronsilaw Malinowski. Classic study of the methods of tilling the soil and of agricultural rites in the Trobriand Islands of Melanesia. Author is one of the most important figures in the field of modern social anthropology. 143 illustrations. Indexes. Total of 911pp. of text. 5⅝ x 8¼. (Available in U.S. only)
23597-1 Pa. $12.95

CATALOGUE OF DOVER BOOKS

THE STANDARD BOOK OF QUILT MAKING AND COLLECTING, Marguerite Ickis. Full information, full-sized patterns for making 46 traditional quilts, also 150 other patterns. Quilted cloths, lame, satin quilts, etc. 483 illustrations. 273pp. 6⅞ x 9⅝.   20582-7 Pa. $4.95

ENCYCLOPEDIA OF VICTORIAN NEEDLEWORK, S. Caulfield, Blanche Saward. Simply inexhaustible gigantic alphabetical coverage of every traditional needlecraft—stitches, materials, methods, tools, types of work; definitions, many projects to be made. 1200 illustrations; double-columned text. 697pp. 8⅛ x 11.   22800-2, 22801-0 Pa., Two-vol. set $12.00

MECHANICK EXERCISES ON THE WHOLE ART OF PRINTING, Joseph Moxon. First complete book (1683-4) ever written about typography, a compendium of everything known about printing at the latter part of 17th century. Reprint of 2nd (1962) Oxford Univ. Press edition. 74 illustrations. Total of 550pp. 6⅛ x 9¼.   23617-X Pa. $7.95

PAPERMAKING, Dard Hunter. Definitive book on the subject by the foremost authority in the field. Chapters dealing with every aspect of history of craft in every part of the world. Over 320 illustrations. 2nd, revised and enlarged (1947) edition. 672pp. 5⅜ x 8½.   23619-6 Pa. $7.95

THE ART DECO STYLE, edited by Theodore Menten. Furniture, jewelry, metalwork, ceramics, fabrics, lighting fixtures, interior decors, exteriors, graphics from pure French sources. Best sampling around. Over 400 photographs. 183pp. 8⅜ x 11¼.   22824-X Pa. $6.00

Prices subject to change without notice.

Available at your book dealer or write for free catalogue to Dept. GI, Dover Publications, Inc., 180 Varick St., N.Y., N.Y. 10014. Dover publishes more than 175 books each year on science, elementary and advanced mathematics, biology, music, art, literary history, social sciences and other areas.